Kathy Sylva is a Fellow of Jesus College and a Lecturer in the Department of Social and Administrative Studies, University of Oxford. Prior to her work with the Oxford Preschool Research Group she investigated the developmental importance of play, carrying out experimental studies at Harvard on the play of three- to five-year-olds, and later conducting observations, in collaboration with Jerome Bruner, on mother-baby play and language learning.

Carolyn Roy is currently researching into the development of language, visual perception and learning in the early years, and is based at the Netherlands Institute for Advanced Study in the Humanities and Social Sciences. Besides working with the Oxford Preschool Group she also collaborated with Professor Bruner on communication and language development in very young children.

Marjorie Painter is a Lecturer in Education at St Mark's Teacher Training College, Embu, Kigari, Kenya. She has previously been Principal of Wellgarth Nursery Training College, in London, and Senior Lecturer in Education at Oxford Polytechnic/Lady Spencer Churchill College of Education. She has thus taught educational methods to students of teaching, nursery teaching, and nursery nursing.

Oxford Preschool Research Project

Childwatching at Playgroup and Nursery School

Kathy Sylva, Carolyn Roy
and Marjorie Painter

GRANT
MCINTYRE

First published in 1980 by
Grant McIntyre Ltd
39 Great Russell Street
London WC1B 3PH

Hardback ISBN 0 86216 002 2
Paperback ISBN 0 86216 003 0

British Library Cataloguing in Publication Data

Sylva, Kathy
 Childwatching at playgroup and nursery school. – (Oxford Preschool
 Research Project; 2).
 1. Nursery schools – Great Britain
 2. Play groups – Great Britain
 3. Child psychology – Great Britain
 I. Title   II. Roy, Carolyn
 III. Painter, Marjorie   IV. Series
 155.4'23   LB1140.2

 ISBN 0–86216–002–2
 ISBN 0–86216–003–0 Pbk

Text set in 10/12 pt VIP Times, printed and bound
in Great Britain at The Pitman Press, Bath

Contents

I cannot help but feel – and I do not have enough evidence to call it a conclusion – that childwatching of a sympathetic yet careful kind can go a long way towards helping us think about child care more in the spirit of gentle problem solving and less as an excercise in ideological projection.

JEROME BRUNER
Gilchrist lecture, 1978

Foreword by Jack Wrigley

In 1971, when a massive expansion of nursery education in Britain was proposed, there was relatively little easily available evidence to suggest how best this should be done. Consequently the Department of Education and Science and the Scottish Education Department initiated a programme of research on nursery education to answer practical questions about provision and to study the effects of expansion. The Educational Research Board of the Social Science Research Council saw the need for a complementary research programme concerned as well with some more fundamental issues which covered the whole range of preschool education.

The work was coordinated in the Department of Education and Science by a management committee on which the Schools Council and SSRC were represented. The original idea, that SSRC should concentrate on fundamental research while DES funded more policy oriented and practical work, proved too simple. What quickly emerged was a view that much of the fundamental work on preschool children had already been carried out. What was lacking was the dissemination of that knowledge and its implementation in the field. Within SSRC a preschool working group was given the task of commissioning projects, and the work of the Oxford Preschool Research Group, under Professor Bruner, reported in this series of publications, was the main element in the first phase of the SSRC programme.

Professor Bruner had already accomplished distinguished fundamental work in this field and was therefore well placed to make the point of the need for dissemination and implementation. Despite the many changes in the economic and political scene in the 1970s the original gap in knowledge remains important and the results of the SSRC research programme will do much to fill the gap. In particular, Professor Bruner's work in Oxfordshire has great value for the rest of the country. The publications of the Oxford Preschool Research Group, together with the results from other participants in the programme, will help give a firmer base on which to build for the future.

Jack Wrigley
Chairman
SSRC Educational Research
Board Panel on
Accountability in
London, 1979   Education

Foreword by Jerome Bruner

This book is one in a series that emerges from the Oxford Preschool Research Group. Like the others in the series, it is concerned with the provision of care in Britain for the preschool child away from home and is the result of several years of research devoted to various aspects of that issue. There are few more controversial and crucial issues facing Britain today. The objective of the series is to shed light on present needs, on the quality of care available and on the extent to which this care meets these needs. The general aim is to provide a basis for discussion of future policy.

The studies have all been financed by the Social Science Research Council of Great Britain. They were commissioned in 1974, a year or two after Mrs Thatcher's White Paper, *Education: a Framework for Expansion,* was published, at a time when it was thought that there would be a publicly financed expansion of preschool care and education in Britain. Since that time events have caught up with the enterprise and Britain finds itself in a period of economic stringency during which many of the hoped-for changes will have to be shelved until better days come again. Nonetheless, the studies are opportune, for careful study and planning will be necessary not only to meet present needs with reduced resources, but to shape policy and practice for an improved future service on behalf of children in Britain and their families.

Developmental studies of the past two decades have pointed increasingly to the importance of the opening years of life for the intellectual, social, and emotional growth of human beings. The books in this series, it is hoped, shed light on the practical steps that must be taken to assure that the early years can contribute to the well-being of a next generation in Britain.

Jerome Bruner

Oxford, 1979

Acknowledgements

There is a strong family resemblance in the acknowledgement sections of books on educational research. Teachers are thanked for their assistance, children praised for their ingenuity – even classroom pets come in for mention. We are pleased to continue this tradition, with extra thanks to Linnet McMahon, Martha Kempton, and Terry End for helping design and conduct the research in Oxfordshire. The Miami study was undertaken by Marjorie Walker as part of a dissertation at the University of Miami. Kenneth Macdonald worked hard to analyse the data, bringing humour to a dry exercise and finding patterns in the numbers that we had not seen. Lynda Gilbert provided valuable criticism on early drafts and prepared the case study in Chapter 7. The entire manuscript was shepherded through cycles of typing and revision by Jackie Evans.

The Oxford Preschool Research Group, under the leadership of Jerome Bruner, served as sounding board for ideas and plans. Miriam Harris helped to organize meetings with teachers and playgroup leaders to plan the research. During these meetings, Avril Holmes and Linnet McMahon saw the value of systematic observation in everyday practice and invented imaginative ways to teach others to observe. Many people were part of the Preschool Research Group and almost as many contributed to the target child studies. We close with the names of those who helped us most: Sanchia Austin, John Coe, Yvonne Cranstoun, Judy Dunn, Harry Judge, Joan Lawrence, Evelyn Phelps-Brown, Teresa Smith, Ann Thompson, Barbara Tizard, Chris Wells, and David Wood.

1

Does preschool experience matter?

This is a modest book. It explores some of the influences on children's actions, talk and social relationships while at playgroup or nursery school. Most of its findings stem from an observational study of 120 children between the ages of three and five in Oxfordshire. A similar investigation was afterwards conducted in Miami, so we can compare the British and American findings to highlight differences in preschools, bringing the obvious out of shadow and showing strengths and weaknesses in a bold light.

The British study was one of several investigations carried out under the auspices of the Oxford Preschool Research Group, founded by Professor Jerome Bruner and supported by the Social Science Research Council. We, the authors, led a team of more than a dozen teachers, playgroup supervisors, and researchers all looking into preschool practice. Though some worked officially for the Research Group, most continued in regular employment while contributing time and intuitions for the sole reward of satisfying their curiosity about children. For more than a year our research team observed in preschools, talked with staff members, and argued amongst ourselves. By this process we designed a research tool satisfying two criteria; it met the scientific standards of the psychologists, and yet was uncomplicated and practical enough for a modified version to be used by practitioners for their own consumption in everyday settings.

Why then the modesty? After all, the target child method as it became known, has proved a sturdy hybrid, yielding new information about preschools and continuing in use on training courses and in ordinary classrooms. Perhaps we remain cautious, as good scientists should, because we know the causes of children's behaviour to be complex, and to include nutrition, intelligence, temperament, home background and neighbourhood, as well as factors within the preschool. Unfortunately, a study on the scale of ours could not cover even these relatively stable factors. Yet there will be temporary ones as well: how a particular child acts on Thursday morning may reflect his mother's bad mood as she dragged him late to school or his own excitement because tomorrow he's getting a puppy. The teacher or playleader often knows some 'historic' biographic detail and sometimes she can guess about the more immediate influences on today's actions. But even the involved and caring staff member cannot always know that John abandons a puzzle in frustration this very minute because a few minutes ago Stephen took the racing car he wanted.

In our study we conducted 240 observations of children (two each of our 120) as they went about normal routine at preschool. We repeated the procedure in Miami. These observations tell us about *some* effects of the preschool environment on children's play. They make a contribution to the jigsaw puzzle of why a particular child acts as he does, but we are well aware of the pieces still unknown.

Another source of modesty is the difficulty of translating general research findings into practice with particular children in specific situations. We make recommendations on the basis of our findings, as this was our original mandate. But we make them knowing that they cannot possibly amount to a guide. We believe our findings and recommendations to have some general applicability to other preschools but the genius in using them lies in knowing which bits fit a given instance. Our work is now done, but the reader must sift, pull apart and assemble pieces afresh.

We view our findings as the basis for further research – not the formal kind we report here but the informal methods practitioners use in evaluating what they currently do and in planning what to do next. Articles in scholarly journals often end with the sentence 'further research needs to be done' and this has become an 'in joke' amongst students as well as the researchers themselves. We end with the same statement, but for us it's a genuine plea. The research we favour should take place in every preschool and follow the age-old canons of exploration and inquiry. First, specify the question. Then make clear the objective procedure for its answer. Finally, collect the information and interpret its meaning in light of the original query. These steps may appear tedious or unnecessarily 'scientific' but they're the only possible guarantee of discovering a truth that runs counter to intuitions or to traditional dogma. Hunches and received wisdom serve well as everyday guides but they quickly acquire halos unless put regularly to the test of objective scrutiny. *Observing Children* in Appendix A is a guide to teachers and play leaders who wish to engage in do-it-yourself research.

This book draws on the research findings of two target child studies to evaluate the intellectual, linguistic, and (to some extent) social benefits of experience in preschools. Before turning to them, however, we look at three strands of previous inquiry into the effects of preschool. They use different methods, stemming partly from different intellectual traditions and partly from different goals. We attempt nothing systematic here by way of review but provide some examples to show how various have been the answers to questions about the value of preschool.

Pioneers in the nursery movement

The founders of this social movement wrote convincingly of the ways that nursery school opened the eyes of young children – kindling curiosity as to how the world works – and also instilled self-respect with each new competence. Early pioneers used no statistical tests to prove their point; there's never a 'control group' mentioned. Instead, their method consisted of painstaking and compassionate observation of how children fared each day, the kinds of play they invented, questions they asked, things they argued over, and skills they developed while exploring the nursery cupboard.

Contemporary inheritors of these traditions continue to look, for example, to Montessori for guidance about materials and learning tasks. And those concerned with the relationship between social inequality and preschool continue to find inspiration in the work of the McMillans.

Perhaps the greatest source of guidance about everyday practice, at least for British teachers, is the work of Susan Isaacs. Her careful records of the Malting House School are classic and still widely read. In them she reports detailed observations on the intricacies of children's interactions with one another, showing a subtle understanding of their thoughts and feelings. Best of all are her observations showing the great help to children's growth of an 'informed' relationship with the adult. *Social Development in Young Children* (1933) reminds even the most vociferous in the 'hands off children' brigade that exploratory behaviour *on its own* will not guarantee the development of concepts. This theme is renewed by Webb (1974) who restates and expands the thesis that conceptual thinking is best nurtured by informed adults talking with children about their self-initiated activities. Webb agrees with Peters (1966) '... Ideas are inert if they are not concretely related to relevant experiences; but experiences themselves are structureless without the differentiation picked out by language.' Contemporary workers pay tribute to Isaacs for her emphasis on the caring adult as gentle tutor helping to give linguistic form to practical experience.

On what authority did Montessori, Rachel McMillan, and Susan Isaacs make their claims? The answer is not simple, for although their methods of investigation hardly meet today's standards of scientific inquiry they attempted objective observation, made careful records and brought them before public scrutiny – the very procedure that 'ought' to be followed in the early stages of scientific investigation. We would like to think that the target child studies continue in this tradition of caring yet sensible observation. We have attempted, however, to make more explicit the nature of the evidence on which we base our claims for the value of nursery school or playgroup. In doing so, we borrow heavily from the natural and social sciences.

Evaluative studies of compensatory preschool education

The second line of inquiry into the effect of preschool is more systematic, scientifically 'respectable' and certainly more expensive! Its best known examples are the evaluative studies of the American Head Start programme, although there are British variants as well in the Educational Priority Areas (Halsey, 1972). Vast nursery programmes were devised, almost overnight, during the late sixties, followed by careful study of their consequences when children entered formal school. At first there was the well publicized failure of children in compensatory preschool programmes to retain their early edge over peers who had not attended nursery school. Most frequently cited were early gains in IQ followed by gradual 'wash out'. (See Barbara Tizard, 1975.) Soon emphasis shifted to the *kind* of programme offered as it became clear that some succeeded while others did not. Preschool experience does 'matter' – but not all of it.

We'll begin with the best known of the longitudinal studies because its results are unequivocal (Weikart, Epstein, Schweinhart and Bond, 1978). From the Introduction:

> The Ypsilanti Perry Preschool Project, examined the impact of preschool attendance on school performance with the goal of reducing school dropout rates and juvenile delinquency. The basic findings from that project after 15 years of longitudinal study of the 123 participating children indicate that (1) experimental-group children significantly out-score control-group children on standardized achievement tests at eighth grade, nine years after the end of the programme; and (2) experimental-group children are significantly less likely to have been retained in grade or placed in special

education programmes throughout their elementary-school years than children in the control group. In addition, an economic analysis of the Perry Project shows that the total cost of the project was more than recovered, primarily from savings which resulted because students with preschool required less costly forms of education as they progressed through elementary school.

Having demonstrated that thoughtful, innovative nurseries could make positive and lasting differences in the lives of children from disadvantage – no surprise to Rachel McMillan – Weikart and his colleagues conducted a kind of study never attempted at Malting House or Deptford. They instituted three nurseries, radically different in orientation but each staffed with experienced and committed teachers. They then randomly assigned young children to the three with the obvious hypothesis that children assigned more or less by lot should act quite differently after two years in given nursery programme. Those who had participated in the Piagetian 'cognitive' programme were expected to score high on intellectual development, those in the concentrated language one (Berreiter and Engelman, 1966) should show higher linguistic scores, and those in the traditional scheme should show evidence of the flowering of the 'whole child'.

But two years on, the results found Weikart surprised. Although at first there were some differences between children from the three programmes, these soon washed out, leaving general gains for all children but none specific to the kind of preschool they had attended. Weikart claims that this study gives 'weight to the idea that the abstractions we call "educational models" are not extrinsically "effective" but become so through the human effort expended in making them real'.

In the absence of information about what the children actually did all the days they went to school, we don't know for certain which kind of programme they experienced. It's a well-known fact that chefs from differing traditions of *haute cuisine* can be indistinguishable in the kitchen. Perhaps the commonsenses of good cookery transcend the formal models. But if this be true, we'll have to make detailed study of who does what, where, and how in the kitchen as well as in the preschool in order to understand what really 'works'.

The Weikart experiments were not unique, and many similar studies were conducted in the U.S. and in Britain (see Smith and James, 1975). Because the Americans have provided the most thorough long-term investigations, their Head Start research will be summarized.

The Consortium for Longitudinal Studies analysed the results of twelve American experiments in preschool intervention. All concentrated on children from low-income families and all were planned from the beginning in a way that enabled careful measurement of the effects of programmes on children's subsequent academic performance. In addition, each documented the nature of the intervention (e.g., home visiting scheme, Montessori curriculum) so that consequences might be matched to prior intervention strategies. The results concerning effectiveness of the twelve programmes can be neatly summarized (Lazar and Darlington, 1979).

(1) Early education significantly reduced the number of children from low-income families assigned to special education classes.

(2) An 'average' effect (across projects) of preschool experience reduced the incidence of grade failure among children from low-income families.

(3) Children who participated in preschool intervention programmes were more likely than control children (children who had no preschool experience but who were similar on factors such as IQ, home background, age, sex, neighbourhood) to meet at the least the minimal standards of their schools.

(4) Children attending preschool did not score higher on IQ tests (beyond age 13) than children who had not but *did* score higher on achievement tests in mathematics.

(5) In the preschool sample, mothers' aspirations for their

children rose relative to the children's own aspirations. Further, children were more likely to give achievement-related reasons for being proud of themselves. Older 'treatment' children rated themselves as better students than their peers with no preschool experience and tended to have more realistic vocational aspirations. The Consortium concludes:

> Considering that these results were found 10–15 years after participating in preschool, they lend some credence to the investigators' early hopes that both performance and attitudes could be changed and the changes would persist.

Most of the studies in this second strand of inquiry suffer a common flaw; they tell us much about the 'official' programme on offer but not much about what the children actually did while participating in it. In other words, the curriculum manuals are explicit as to their methods and goals, but what about the children? Rarely was systematic observation undertaken to see how youngsters themselves took to the shiny new methods. In other words, effectiveness was tested after the fact and we have no way of knowing which part or parts of the programme really 'worked' with the children.

Observational studies of children's behaviour in preschool

The third approach to assessing whether preschool experience matters to children is the one used throughout this book. Instead of exhortation on the basis of anecdote, or condemnation or applause on the basis of testing, observational research is undertaken *in vivo* as children go about their everyday activities at preschool. Like the Head Start research, it is statistical and formal, but unlike it, information is gathered *while children participate* in the programme, a far cry from inferences made afterwards on the basis of tests or school records. (On the other hand, of course, it does not tell us how its 'targets' of investigation will fare as they grow older. It freezes them in time, unless follow-up observations or tests are carried out.)

There are many ways to conduct observational research and a quiet revolution in method has occurred in the last decade, spurred by advances in the science of ethology. Interested in the biological adaptedness of species and the evolution of behaviour, ethologists devised ways of studying individual animals as well as groups – often in the natural habitat. McGrew (1972) and Blurton-Jones (1972) were two of the first to apply ethological methods to the study of children at preschool. McGrew has given us fine-grained detail concerning children's actions on their first day at school, as well as the changes in social behaviour that follow soon thereafter. And, more recently, Roper and Hinde (1978) have looked at patterns of social participation to find, for example, that individual children were consistent across play situations in how much they talked or interacted with others. Studies like these provide a wealth of descriptive detail and some clues about the development of social relationships. They do not, however, explicitly answer the question 'does preschool experience matter?' for their research goals have never been 'educational'.

There have been many observational studies with explicit and practical goals such as 'who thrives in group day care?' (Prescott, Jones, Kritschevesky, Milich and Haselhoef, 1975) or 'should toys be kept on open shelves or stored in cupboards?' (Montes and Risley, 1975). But there have been few observational studies with sufficient boldness – perhaps madness – to investigate how preschool 'matters'. Tizard, Philps and Plewis (1975) observed 109 children, one at a time, and on ten occasions, in order to estimate the intellectual 'level' of their play. Unfortunately, they concluded with sadness that much play, at least in the centres they visited, was brief and very simple. Where are the lively, curious children described by Susan Isaacs? The young child who asked her why his two eyes didn't see two different things? Can the scientific method ever discern a child's thought, curiosity or joy by merely watching him? And, more importantly, can it ever show which people and objects he daily confronts help him to develop skills for intellectual coping?

Enter the target child technique. It has its roots in science, to be sure, but focuses on the child in his routine environment, playing with everyday materials, and talking with daily companions. This method, dressed in both its 'scientific' and 'practical' garb, makes an effort towards objectivity. We admit it tells only half the story: we don't know what target children thought of us as we chased them hither and yon. We don't know for certain what they were feeling, nor their intentions. But children of this age communicate much about their inner thoughts and emotions by overt behaviour. This we could see, record, and later analyse. If total objectivity had been our goal, of course, we would have failed. But luckily we were wiser in defining the ends of our work. By seeking objectivity, we confronted both our own prejudices as well as the limitations of behavioural study. We'll return to this in Chapter 3.

Our methods differ in motivation from those of child study described early in the chapter because the hardy pioneers usually had axes to grind. The target child method, on the other hand, counts its methodological ancestry in ethology while deriving its questions from the field of education. Because of this, our general method is not confined by the need to grind ideological 'axes' or justify expenditures, and allows in some happy instances a fresh eye on children in classroom settings.

We close with cautious optimism. Scientific knowledge about anything so complex as the care and nurture of the young will never achieve the sudden breakthrough we've now grown to expect in medicine. And so we must patiently begin with intuitions, turn them into formal hypotheses, then devise ways of testing them. No study, by itself, will answer the question about the effects of preschool. But many, drawn together and sifted through, form a picture of the reasons children thrive in preschool, the circumstances that help them most, and the future consequences of their daily diet there.

2

Participatory research, or disrobing science

One of the goals of the Oxford Preschool Research Group was to translate the research findings of psychology so that they could inform the practice of those charged with the care and education of children under five. The budding teacher and new parent often think that psychology, the science of human behaviour, must be a goldmine of useful information. Sadly, if they delve into the journals of psychology they emerge baffled or, even worse, angry.

Americans are not famed for their eloquent use of the English language but occasionally show a flair for journalistic punch. In his presidential address to the American Psychological Association more than a decade ago, George Miller put the question nicely: WHY CAN'T WE GIVE PSYCHOLOGY AWAY? Presidents before him had crept softly 'round the issue of relevance to practical matters'. They occasionally exhorted their psychological colleagues to 'turn the findings of psychology to problems of social need'. Or, if they were applying for research funds, proudly announced that 'education and child care look to psychology for theoretical and empirical support'. But is this so? It seems to us that the genius of George Miller's phrase was that it let the cat out of the bag. No one wanted the gift.

But why? Perhaps because psychologists have for decades plied their tight little trade in laboratories. Children were studied one at a time, usually for less than an hour, then dismissed. The typical experiment in developmental psychology consisted of the following elements: one child carefully removed from home or classroom, a highly trained adult who lavished full attention on the experimental 'subject', and a specially designed and unfamiliar task, often requiring the child to negotiate a host of puzzles, problems, or other mental conundrums. Perhaps one of the reasons that teachers find the Piagetian research puzzling is that it too often traffics in what we call the 'stripped down, bloodless experiment'. The Piagetians' pursuit of the formal properties of thought have led them to focus narrowly on a small set of tasks with little meaning to the child. In *Children's Minds* (1978) Donaldson argues convincingly that children's failure at Piagetian tasks may often be attributed not to the child's ignorance but to the way the experimenter frames the instructions, chooses the materials, or interprets the answers. One reason that teachers do not take home psychology books when planning tomorrow's programme may be that its results often run counter to their classroom experience.

As example of such discrepancy, Donaldson takes a hard look at the psychological literature on egocentrism and its opposite, decentration – the ability to take into account somebody else's point of view. This means quite literally recognizing that someone looking at the same thing as oneself but from another angle sees something different. Piaget claims that before the age of eight or nine children cannot 'decentre', but this claim is refuted daily in the preschool as observant teachers will readily testify.

The difference between what teachers and researchers see may be explained by the fact that young children are pretty fair solvers of problems that take humans and human events as the object of knowledge rather than physical facts or logico-mathematical reasoning. Donaldson documents this point by comparing studies by Piaget and Inhelder (1956) with those by Hughes (1977). In his now classic experiment, Piaget places before the child a three-dimensional model of three mountains. He then places a doll across the table from the child and on the other side of the mountains, inquiring 'what does the doll see?' When asked to draw a picture in response, children under the age of six or seven often draw the mountains exactly as *they* view them. Responses such as this are the basis of Piaget's claim that children 'really imagine that the doll's perspective is the same as their own'. Further, it is argued that this experiment shows the child's inability to 'see his own momentary viewpoint as one of a set of possible viewpoints and to coordinate these viewpoints into a coherent system' (Donaldson, p. 20).

Consider now the Hughes version of the experiment on varying viewpoints. He replaced the mountains with a wall-like barrier and the two original 'viewers' (child and doll) by *two* dolls, a policeman, and a young boy. There are several steps in the experiment but one of them is for the child to 'hide' the boy so that the policeman cannot see him. Even three-year-olds are able to take into account the policeman's point of view and so safely hide the boy doll behind a wall. Further, they can succeed at such hiding no matter where they, the child, stand in relation to the two dolls.

Notice that the policeman-and-boy task is one likely to make sense to children. We hope that not many of them have hidden from constables but know that *all* of them have hidden from someone. Although the Hughes task is not as difficult as Piaget's mountain one because the child is asked to *use* information rather than *reproduce* it, his results put a large dent in Piagetian theory and remind psychologists that they cannot confine investigation of children's thought to experiments with little meaning to children nor connection to their understandings about human intentions and events in the everyday world.

There is yet another reason why psychology has been little help to the practitioner and this is due to one of its favourite methods of research. Jack Tizard, in a Presidential address to the British Psychological Society (1976) concluded that the discipline failed to have significant impact on social policy in part due to its devotion to the 'epidemiological model' of inquiry. First of all, what is that? An index case of dysfunction is located, say a patient with a chronic ailment, and he is matched to a 'control' case who does not suffer from the same complaint but who is similar to the diseased man in other ways, such as sex, age, or occupation. Now imagine that most, or even all, of the index cases were discovered to have had a rare childhood disease, whereas the controls did not. The conclusion usually drawn is that the chronic complaint seen in the adult is the consequence of the childhood illness which, although cured, left an organic weakness.

The epidemiological model has been a great boon in medicine and was borrowed wholesale by psychology. A typical investigation reported by Professor Tizard is the use of the index and control design to examine the causes of psychological dysfunction. He takes the case of absconding from an approved school. Psychologists have spent much time discovering the 'personality structure' of those who abscond and those who don't. It's easy to design the study: first, find some index cases – the absconders – and then match them to children in an approved school who stay put. After controlling for age, sex, IQ, and school, the researcher is left with rather modest differences between absconders or non-absconders on tests of personality.

What conclusions can be drawn from this kind of exercise? First of all, that the cause of the observed dysfunction lies within the individual, and second, that there is very little the institution can do except discover the incipient index cases, those we might claim to be incubating dysfunctional behaviour, and be alert to the next runaway.

The central problem with this design, and it is still in wide use, is that matching in this way (locating control cases who are alike on a variety of variables) takes out of account the effects of those dimensions that form the basis for matching. Going back to the case of school absconding, if we had located three absconders from school A, two from B, four from C, and so forth, suitable control cases would have been found in equal numbers from the very same schools. Suppose that schools A and B are excellent, whereas C and D are shocking. If we transferred the entire population of A to C, there might well have been even more absconding but there is no way our original design could tell us this. And, Clarke and Martin (1975) do tell us that the rates for absconding are up to six times higher in some approved schools than in others where all serve pretty much the same kind of population and community.

The case may be extrapolated to preschool. Suppose a psychologist is interested in children who fail to thrive at school. He locates index cases, matches them with suitable controls from the same schools, then studies family records to conclude that the failure to thrive is the consequence of a lack in early mother-infant bonding. Perhaps some of the preschools attended by the children do a fine job of helping them to concentrate, share with their mates, and so on, while others exacerbate their problems. Such a fact, if it were true, would never emerge from the study because the school, as a contributing factor, has been controlled by the matching.

In sum, then, the manner in which a psychologist poses his question, and the data he collects, determine the range of his answers. One favourite research technique can tell us about traits inherent in the individual suffering 'dysfunction' but little about the influence of factors associated with the matching – often the factors in the immediate environment. But these ones are perhaps the most interesting because they are the ones that practitioners can actually alter.

Luckily, this brand of myopia is getting cured. Michael Rutter and colleagues in *Fifteen Thousand Hours* (1979) take as their unit of analysis the *school* itself and look directly at it, its effect on all manner of pupils and not just troublesome ones. And the cheering finding that emerges from that study is the fact that the positive characteristics of secondary schools can have a beneficial effect on their pupils, despite old buildings, neighbourhoods with high crime rates, and pupils from families with histories of adversity.

Our study did not focus directly on the organization of preschool, but looked instead at the *interaction* between children and what was on offer there. We looked at the situational factors that helped children – all children – to thrive there.

Pausing a moment both to review the thesis so far and to look ahead, we argue that there are at least two methodological reasons why it is difficult to give psychology away to teachers of young children. First, the failure of the index-matched control design to take account of the effect of the immediate environment, and the failure of the stripped down, bloodless experiment to take into account the child's everyday experiences.

A third reason gets closer to the heart of the matter, and that is the huge chasm between what works for the individual child and what *can work* in the normal group situation. This obvious point need not be laboured here, but any 'suggestions' from science that dictate an adult to every child, quiet throughout the day, or expensive materials, will be the butt of practitioners' ironic laughter.

We have gone to great pains to show why psychological science, in its disinterested way, has not had a great impact on preschool practice. Teacher training pays it lip-service but in day-to-day planning the typical practitioner has had little recourse to its findings. We do not argue that they are irrelevant, for we've learned much about the development of thought, language, and even friendship. What we *do* argue is that the ties between psychology and teaching practice have been tenuous and fragile. The teacher, if intrepid, dips into the literature in hopes of finding something useful. The gold is indeed there but the research has been designed with disinterested questions in mind. Studies are geared towards 'finding out', in the purest sense, not towards answering questions of interest to persons responsible for care.

The Preschool Research Group tried valiantly to work in a different scientific style. It certainly didn't wholly succeed, and its veterans sport their scars, but it struggled to carry out 'participatory research' where the collaboration between the seekers and consumers of information made the distinction irrelevant to daily work and the research process a joint enterprise. In this collaborative work, the investigation is a joint venture between researchers (people with academic credentials in formal science) and practitioners (people with skills in a real-world domain such as education or social work). It takes two forms, roughly characterized by different balances of power. The less radical form, called here Model 1, is usually conducted by a interdisciplinary team consisting of people from both camps. The opinions of the practitioners are taken seriously and they prepare reports on practice as well as liaise with institutions such as schools or hospitals. But because research is a highly skilled enterprise that is financially dependent on outside bodies with rigorous – often traditional – views of science, decisions concerning the research are firmly in the hands of the scientists.

Model 2, usually smaller and more local, puts the shoe on the other foot where decisions are concerned. In this model, practitioners decide on goals, confer on methods with researchers and decide for which audience the research is geared. Model 2 is far less common and anyone wishing to attempt it usually encounters stony silence when seeking financial support. Why? Perhaps because its effectiveness is more difficult to evaluate. This does not mean that the work performed by those following the second model is not worthwhile, only that the *products* of their research often do not conform to traditional criteria for evaluation.

The Oxford Preschool Research Group, of which the target child team was but one part, experimented with a variety of means for establishing joint research ventures between academics and practitioners. Jerome Bruner discusses in *Under Five in Britain* (1980) how each of them fared. He documents where they failed, and why, as well as their partial success.

The target child project, oddly enough, was both Model 1 and 2. When the goal was formal research into the effect of preschool, it operated according to the Model 1. When choosing which statistical tests to apply, it's unwise to ask the opinion of a playgroup supervisor – unless she is a rare specimen of her species. Conversely, when experimenting with ways to use child-observations more effectively in the playgroup or classroom, the opinion of the scientist is not the first to be sought.

Although most of the material in this book emanates from the team when wearing its Model 1 hat, the observational guides intended for practitioners (and written by the Model 2 team) appear in Appendices A and B. The great fun in the entire project was that all of us – psychologists, teacher-educators, teachers, and playgroup workers – attended the same meetings and sat in the same chairs each week. Our research 'hats' influenced discussions and lent humour to the serious work, but they rarely interfered with the agenda of the day. In fact, the frequent role-swap probably served to sharpen our minds and forced us to articulate our differing use of language.

We hope that our status as both a Model 1 and 2 participatory team makes our findings useful to people who work each day with children. Our methods, adapted originally from ethology, had to be tailored to preschool settings.

The questions we asked were surely alive in the minds of teachers and playgroup workers for most of them came from these very sources. But the tools used in analysing the data and our interpretations of numerical patterns are the legacy of formal science. We hope they are not so 'hard' as to obliterate the lively human beings they represent.

Wood and Harris (1977) describe two ways, amongst many, in which research findings, no matter how sensibly drawn, are bound to disappoint the practitioner. First many seem commonsensical. 'We knew that all along.' This is often true. In fact, one would heartily distrust a science whose findings were always at odds with practical experience. We ask of science only that it occasionally surprises us and makes us scrutinize commonsense truth. The problem with commonsenses is that they are sometimes incompatible and rarely put to test.

The second reason that Wood and Harris believe practitioners to resist research findings is that it, perforce, deals in statistical probability. 'Children of certain characteristics usually respond in a definite way when under the sway of Factor X'. Statements such as this, even if they are based on a firm statistical likelihood, can never make an exact prediction about Jessie, the girl who causes trouble every day. But they do provide clues for further investigation, and armed with the findings from Oxford and Miami, as well as the guides in the appendices, preschool research can now 'go local'.

3

The target child study in Oxfordshire

What did we study, and how?

The Preschool Research Group set out at first to study concentration, by which we mean focusing one's attention on some act or thing in a sustained way. A child may concentrate on his own actions, those of others, or objects and events around him. Concentration has two components: one ability to sustain attention, and the other the capacity for commitment to one's actions. In practice, it is easier to design measures of the first component, but there are objective signs of the second as well.

Why concentration? For several reasons. First, because most people concerned with the care and education of the under-fives would agree on its value. No matter what views they took on self-expression, discipline, 'hot house' teaching or the like, few would disagree that by five a child ought to control his attention such that he can pursue plans of his own choosing and even those set for him by others. Secondly, we were keen to focus on an area where any advances we might make could be turned to practical benefit. Though everyone might believe in promoting concentration, the same could not be said of for instance promoting sterotypical sex differences!

Our first clearly defined research goal concerned factors in the preschool that encouraged or hindered concentration in young children. We wished to explore materials, events and interactions that were most often associated with periods of sustained attention to some action or event that earned the child's respect. This did not mean that we viewed concentration as the single most important issue at preschool, nor even that we valued cognitive skills at the expense of social or emotional ones. But we had to begin somewhere and concentration provided an excellent starting point for a study of the effect of preschool on children's development.

Psychologists before us had studied it. There are laboratory studies that look at perseverance in mechanical problem-solving (Sylva, 1976) as well as block-building (Wood, Bruner and Ross, 1976). Although interested in children's attention to formal tests of skill, we were also keen to study their concentration during more relaxed activities such as water play or chat. Thus it was clear from the very beginning that we would have to conduct our studies in the nursery and playgroup setting itself if we wished to discover what aided or hindered concentration in the child's everyday surroundings.

The kinds of question one can ask, and the nature of their answers, are to a large measure determined by how one goes about sampling and interpreting behaviour (Tizard, 1975). Having rejected an experimental approach, we turned towards observational methods. Richards (1974) has pointed out that one of the strong suits, or at least one of the passions, of British psychology has been an ethological approach to the study of child development. Because of this, we were able to seek the advice of nearby researchers experienced in observational studies of preschool children. The methods we were later to design owe much to discussions with Corinne Hutt at Keele, Judy Dunn at Cambridge, and Barbara Tizard in the Thomas Coram Research Unit.

To begin, we visited nursery schools and playgroups, experimenting with a variety of ways of recording children's concentration. We considered the use of video cameras and recorders, but quickly rejected them. Our goal from the very beginning was to develop a research tool that could be used by teachers and play leaders in their own settings. The expense of video equipment, coupled with the need for time-consuming analysis of the tapes, made it an unlikely classroom tool. Indeed, we finally concluded that the 'tunnel vision' of the video camera made it too bulky a recording device for the busy preschool no matter what the constraints of time and money. This is examined in detail in Chapter 10 where we discuss inter-observer reliability.

After the brief flirtation with video recording, we found ourselves relying on the intelligent observer and her pencil. But is it more fruitful to observe one child at a time or to scan an entire group? Should one rely on check-lists, or make running notes instead? Is it better to observe continuously or to sample from time to time? And how long is 'long enough' for a single observation?

After months of study and experiment, we decided to adapt to our purposes the 'focal animal' technique originally developed by ethologists (Altmann, 1974). Concerned with the evolution of behaviour they sought precise information on the ways that animals adapt to the environment. Although ultimately interested in the behaviour of *classes* of animals, for instance young infants or mature males, they first had to amass quantities of information about individuals.

Who has not been touched by descriptions of the chimpanzee mother, 'Flo', provided for us by Jane van Lawick Goodall (1968, 1975)? Using detailed records on individuals such as Flo, Figan and Flint, primatologists have revealed enormous individual variety in chimpanzee behaviour. Figure 3.1 shows how much six chimpanzee mothers played with their infants. It tells us that chimps vary in how they relate to one another – no surprise! For instance, Mandy does not appear to play with young Jane nearly so much as does Flo with her children.

Figure 3.1 tells us more than how individual pairs get on with one another. It suggests that there is a peak in mother-infant play when the infant is between three and six months old. After this peak, there is a slow but steady decline.

Six chimpanzee mothers cannot tell a conclusive story about anything. But how many pairs does one need to draw conclusions about mother-infant play?

How typical were Flo and Olly and Marina in terms of other chimpanzee traits? The focal animal method, following one animal through time and across many different routine situations, yields a profile of *individuals*. When added one to

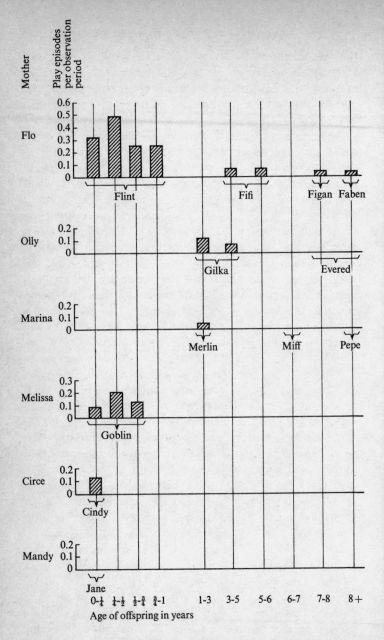

Figure 3.1 *Changes in frequency of chimpanzee maternal play in relation to the age of the offspring*

the other, we get a description of the typical behaviour of a class of animal: how they feed, defend themselves, communicate, and the like. Exceptions there are, and individual style persists even in the lower orders, but the composite picture it affords tells much about a species 'behaviour-in-general'.

It can be seen that this brief look at chimpanzee play raises questions about observational method that will concern us throughout this book. We summarize by saying that the focal animal method collects information from observing individuals in the natural environment. Furthermore, the wealth of data is subsequently categorized in ways that enable general statements such as 'Animals in category X usually act in ways described as Y when in an environment with Z characteristics.' A human translation of this might be 'boys between the ages of four and five years usually concentrate for long periods of time when at the nursery school woodwork bench'.

On location

Our first problem in the preschool was *how much* to record, as well as *which kinds* of things. Researchers have noted scores of different actions: sounds, hand movements, glances and postures. We couldn't capture all behaviour in handwritten notes so had to decide on just a few. After much experiment, we decided on

> The child's task, be it art, or story-listening, or watching others
> With whom he was doing it
> What he was saying and what was said to him
> What materials he used
> What 'programme' was in force at the time of observation; for example, was it free play or group story
> Whether there were signs of commitment or challenge, such as pursed lips or intent gaze

Because our records were made in natural language, they

were not limited to a set of preselected categories of behaviour. Although certain actions and events were systematically noted, as in the list above, observers were free to add anything that seemed important to the child's plans, or the way he carried them out. Thus if the 'target child' (our name for the ethologists 'focal animal') made dough pies while sitting next to another child we noted the dough and the child nearby. But if the child under scrutiny glanced regularly at his mate, absent-mindedly patting the dough while intently observing the other child, we noted details of his visual attention. Thus, an observer might make different notes on two children shaping identical mounds of dough.

Child A	*Child B*
Pats dough into five round shapes. Sits next to Gillian.	Pats dough into five round shapes. Does not look at it. Glances frequently at Pamela (next to her) and at Pamela's dough.

We observed for 20 minutes at a time. After experimenting with both longer and shorter periods, we settled on 20 minutes as long enough to capture most spells of involved play yet not so long as to exhaust the observer. But in practice, observers watched their targets a little longer, beginning several minutes before the formal start in order to make sense of the initial activity, and continuing after the formal end as long as necessary to understand where the child was 'heading' at the close of the observation period.

Although the method we designed is straightforward and can, in principle, be attempted by any classroom teacher, it takes weeks of practice to sharpen concentration and develop the capacity to summarize complex scenes in a few telling words. As a matter of fact, the three observers who gathered the data for the Oxfordshire study soon developed idiosyncratic shorthand for commonplace actions. Knowledge of the kinds of analyses to be performed afterwards also aided in the decision as to what to record, but this takes us ahead in the chapter.

The observer added notes to the bottom of the sheets concerning weather, information from staff members about previous activities, or events occurring at a distance from where the target child played, and, having completed the timed record plus extra notes, left the preschool to analyse the behavioural record.

We were surprised at how much the written record could catch of the child's actions. The human ear proved adept at filtering out irrelevant conversations while focusing on the (often) barely audible speech of the target child himself. We sharpened our peripheral vision so that we could move aside adroitly if another child careered into us on his tricycle, still making notes while executing the defensive manoeuvre.

There follows a sample record taken from our Oxfordshire study. The target child is referred to throughout as TC. Other abbreviations include C for another child, S for staff member, and → for an utterance addressed towards the person at the right of the arrow.

Minute	Activity record	Language record
11.0	Goes over to watch s selling cakes. Yawns, looks at home corner, runs back to join 2 cs on steps.	
11.5	Puts hat on. Makes 'fire engine' noises.	TC → CS (about hats) TC + CS: 'Dor dor dor dor.' TC → C: 'What's here?'
12.0	TC with 2 cs on steps	C → TC: 'Here's mine.' (showing a toy)
12.5	Talking and moving with the 2 cs, playing on steps.	S → CS: 'What have you there?' TC → S: 'Fire engine.'
13.0	Places large cardboard box beside steps, throws hat off. Steps carefully from top of steps onto cardboard box.	TC → C: 'Step on it.' C → TC 'I want to come down.' hollow box

13.5	Goes up steps and climbs down onto cardboard box again. Crawls in hollow area under steps with c.	TC → C: 'Can I come in?' C → TC: 'Yes.'
14.0	Then gets out and allows other c to go in hollow. c pushes box away.	TC → C: 'Shall I do it for you?' TC → C: 'Don't do it.' C → TC: 'It wasn't me, it was Simon.' TC → C: 'Stop it.'
14.5	Leans over edge from top of steps. cs below push box away, then back. TC climbs carefully and gingerly from top of steps onto box.	TC → C: 'Stop it Simon.' TC → C 'If you do it . . . I'm going down – don't push will you.' C → TC: 'No.'
15.0	Fetches large egg-box carton. Places it below steps. Goes up stairs and climbs down into carton.	TC → C: 'I'm going up stairs.' TC → C: 'I'm going up stairs.'
15.5	c gets in carton. TC pushes him in, then watches.	TC → C: 'Shall I do it for you?'
16.0	Takes another box from other 2 cs. Watches 3 cs with boxes.	C → TC: 'Get another box.' TC → CS: 'We need that box.'
16.5	Leaves, goes to nearby playplax on table (2 cs). Places one ring on another, then examines other pieces of construction material and tries to fit them together.	
17.0	Works with construction kit. (1 other c)	
17.5	Runs down room to fetch woodwork (which he made earlier – he has seen s setting up woodwork bench).	
18.0	Holds his woodwork (complicated – several pieces nailed together). cs bring big cartons near woodwork bench.	TC → CS (about boxes)

18.5	Picks up and holds saw. Tentatively starts to saw cardboard box – stops. (s and 3 cs fixing up bench.)	
19.0	Holds wood over vice. Unscrews vice, wood slides in, then tightens vice.	
19.5	Saws top of block, which wobbles badly. c watches him and wobbling wood.	TC → C: 'Falls off.' (about woodwork)
20.0	Holds onto vice and stretches arm to reach something (without letting go of vice). c tries to get vice.	TC → C: 'No!' s → TC + c: 'Only two at a time on the bench.'
20.5	Hammers nail into top of his woodwork (held in vice). Watches 2 others.	

Coding the records

Hundreds of records such as these, fascinating in detail and filled with personal style, baffle the serious student. Which ones are 'important'? Which typical? And how to summarize all of them? In order to make comparisons across children, situations or time, some detail must be ignored and some framework applied that highlights the essential. For example, the raw records often provide splendid detail about the way a particular child held a hammer at the woodwork table. In addition, the observer often drew pictures showing the final construction. But if we were to treat tapping nails with a hammer, screwing down a vice, making a tower out of lego, and countless other constructional activities, as separate events it would be impossible to make generalizations about 'five-year-old boys' or 'children working in pairs'. Once we group together the several kinds of constructional activity, we can investigate the kinds of children (say, older boys) who perform it and the kinds of talk (say, one-off utterances) that accompany it. Working closely with teachers and play leaders, we developed a network of categories of behaviour that enabled us to group together instances of uniquely different play on the basis of some essential characteristic that they shared.

However, before trying to categorize the behaviour of children, we had to break the observations into manageable chunks of time. After much discussion, we decided that the half-minute time interval our observers found so comfortable would serve as the fundamental building block of the study. Decisions as to what was essential about a particular bit of play or social interaction are made for 30 seconds at a time.

Returning to the sample record on pages 25–7, it can be seen that the interval between the second half minute (Minute 11.5) and the end of the second minute (Minute 12.5) was devoted to *pretend*. It concerns fire engines and fireman's hats but its essence is the transformation of reality. As such, it is similar to other play episodes where one thing is made to stand for another. Page 29 shows how the half minutes of an observation are categorized according to their essential activity.

And further in the record, three and a half minutes are devoted to a category called small scale construction. (Note that large scale construction requires child-sized units such as packing crates or large wooden planks.)

The activity categories are but one type of analytical coding. We had four major categorical systems, discussed separately below. The first three use what we've called earlier the 'half-minute building block'; the fourth ignores it in the interest of thematic continuity.

Action codes

This set of categories, discussed above, concern the child's actions. It includes traditional nursery activities such as pretend, manipulation, or gross motor play. It also includes

Minute	Activity record	Language	Activity category
11.5	Puts hat on. Makes 'fire engine' noises.	TC → CS (about hats) TC + CS: 'Dor dor dor dor.' TC → C: 'What's here?'	Pretend
12.0	TC with 2 CS on steps	C → TC: 'Here's mine.' (showing a toy)	Pretend
12.5	Talking and moving with the 2 CS, playing on steps	S → CS: 'What have you there?' TC → S: 'Fire engine.'	Pretend

Minute	Activity	Language	Activity category
17.5	Runs down room to fetch woodwork (which he has made earlier – he has seen s setting up woodwork bench).		Small scale construction
18.0	Holds his woodwork (complicated – several pieces nailed together). cs bring big cartons near woodwork bench.	TC → cs (about boxes)	Small scale construction
18.5	Picks up and holds saw. Tentatively starts to saw cardboard box – stops. (s and 3 cs fixing up bench.)		Small scale construction
19.0	Holds wood over vice. Unscrews vice, wood slides in, then tightens vice.		Small scale construction
19.5	Saws top of block, which wobbles badly. c watches him and wobbling wood.	TC → c: 'Falls off.' (about woodwork)	Small scale construction
20.0	Holds onto vice and stretches arm to reach something (without letting go of vice). c tries to get vice.	TC → c: 'No!' s → TC + c: 'Only two at a time on the bench.'	Small scale construction
20.5	Hammers nail into top of his woodwork (held in vice). Watches 2 others.		Small scale construction

more domestic activities such as eating, tidying, washing or dressing. Lastly, some of these categories are 'inactive' or empty, such as waiting, watching, or 'cruising' about.

The main activity occasionally contained a short interval of something else inside it. For example, a child might stop painting for ten seconds to tie his shoe lace. Or, he might cease climbing on a frame to answer a question put to him by a passing mother. If the 'break' was less than 15 seconds, we ignored it in the primary coding but noted its content elsewhere as an 'embedded activity'.

Sometimes a child engaged simultaneously in different tasks. We then decided rather arbitrarily that his primary activity was the one with more cognitive challenge, and called the descant behaviour an 'embedded' activity. Because our initial research goal was concentration, we were keen to document activities rich in intellectual challenge. Therefore, a child who hummed a song to herself while completing a difficult jigsaw was coded as engaging *primarily* in complex manipulation; we called the song a subsidiary embedding.

A full list of *activity* codes follows, along with the proportion of total time they occupied in the sample. These categories were the ones used in the Oxfordshire (240 observations) study, and are slightly different from the ones practitioners use when conducting their own target child research. The abbreviated list of activity categories appears in *Observing Children* in Appendix A.

1 *Gross motor play* (9·8 per cent of sample, most common in group play): active movement requiring coordination of larger muscles – such as running or climbing

2 *Large scale construction* (0·9 per cent, group): arranging and building dens, trains, and so on, with large crates or blocks

3 *Small scale construction* (4·3 per cent, parallel): using table-top construction materials such as lego bricks and meccano, or hammering and nailing

4 *Art* (8·3 per cent, parallel): 'free expression' creative activities such as painting, drawing, cutting, sticking

5 *Manipulation* (12·0 per cent, pair): mastering or refining manual skills requiring coordination of small muscles (like hand/arm) and the senses, as in handling sand, dough, clay or water. Also sewing, gardening, arranging, sorting or handling objects

6 *Structured materials* (4·5 per cent, parallel): the use of materials with design constraints, such as jigsaw puzzles, peg-boards, templates, picture- or shape-matching materials, counting boards, shape-posting boxes, bead-threading, sewing cards; or board games such as dominoes, picture lotto, snakes and ladders

7 *Pretend* (10·4 per cent, group): transformation of everyday objects, people or events so that their meaning took precedence over reality

8 *Scale-version toys* (2·3 per cent, pair): arranging miniature objects such as dolls' houses, farms, zoo or fort sets, or transport toys including train tracks. This category did not include the use of larger representational toys such as prams, dolls or dishes. When miniature objects were used as props, we categorized the play as *pretend*

9 *Music* (0·3 per cent, parallel): attentive listening to sounds, rhythms or music; playing instruments, singing solos, dancing to music

10 *Informal games* (3·1 per cent, group): a play situation, with or without language, where the child was playing in an informal game with one or more others. These were spontaneously and loosely organized; following one another around while chanting, hiding in a corner and giggling, or holding hands and jumping were all examples

11 *Social play with spontaneous rules* (0·8 per cent, group): spontaneous play with others, not at a traditional game but where there was some structure or set of rules. The structure was invented on the spot by the child and often included turn-taking

12 *Non-playful interaction* (7·0 per cent, pair): social

interaction, verbal or physical, with a child or adult, such as borrowing, seeking or giving help or information, aggressive behaviour (not play-fighting), teasing, being cuddled, or comforting. (Note that *non-playful interaction* was used only when the child was not engaged in another task code category; if he was doing a puzzle while chatting to a friend, that was coded as *structured materials*)

13 *Three Rs activities* (0·6 per cent, parallel): careful, genuine attempts at reading, writing or counting

14 *Examination* (1·5 per cent, pair): careful examination of an object or material; for instance, looking through a magnifying glass. This category included attentive looking at books. It differed from *manipulation* in that the looking, smelling or tasting were more important than the handling

15 *Problem solving* (0·2 per cent, pair): the child solved a problem in a purposeful way using logical reasoning; for example, he looked to see why something wouldn't work and then repaired it

16 *Adult-directed art and manipulation skills* (0·6 per cent, pair): mastering and refining skills and techniques under adult direction and sometimes with an adult-determined end-product, such as tracing or directed collage. The emphasis was on learning or improving skills

17 *Rough-and-tumble* (1·3 per cent, pair): informal, spontaneous play involving body movement in social interaction, as in play-fighting, chasing and catching, or jostling in a mob

18 *Organized games with rules* (0·1 per cent, group): formal games involving body movement (not board games, which are *structured materials*), with structure and rules not spontaneously invented but dictated by an adult or by tradition. It included formal skipping, ball games, circle games, skittles and hopscotch

19 *Adult-led group activities* (7·7 per cent, parallel): a

large group of children under the leadership of an adult listened to stories, rhymes or finger-plays, watched television, or watched a planned demonstration (such as nature table, making popcorn). The children were always 'parallel', either passively absorbing (for instance a story) or active but in unison (as in singing or music-and-movement)

20 *Watching staff* (4·0 per cent, parallel): watching or listening to an adult or adult-directed activity

21 *Watching peers* (2·9 per cent, parallel): watching or listening to another child or group of children

22 *Watching events* (2·5 per cent, parallel): looking around in general, or watching something specific; for example scanning the room or casually looking at a picture without attentively examining it

23 *Waiting* (1·4 per cent, parallel): inactively waiting for someone or something specific

24 *Purposeful movement* (3·0 per cent, solitary): movement directly towards an object, person or place; for instance going outdoors, crossing the room to another activity, or searching for a dropped object

25 *Cruising* (2·0 per cent, solitary): active movement around from one thing to another, or purposeful looking around and apparent searching for something to do

26 *Aimless standing around, wandering or gazing* (1·0 per cent, solitary): not actively engaged in a task or watching a specific event, nor moving purposefully, but rather 'vacant'

27 *Individual physical needs* (2·8 per cent, solitary): attending to some private bodily need, such as toilet, washing, dressing, nose-blowing. This category did not include routine activities that were part of the group's programme, such as milk-time, even if the individual could choose when or whether to have milk

28 *Group routine* (4·3 per cent, parallel): non-playful

or domestic activities that were part of daily programme, like milk- or snack-time, rest periods,
group tidying up, arrival and departure. This category included tasks assigned to an individual for the
group, such as laying tables, handing out materials,
cleaning or routine assembly of materials in preparation for an activity

29 *Distress* (0·1 per cent, group): seeking comfort or
attention from an adult or other child. The child
must have shown visible signs of distress or made a
visible bid for comfort, by way of for example
prolonged crying, wanton destruction of materials,
or social withdrawal

30 *Other activity* (0·0 per cent, —) other play or
non-play activities not classifiable in the above
categories

Each of these categories could include talk. Even if it
appeared that social interaction was more important to the
child than the task, the appropriate activity code was used
and the social side to the behaviour was picked up elsewhere.
Agreement between observers as to the use of categories was
exceptionally high and is discussed in Chapter 10.

Social codes

In addition to categorizing the activity that each child carried
out in each half-minute unit, we coded the social setting in
which it occurred. We noted whether the child was interacting with others, was near others but not interacting with them,
or was alone. Naturally we differentiated between interaction with peers, members of staff and casual visitors, as well
as parents. In addition, we noted the size of the group, small
or large. It can be seen that the activity code told us what the
child was doing while the social code told us whom he was
doing it with.

Language codes

Again we used a separate coding system to note the target child's language as well as the speech addressed to him. Because our handwritten observations did not allow precise recording of each utterance, we described the child's language in rather broad categories. These included: the number of utterances the target child addressed to others, the number of utterances addressed to him, the status of the speakers and the listeners (adults or other children).

Play bouts

The objective of the three coding schemes discussed so far was to describe with precision the child's moment to moment behaviour. Thus, a child who made a wooden aeroplane was considered to engage in *construction* whereas the same child painting the aeroplane was thought to engage in *art*. Exact categorization such as this allows fine discriminations and tells us when construction ended and painting began. However, it does not do justice to the unity of the activity.

In our fourth coding scheme we looked for longer spells of related activities and called them 'bouts'. The child who first constructed, then painted the aeroplane was considered to engage in a long bout of coherent play. Contrast it with another child who left the milk table and went to the woodwork bench. Here he constructed an aeroplane. Then he left the bench, cruised around the room for a minute, and finally began an easel painting. In the case of this second child there were *separate* bouts for the *construction* and the *art* as they were not part of a unitary theme.

Two more contrasting examples should clarify the difference between a bout of related activities and several different bouts of sequentially organized but not thematically structured activity.

A child climbs up and slides down the slide, goes over to a large barrel and wriggles through it, then goes off to

> climb along a raised plank. All of this sequence involves body movement, but there are three separate themes.

but

> A boy is with two friends playing 'follow-the-leader'. He follows his friends up and down the slide, through a barrel, along a plank. Here there is only one theme, with the different movements tied together by the flow of the follow-the-leader game.

The bout coding allowed us to string together related activities and it also allowed us to include preparations and discussions as part of larger themes. The child who spent several minutes putting on an apron was considered to be engaged in a bout of art that extended from the preparation through the execution and concluded with a discussion of the painting with an adult. Note that in the activity code these half minutes would be assigned to *individual needs* (apron), *art* (painting) and finally *non-playful interaction* (discussion with adult). The two different coding schemes, activity and bout, enabled us to look at separate bits of the behaviour as well as the thematic unity of them.

On page 38 appears a fully coded observation showing activity coding, social coding, language coding, and bout coding. Lines separate the bouts.

In our study, the people who made the observations in preschool were also the ones who coded them afterwards. This has two advantages; first, they coded immediately after observing and still had visual images fresh in their minds as well as recourse to details of setting they had not recorded on the spot. The second advantage is more profound. Formal observation is a far cry from casual watching. No one, even the most innocent, watches with an open mind. All of us select bits of activity as 'interesting' or 'important' and exclude the rest. We are often unaware of the process of selecting and interpreting but it is always with us. The focal animal technique, modified by us and re-christened 'target child', makes explicit the nature of its lenses. Observers cum

Minute	Activity record	Language record	Activity	Social	Bout
1.	TC picks up construction toy and sucks it. Examines plastic spanner (Wearing plastic hat).	C→TC	Manipulation	Solitary	*3 minutes*
	Listens to C and looks at observer. Smiles, waves hat, picks at face.	C→TC (about observer – looking at me through a playplax construction)	Watching events	Child pair	cruising
2.	Takes object out of box of construction toys. Goes off with C.	C→TC TC→C C→TC: 'Play something.'	Manipulation	Child pair	
	Touches birds' nest on nature table. (C goes on looking through playplax telescope!) Stands by group of Cs at book table.	TC→C (about nest)	Cruising	Solitary	
3.	Runs off with C. Returns alone to construction table. Takes plastic screw.	C→TC	Cruising	Solitary	
	Puts it down. Picks out playplax. C returns. TC skips off with C, to book table.	C→TC (about me, observing) 'Let's go …'	Purposeful movement	Child pair	
4.	Sits down at book table. Sucks plastic toy. Looks at book on space.	TC→C (about picture of the moon) C→TC	Examination	Child pair	*½ minute* looks at picture book

	Activity	Language	Waiting	Parallel to small group
	Watches assistant supervisor bringing milk in cups on tray to the table.			*4½ minutes 'buying' cake and snack*
5.	Gets up from table with others. All go to next table where s is sitting with cakes, cash register and tray of toy money.	s→TC + cs: 'Before you have your milk today you have to go to the cake shop and buy your cake.'	Three Rs	Small group with adult
	Watches s talking to c about 'buying' cakes, and waits for his turn.	s→TC + cs (giving them money and explaining about 'buying' their cakes)	Three Rs	Small group with adult
6.	Waits and watches others. TC's turn comes. s gives him money, he 'pays' her and takes a cake.	s→TC (about buying his cake)	Three Rs	Pair with adult
	Returns to milk table with cake and 2p in hand. (Asst. Supervisor and 4 cs at milk table)	s→TC: 'Two pence change.'	Three Rs	Small group with adult
7.	Sits at milk table.	s→TC: 'Is this your cake Darren? How much did it cost you? You don't know?'	Group routine	Pair with adult
	Eats cake, holding 2p in hand at same time.	(s→cs)	Group routine	Parallel to small group; adult near

Minute	Activity record	Language record	Activity	Social	Bout
8.	Eats his cake.		Group routine	Parallel to small group: adult near	
	Gets up, picks up hat. Goes off. Taps c on arm, at construction table. Wanders, turning around slowly.	TC → c: 'Look, I got money.' c → TC: 'Where did you get that?'	Non-playful interaction	Child pair	
9.	Stands at jigsaw table (1c) Wanders off.		Aimless standing etc.	Solitary	*1 minute* wandering
	Wanders around room.		Aimless standing etc.	Solitary	
10.	Picks up telephone receiver. (Telephone in 'pretend' area of 2 sets of steps and carpet).	TC → c (on phone)	Informal games	Child pair	*½ minute* on phone
	Watches c talking to his mother. Wanders off again, slowly crossing room.		Watching events	Solitary	
11.	Goes over to watch s selling cakes. Yawns, looks at home corner, runs back to join 2 cs on steps.		Cruising	Solitary	*1 minute* cruising

	Puts hat on. Makes 'fire engine' noises.	TC→CS (about hats) TC + CS: 'Dor dor dor dor.' TC→C: 'What's here?'	Pretend	Small group	1½ minute 'fire engine'
12.	TC with 2 CS on steps.	C→TC: 'Here's mine.' (showing a toy)	Pretend	Small group
	Talking and moving with the 2 CS, playing on steps.	T→CS: 'What have you there?' TC→T: 'fire engine'	Pretend	Small group
13.	Places large cardboard box beside steps, throws hat off. Steps carefully from top of steps onto cardboard box.	TC→C: 'Step on it.' C→TC: 'I want to come down.' [hollow box]	Gross motor play	Small group	3½ minutes climbing on steps and box
	Goes up steps and climbs down onto cardboard box again. Crawls in hollow area under steps with C.	TC→C: 'Can I come in?' C→TC: 'Yes.'	Gross motor play	Small group
14.	Then gets out and allows other C to go in hollow. C pushes box away.	TC→C: 'Shall I do it for you?' TC→C: 'Don't do it.' C→TC: 'It wasn't me, it was Simon.' TC→C: 'Stop it.'	Gross motor play	Small group
	Leans over edge from top of steps. CS below push box away, then back. TC climbs carefully and gingerly from top of steps onto box.	TC→C: 'Stop it Simon.' TC→C: 'If you do it.... I'm going down – don't push will you.' C→TC: 'No.'	Gross motor	Small group

Minute	Activity record	Language record	Activity	Social	Bout
15.	Fetches large egg-box carton. Places it below steps. Goes up stairs and climbs down into carton.	TC→C: 'I'm going up stairs.' TC→C: 'I'm going up stairs.'	Gross motor play	Small group	
	C gets in carton. TC pushes him in, then watches.	TC→C: 'Shall I do it for you?'	Gross motor play	Small group	
16.	Takes another box from other 2 cs. Watches 3 cs with boxes.	C→TC: 'Get another box.' TC→CS: 'We need that box.'	Large-scale construction	Small group	
	Leaves, goes to nearby playplax on table (2 cs). Places one ring on another, then examines other pieces of construction material and tries to fit them together		Small-scale construction	Small group	*1 minute* playplax construction
17.	Works with construction kit. (1 other c)		Small-scale construction	Child pair	
	Runs down room to fetch woodwork (which he made earlier – he has seen s setting up woodwork bench).		Small-scale	Solitary	*3½ minutes* woodwork

18.	Holds his woodwork (complicated – several pieces nailed together). cs bring big cartons near woodwork bench.	TC → cs (about boxes)	Small-scale construction	Small group
	Picks up and holds saw. Tentatively starts to saw cardboard box – stops. (s and 3 cs fixing up bench.)		Small-scale construction	Small group
19.	Holds wood over vice, Unscrews vice, wood slides in, then tightens vice.		Small-scale construction	Small group
	Saws top of block, which wobbles badly. c watches him and wobbling wood.	TC → c: 'Falls off.' (about woodwork)	Small-scale construction	Child pair
20.	Holds onto vice and stretches arm to reach something (without letting go of vice). c tries to get vice.	TC → c: 'No!' s → TC + c 'Only two at a time on the bench.'	Small-scale construction	Child pair
	Hammers nail into top of his woodwork (held in vice). Watches 2 others.		Small-scale construction	Child pair

coders knew fully the network of categories that were to be applied later to the records. Thus prepared, they sharpened their sights for details of children's actions and attention that would provide firm evidence for saying that a particular child was 'watching another child with active attention' or merely 'aimlessly staring'. And there *are* behavioural clues to this distinction. The former child will shift his position if someone interferes with his line of vision. Indeed if he is listening to the other child, he will often gesture, smile or pause in keeping with the other's talk. The passively staring child takes no notice of junctures in another child's activity.

The coding schemes described were devised initially to study concentration. One of the questions we asked concerned the effect of different activities on how long a child stayed at one thing. After coding the records for activity, it's a simple matter to calculate mean lengths of different behavioural categories. In this way we discovered that art activities capture children's attention for the longest periods.

Other initial queries concerned the role of the adult in prolonging attention. Comparing half-minutes where an adult is present in the social code with those where she is not, we found that adults have a beneficial role in extending concentration – but in some kinds of activities more than in others. While examining the social code, we were able to assess the effect of play with other children on concentration as well.

It took us more than a year to shape and polish the method of observing and coding. While conducting trials in a variety of preschools, we chatted with staff about the research. We met regularly with teachers and play leaders, sharing our methods when people were interested and encouraging them to conduct their own observations. From this year of collaboration, we learned that our original research questions focused too rigidly on concentration. Having devised a research tool sensitive to many factors in the preschool day, we were getting poor value for money in breadth of our results. Therefore, we turned to other aspects of behaviour in preschool.

Trial studies convinced us that target child observations could shed light on complexity of play as well as its extent. To this end we added measures of cognitive challenge. The factors that foster it are described in Chapter 4, along with our ways of measuring it.

The sample

We turn now to the children and the preschools where we conducted the formal observations begun after the first year's experimenting was over. At the time of our study, 1976–8, Oxfordshire had 28 state-maintained preschools; exactly half of these were nursery schools and the others were nursery units within larger first schools. Although it is difficult to obtain precise figures for playgroups, which mushroom and disappear more casually, there were about 120 playgroups registered on the Social Services lists, most of which were affiliated with the Pre-school Playgroups Association (PPA).

As usual, research funds were limited and we had only three part-time observers to conduct the formal study. One was a trained teacher, one a playgroup supervisor, and the other a psychologist. We decided to look with equal attention at the three kinds of preschool: nursery school, class, and playgroup. We decided also to divide our attention equally between young children (three and a half to four and a half years) and older ones (four and a half to five and a half).

Age range	Nursery schools ($N = 6$)	Nursery classes ($N = 6$)	Playgroups ($N = 7$)
$4\frac{1}{2} - 5\frac{1}{2}$	20	20	20
$3\frac{1}{2} - 4\frac{1}{2}$	20	20	20

Table 3.1 *The sample summarized (each group was divided evenly between the sexes)*

Were the 19 centres typical of others in the country? We did not choose our centres randomly, as some were eager to collaborate in the study while others remained cool to outside research. Although to some extent the 19 centres in the sample were self-selected, great effort was made to ensure that city, suburb and rural centres were represented within each of the three statutory categories. The final sample included nearly half of the state maintained nurseries in the county but less than a tenth of the registered playgroups. We are satisfied that the state sample is fairly representative of the others in Oxfordshire but admit that our playgroups are probably drawn from amongst the better ones; that is, most had well-established histories and highly trained staff.

Although the centres studied were far from a random sample in the county, the individual children were selected on a random basis. We excluded children with obvious physical handicaps or children who had started at preschool less than one month previously. Having done this, we drew randomly from the registers.

How typical was our sample?

Questions concerning similarity to the rest of the nation are more difficult to answer. Is any county like any other? Oxford has long been proud of its nursery schools. There was not an over-abundance of state provision, and there is even less in 1980, but in general, nursery schools were stimulating places for children. The county also has a resourceful and energetic playgroup network that is up-to-date in training and organization. In sum, the county probably resembled others with a solid, but thin, state programme supplemented by a vigorous voluntary network.

And now analysis.... When still a graduate student, one of us attended a course on computer analysis of behavioural data. During practical class devoted to means of entering numeric data into the computer, the lecturer announced

'After the last number is entered into the machine, push the button labelled PUBLISH RESULTS'. The class laughed politely, little realizing how great is the gap between putting the numbers into the computer and completing analysis of the results. Early findings are often puzzling and seem thin. Were our questions the most important ones? Were the measures appropriate? This chapter has outlined the bare bones of our research questions and methodology. Over the course of the project we enlarged both but these modifications and additions will be discussed in the following chapters where we describe in detail our findings.

With this description of the schools and children we observed, as well as the method used to study them, we turn to results concerning concentration, social skills, language, and intellectual complexity.

4

Complex and simple play

Is all play equally valuable? Everyone knows that play may be rich and imaginative or boring and stereotyped. Parry and Archer (1975), among others, are concerned with this important difference:

> There are two levels of play. One merely keeps children occupied; the other contributes to their educational development. Teachers in nursery schools are concerned with play at the latter level.

Despite warnings to teachers, many researchers (Tizard, Philps and Plewis, 1975; Hutt *et al*., 1977) have found play in the preschool to be more 'occupying' than 'educational'. Is this because teachers and play leaders can't tell the difference? Or because they don't know how to encourage more imaginative and complex play?

In our work in preschools we found teachers and play leaders loath to deprecate the value of any child's play. While they were quick to applaud the creativity or perseverance of an individual, they rarely judged his play as tedious or lacking in sparkle. On the whole, adults who work with children are positive in approach; they lean over backwards to find something of value in each child. If he stands against the garden fence for ten minutes, staring absently around him, they claim he 'is learning by observing'. If he repetitively pats dough into balls, they say that 'the new baby at home is causing him to regress and he needs this simple act'. In other words, all that the child does at preschool (provided it isn't positively anti-social) is construed as valuable and necessary to his development.

Surely this attitude towards children's play is desirable. Formal school looms ahead and there is plenty of scope there for evaluative yardsticks. Most fair-minded people would like the preschool to protect the child from negative judgements and feelings of failure. But it does not follow that evaluations of play ought never to be made. If we refuse to say 'X is better than Y' we cannot systematically encourage X nor indeed investigate its properties.

Objective science has much to offer here. The teacher sees each of her charges as an individual and, naturally, wishes to give all of them the benefit of every doubt. But staff members could be trained to look more closely at children's behaviour, noting examples of stretching, worthwhile play. There is an important distinction between *condemning the child* and *evaluating his play*. In order to nurture a child's growth, the would-be nurturer must make the 'X is better than Y' claim – even if only implicitly. And indeed, staff members who say they identify only the positive are trafficking in sophistry. To cite something as a plus tells us that a yardstick of some kind has been used.

How does one evaluate play?

Having noted that some measures of play are necessary, and indeed are used implicitly, we turn to distinguishing features of play that is worthwhile. Parry and Archer (1975) tell us:

> The difference between the two levels of play is not easy to detect. Play can sometimes look good with the children actively involved, and yet lack the elements which contribute towards educational growth. In assessing the value of play situations, teachers should look for the security of the children within the groups and among known peers, for a continuity of care, interest and involvement from adults sharing the situation, for the appreciation of the importance of progression, extension and challenge for each child, for possibilities of a sense of achievement among the children and for ample time in which to explore a situation thoroughly.

Sadly, their description provides little guidance in deciding whether a definite slice of child's play is of an 'occupying' or an 'educational' kind. It fails to draw clear distinctions between the different kinds of 'stretch'. An example may clarify. Imagine an 'only' child on first entry into playgroup. He is shy with others and unable to make known his wishes or defend himself. He approaches another child, a sturdy confident boy riding a tricycle, and asks for a turn. This brief move in a social interaction hardly appears complex but the planning behind it may have been sophisticated. Even more, it may have taken a week of summoning courage to encounter so dominant a child. On balance, it appears that this half-minute interchange was indeed stretching for the shy newcomer.

But how was he stretched? He conducted a manoeuvre requiring social skill and bravery as well. We can all applaud the newcomer as well as the adults or programme that helped him to achieve the triumph. We can see that a variety of competences were brought into play: cognitive (planning how to make the request), social (making it in a positive, firm way) and emotional (maintaining feeling of confidence in the outcome). It is difficult to untangle three skeins, but in this chapter we try.

Could the observer know for certain whether the request for the tricycle was difficult or easy to make? Probably not. Especially in the case of a newcomer the teacher or play-leader might not recognize signs of effort. A furrowed brow on one child does not signify the same as a frown on another. It is for this sort of reason that most practitioners throw up their hands at the futility of making judgements about what goes on inside the heads of children. Unfortunately, the policy of giving each child the benefit of a doubt means that relatively futile play continues day after day unnoticed and unhelped.

As researchers we were not daunted by the formidable problems of evaluating play. Young children often tell the observer about their thoughts by overt actions. We decided to look directly at cognitive stretch. This does not mean that we discredited the value of emotional and social development, only that we turned the scientific searchlight on one of the three skeins. When social and emotional factors impinged on the child's play, and they did so all the time, we tried to study them as well.

Our point of entry, so to speak, into the child was his intellect. We made this choice for three reasons. First, as cognitive psychologists we felt it was our strong suit. Secondly, it is easier to judge cognitive complexity than emotional state from a child's actions. Lastly, psychologists and practitioners can agree on certain intellectual goals for the preschool whereas it is difficult to agree on which feelings are desirable or even appropriate. We turn now to our means of evaluating the educational quality of children's play.

Many researchers have attempted to classify children's play according to its complexity (Lunzer, 1959; Tizard, Philps and Plewis, 1975). Most of these attempts, either explicitly or implicitly, rely on notions of *differentiated sequence* or *transformation*, and have produced complicated rating scales.

Differentiated sequence

Take the former first. When several actions (including sentences) are strung together such that each one builds upon the one that precedes it, they form a contingent progression. This is in sharp contrast to a sequence of unrelated or repetitive acts. Imagine a child, Peter, who pushes a toy car along a track. Compare this simple act with that of another child, Paul, who carefully lays the track, propels the car along it for a while, then adds a bridge or tunnel before pushing the car again. If the children are the same age, we can state with confidence that the car task was more challenging to Paul than to Peter.

But are we certain? Perhaps Peter was recollecting an earlier conversation while absent-mindedly pushing his car.

It is *possible* that he was engaged in complicated thought in this example but children usually give evidence of this, for instance by talking to themselves, or frowning concentratedly. A child absent-mindedly pushing a car has about him a vacant facial expression and a relaxed posture. What we know for certain is that Peter's *task-oriented* behaviour was simpler than Paul's. In other words, we know for a fact that Paul engaged in long-range planning and organizing of behaviour whereas we are not certain about Peter's mental processes. In our assessment method, we gave 'credit' for behaviour that was apparently complex and remained open about the rest. We did not conclude that Peter's behaviour was simple, only that Paul's was observably complicated.

But recall the Parry and Archer quotation at the start of the chapter. They mention the security of the child in assessing the complexity of play as well as his sense of achievement. These are important, to be sure, but we found them difficult to assess. Perhaps Peter was feeling insecure and this led to rather stereotyped play. Conversely, Paul may have been copying a car-and-track set-up he assembled yesterday and therefore felt very little pride at this, his fifth go-round. But feelings of contentment, safety, or even achievement are difficult to observe. We think that they are important and intuitively believe them to be prerequisites to competent thought. But observable clues to them are elusive. Peter's smile might signal a feeling of security but perhaps not.

So in the end we adopted a strict behavioural definition of cognitive complexity. It is extremely task-related and relies on empirical evidence of contingent sequences of behaviour. We did not second-guess a child's secret feelings nor his secret thoughts. Instead we noted his actions. Thus, we recorded how carefully a child wielded the paintbrush, whether he was resistant to distraction as he concentrated or was quick to fly off to something else. These are behavioural signs of an inner process and we used them in assessing complexity. Primary evidence, however, was in the task-related behaviour itself. We readily admit that some children may have been thinking in complex ways that we could not pick up in our observations.

Transformation

There is another way of conceiving complexity in children's play and this one concerns *transformation* of materials or people. It is seen most often in children's make-believe. This, too is not easy to spot. One object or act is made to represent another. Indeed it is not merely representational, it achieves some functional equivalence as well. This kind of 'double-knowledge' requires complex thinking that treats two substances as though they are alike while at the same time really knowing the difference.

How did we sort the behaviour we had coded?

Thus our theoretical stance towards complex play was double-barrelled; the first definition focusing on the sequential nature of play behaviour and the second on its transformational potential. Unfortunately, when it came to sorting actual behaviour into one camp or the other, we encountered severe difficulties. Theoretical distinctions such as have been discussed do little more to guide the critical observer than those of Parry and Archer. We needed more detailed definitions and turned to experienced practitioners for advice.

We asked them to go into schools and playgroups (not their own) and collect instances of both rich and simple play. With no personal knowledge of the children, none whom they saw as favourites or nemeses, they judged some play as complicated or imaginative, and other as ordinary or dull. These samples included not only art and make-believe, but 'chats' and adult-led activities as well. Together, researchers and preschool staff sat down to analyse the wheat and the chaff. Here are examples drawn from construction play and vehicle riding.

CONSTRUCTION PLAY

High level of challenge

A child is at the lego table. He roots in the box of lego bricks and selects a base plate. He carefully fits bricks onto the base, choosing them from the box. He continues this careful building, looking in the box to find the 'right' bricks, not just using any brick. Although his construction doesn't look like a representation of a real-life object to the adult observer, the child is systematically and purposefully following some plan of his own design.

Ordinary play

The child at the lego table takes apart apart some bricks and scatters them on the table. He builds a 'tower', taking bricks from the table as they come to hand. He stacks bricks one above the other with ease, then takes them apart, builds another tower in the same way. He is engrossed and systematic in his actions, but the activity is routine, repetitive; he doesn't add any new elements or combine ideas, and he is rather 'slapdash'.

VEHICLE RIDING

High level of challenge

A child is riding his tricycle around the playground when suddenly the trike stops moving although he is still pedalling. He pedals for a moment, looking down at the wheels. He dismounts and squats down, examining them. He turns the pedals, touches other parts, looks at them. He sees that the chain has come off and carefully tries to fit it back in place. He is solving a problem; his activity is complex, combining ideas, goal-directed, purposeful, systematic.

Ordinary play

A child grabs a tricycle and pedals round and round the playground. He is clearly adept at cycling, it requires little or no mental effort from him (only physical effort), and he isn't trying to steer the trike around a particular course of obstacles; rather he appears to be simply 'letting off steam'. His activity is routine, repetitive, familiar, and not cognitively complex.

The job of practitioners had been to identify examples of both rich and poor play. It was the task of the Preschool Research staff to see if their intuitive judgements were in keeping with theoretical distinctions just discussed. Luckily the theoretical definitions of complexity stood up to empirical test. Play the observers judged as stretching *was* either sequentially organized and elaborated, or else contained symbolic transformation. Often both, of course. Psychological theory worked well after the fact whereas it had been of little help in making the primary judgements. Why?

The main usefulness of psychology theory was in providing a level of *abstractness* that transcended the peculiarities of diverse activities such as skipping, arguing, being a fireman, and receiving instruction about the use of scissors. But it is very difficult to use abstractness in the opposite direction – as a concrete guide in judging specific instances. We believe we developed a yardstick that combined the intuitions of practitioners with the rather dry definitions of psychology.

We took next the samples provided by teachers and playleaders. Looking at each of the 30 categories listed in Chapter 3 we found that many of them did not easily fall into the complex or ordinary division, often because the child was silent, as for example the watching categories or while listening to a story. Rather than second-guess a child's thoughts when we had no observable evidence, we decided to score cognitive challenge in only 12 categories (the first group on the list in preceding chapter). When we looked hard at examples of both high and low challenge in these 12 categories, we were disappointed to discover no all-encompassing definition of challenge that would fit every behavioural group. Finally, we decided that each category would have to be judged according to independent rules so that, in effect, we devised a large manual that dealt separately with each category that was amenable to subdivision into challenging and ordinary levels. Some samples follow.

CHALLENGING

Manipulation

TC fills a bottle then pours its contents into a cup. He puts a plastic saucer in trough – it floats. TC pours water onto the saucer from the cup and watches it sink. He fills the cup again, sets the saucer to float, pours water onto it this time through a funnel, slowly and carefully, watching intently. He puts the cup in water so that it floats. Again he pours through the funnel to sink the cup. He looks around for other objects – fetches things from other tables and tries them in the water, separating those that float from those that sink.

ORDINARY

TC is at the water trough with other cs. All dabble their hands in the water. TC takes a bottle, holds it under water to fill it, pours it out, fills it and pours it out again. c splashes him, TC splashes back, they all splash. TC fills the bottle and pours it out again, fills a cup and pours that out too.

CHALLENGING

ORDINARY

Small scale construction

TC takes two blocks of wood, large and small. He holds the small block over the large, selects a nail from the tin, and hammers it through, joining the two blocks. He pivots the small block around. He takes another nail: 'I'm going to hammer it so it can't move.' He hammers the nail in but it doesn't go in far enough to pierce the block underneath. He takes that nail out and selects a longer one. He hammers it carefully, and looks as if to see that it's gone right through. He tests to see that the two blocks are now anchored and don't turn. He takes a bottle top and hammers it on top, embedded in the wood.

TC and others are at the woodwork table with wood blocks, hammer, nails, and so on. TC takes a block of wood, hammers a nail into it, banging hard and laughing with the others. He takes another nail and hammers it hard repeatedly. All the CS hammer and make a lot of noise. TC takes a nail out of the wood and hammers it in again.

Structured materials

TC selects a jigsaw from the shelf, looks at it, takes it to a table and empties it out. He looks at the pieces, and fits them together carefully. He looks for the 'right' piece on the table each time. He tries to fit a piece in the wrong place, takes it out and tries another piece which won't fit either. He returns to the first piece and tries it in various places until it fits. He completes the puzzle, and goes to choose another from the shelf.

TC is at the jigsaw table. He empties a jigsaw onto it, takes the pieces and rapidly fits them into place with ease. He empties another jigsaw onto the table, and chews a piece as he watches CS at a neighbouring table. He slaps pieces into the jigsaw, frequently looking up at the nearby CS. He tries to put in a piece upside down; and presses down on it with his hand to force it into place while watching the other CS.

Art

TC takes paper and a pen, and colours in 'blobs' with apparently random scribbles but carefully. He takes another colour and fills in a corner. He fills in another corner with a new colour. He takes a stapler and puts staples down one side, then adds a strip of Sellotape. He folds paper in half and staples down the ends. Then he takes a pen and draws round staples.

TC is at the table with paper, felt pens, stapler, and Sellotape. TC takes some paper and a pen, and scribbles hard, filling in a large coloured 'blob'. He folds the paper in half, takes another sheet, and does the same again. He holds the paper in half and Sellotapes it down, folds it in half again and tapes it, then folds and tapes again.

Gross motor play

TC walks along a raised plank, clambers from a tressle onto a climbing

TC is at a climbing apparatus – tressles with planks laid across, a climb-

frame. He climbs to the top, turns a somersault over the top bar, hangs by his hands from the top bar, trying to get his feet onto a lower bar. To do this, he has to adjust his position several times before he succeeds. TC wriggles in and out of the bars, sometimes head first, sometimes feet first, using several methods of getting up and down the climbing bars.

Large scale construction

TC and C discuss building a train. Together they arrange a row of large boxes, add a crate on top at the 'front' and a short plank across the crate. TC and C discuss the fact that a train needs wheels. TC runs off and returns with a tyre, leans it against the side of the 'train' like a wheel. Then TC and C together arrange more tyres in the same way.

Pretend

TC and C have constructed a train with large boxes, etc., as in the above example. C climbs onto the front announcing he's the driver. TC climbs on behind and says, 'I bought a ticket. Let's go to the seaside – I've got my spade and we can make a sandcastle and go in the sea.' C calls out 'All aboard. We're going to the sea.' TC pretends to sound the whistle, pulling an imaginary rope, 'Toot, toot!' C drives the train, assisted by TC. Another C bangs into the train with a large cart. TC shouts, 'The train's crashed – get an ambulance!'

Scale-version toys

TC sets up a 'petrol pump' outside a 'garage'. He runs a car up to the pump, pretends to fill it with petrol, and parks it under the garage. He takes another car out, runs it around the floor; takes a lorry out, runs it and crashes it into the car. He takes a pick-up truck out of the garage,

ing frame, a slide with a ladder, and so on. TC climbs up the tressle, walks along the raised plank, climbs up the ladder, down the slide, and back to walk along the plank again. He repeats this several times.

TC is with one other C at the large boxes, crates, planks, and so forth. TC piles boxes one on top of the other, and C knocks them down. Both laugh, and TC rebuilds the pile.

TC is with two other Cs in the playground. One says, 'I'm the Bionic Man' and pretends to hit another with a 'karate chop'. All play-fight, pretending to hit each other and shoot with 'space guns' while shouting the names of the character each is playing – Batman, Incredible Hulk, etc. Their play doesn't develop beyond announcing the role and pretend fighting of a stereotyped nature.

TC is playing with toy vehicles and a garage set. He takes a car out of the garage, and runs it up and down on floor, making 'car sounds' – brrrm, brrrm. He pushes the car along the floor, retrieves it, and pushes it again. He takes another car from the garage, and pushes it along the

CHALLENGING

runs it to the car, hooks it to the 'crashed' car and makes it tow the car to the garage. He sets the car up on a ramp and puts a toy man underneath it. He then returns to the first car.

ORDINARY

floor. He takes one car in each hand and runs them along, banging them into each other.

Music

TC plonks on the piano, making discords, changing the chord each time. He changes to hitting one note at a time, slowly. Then he sings each note he plays. He speeds up the playing and singing, as if it were a proper song. Although it sounds quite discordant, TC is clearly playing and singing a tune for himself and devoting care and attention to it.

TC goes to the 'music corner', which contains a piano, tambourine, triangle, xylophone, etc. TC hammers his fist on the piano, laughs, and puts his hands over his ears. He takes the xylophone hammer, bangs it hard up all the xylophone keys, then up all piano keys, laughing. He leans with hands spread out on the piano. Then he plonks down keys at random, laughing.

Informal games

TC with others arrange an utterly incongruous outfit of dressing-up clothes on a hanger – a cowboy hat with a ballet dress and wedding veil. Instead of just laughing at it, TC takes the hanger of clothes and holds it up against his body, marching around the room to emphasize the absurdity of the outfit and make others see the joke.

Cs are milling around by the dressing-up corner. Cs poke at each other and giggle, TC among them. They try hats on from the dressing-up clothes, laughing at each other. They throw hats to each other to catch, and continue giggling and nudging.

Social play with spontaneous rules

TC and C are at the puzzle table with picture lotto materials. TC invents a game with them, devising his own rules and explaining them to C. They lay out the cards on the table. TC explains that he will cover his eyes while C takes a card and hides it. TC tries to guess which picture is missing. Then C has a turn at guessing.

TC and C are in the washroom. C hops on the square tiles of the floor, avoiding the edges. TC follows, holding onto C. Both hold hands and step around the tiles avoiding the 'cracks' and laughing when the other steps on a crack.

Non-playful interaction

C is at *large scale construction,* trying to move a large tyre. TC comes up.
TC: 'Can I do that too?'
C: 'I'm making a fire engine.'
TC: 'I want to help.'
C: 'You can put the other wheel on.'
TC: 'I saw a big wheel like that. We

TC is building with the large scale boxes, planks, etc. Another C runs up and starts to roll away a tyre that was part of TC's construction.
C: 'I need that.'
TC grabs it back: '*I* need it.'
C: '*I'm* having it, it's mine.'

CHALLENGING

saw big tractors at the farm, at my grandad's farm, and they had big wheels.'

c: 'I've got a tractor at my house. I can ride on it outside.'

tc: 'I've got a big car and my mummy lets me drive it to the park.'

c: 'Did you see the ducks at the park?'

tc: 'I saw the swans too, and we gave them some bread to eat. They were very hungry.'

ORDINARY

tc tries to pull tyre from c's grasp: 'I'm going to tell Mrs Evans.'

(Measures of inter-observer reliability for these and other behavioural categories will be discussed in Chapter 10).

Note again that the kind of 'challenge' noted here concerns the *cognitive* level of the task. Although the child may engage in behaviour that is highly challenging in other ways – as in physical exertion, for example, or in the management of feelings – we focus here on the challenge *of the task* and the way in which it is carried out. We did not have separate definitions of complexity for the two age groups, and the play of younger children may have been scored as ordinary when in fact a seemingly simple action was an achievement for a child of only three.

Unfortunately, some behaviour is inscrutable. Examples of this include watching, waiting, or standing in queue. Indeed rather popular pastimes, listening to an adult watching television, were inscrutable. We debated whether a child so engaged was thinking about the speech or allowing his mind to wander. A local Primary Adviser pointed out to us that the child who appeared to stare aimlessly at the wall might be composing a poem. For reasons such as these, many behavioural categories were not assessed for complexity of task. These included watching for long periods of time, domestic tasks such as tidying-up, and cruising about the room. If a child at one of these was definitely engaged in some more challenging task, such as conducting a complicated conversation while waiting for milk, he was coded as participating in *non playful interaction,* a two-tier category, rather than *group routine* which is undifferentiated as to level of challenge.

In sum, of our 30 behavioural categories, in 12 of them we felt confident enough to assign each sample of behaviour to the 'complex' or the 'ordinary' group. In addition there were categories that might take values ordinary or challenging: *three Rs, examination, problem-solving,* and *adult-directed arts and crafts*. If a child engaged in one of these with evidence of complex thinking, we scored his behaviour accordingly. If he was formally part of one of these activities (e.g. *three Rs*) but engaged in something else (such as watching, waiting, chatting about something off-topic) he was not coded as participating in the challenging category but scored as engaged in that other behaviour. We might summarize the characteristics of high and low cognitive challenge as follows.

HIGH COGNITIVE CHALLENGE (COMPLEX)	ORDINARY COGNITIVE CHALLENGE
Child's activity is:	Child's activity is:
Novel, creative, imaginative, productive	Familiar, routine, stereotyped, repetitive, unproductive
Cognitively complex, involving the combination of several elements, materials, actions, or ideas	Cognitively unsophisticated, not involving the combining of elements
Carried out in a systematic, planned and purposeful manner	Performed in an unsystematic, random manner with no observable planning or purposefulness
Structured and goal-directed – working towards some aim, whether the result is a tangible end-product or an invisible goal	Not directed towards a new, challenging goal, 'aimless', and without structure
Conducted with care and mental effort; the child devotes a great deal of attention is deeply engrossed – takes pains	Conducted with ease, little mental effort, and not much care; the child is not deeply engrossed, his attention may not be entirely on that task
Learning a new skill, trying to improve an established one, or trying novel combinations of already familiar skills	Repeating a familiar, well-established pattern without seeking to improve upon it nor to add any new component or combination

There are behavioural indications of how much the child's task is stretching him. We don't need to guess what he is thinking in order to decide whether or not his activity is cognitively complex; we can see this in his actions and hear it in his talk. We admit, however, that children who verbalize their thoughts (alone or with others) probably had a greater chance of being scored 'complex'.

It will be recalled that the object of the exercise was to find a means of evaluating task complexity so that factors that encourage and hinder it might be identified. Further, we decided that the positive orientation of practitioners, the leaning over backwards to see something valuable in each child's behaviour, was desirable in the preschool but unacceptable in science. In effect, we adopted a stance opposite to that of the practitioners; we called a behaviour high level and challenging *only if we saw positive evidence* of sequential elaboration or transformation. In other words, teachers most likely identify a host of false positives whereas we err on the side of false negatives.

What we discovered

Every evaluative yardstick has its drawbacks and limitations. Having stated some of ours, we continue with a summary of our investigations into rich and imaginative play at preschool. Many factors affect cognitive complexity in play: intelligence, home background, emotional security, to name but a few. We did not set out to study these directly but concentrated on the part the *environment of the preschool* plays in nurturing or hindering children's play. We divide the facilitating factors into those of *task setting* (these include materials and activities) and *social setting*. We shall consider them in turn.

Task settings associated with challenging play

Barbara Tizard, Jerome Bruner and others have written

about the 'received wisdom' in preschool education. In his Gilchrist Lecture (1978) Bruner queried the traditional nursery dogma with its praise of unstructured materials (water, sand, dough) and physical expression (rough-and-tumble play). There is little evidence in the psychological literature that these activities challenge children, and our own data actually refute the claim.

We looked closely at each kind of activity – be it work or play or just horsing around. In some activities, such as *art*, most of the minutes were judged to be 'worthwhile' or intellectually demanding. In other categories such as *gross motor play*, the proportion of time devoted to intellectually challenging activity was much lower. We computed a table of relative 'stretch' for each kind of activity and it appears below as Table 4.1. Here and in Chapter 5 we have refrained

	Activity	Percentage of half-minute observations that were challenging	Percentage of half-minute observations that were ordinary	N
high yield	Three Rs	100 (by definition)	0	55
	Music, when not led by adult	73	26	26
	Small scale construction	71	29	416
	Art, where the child chooses his own medium	71	29	795
	Large scale construction	70	30	88
	Structured materials	69	31	432
moderate yield	Pretend	50	50	999
	Scale version toys	50	50	225
	Manipulation	47	53	1156
low yield	Non-playful interaction	32	68	668
	Informal games and rule-bound games	28	71	85
	Gross motor play	22	78	941
lowest yield	Social play, 'horsing around', giggling	2	98	123

Table 4.1 *Some activities that challenge and some that do not (Note that the pattern is the same for bouts)*

from simple tests of significance. Statistical tests appear in Chapter 10.

The results are clear; art, constructional activities, and structured tasks lead the rest in the opportunity they provide for the child to act at his intellectual best. We believe that these activities all possess a definite goal structure. More interestingly, these same 'high yield' activities usually involve materials that provide real-world feedback. They show the child whether a given sequence of behaviours has 'worked' or hasn't. (Note that the goals were usually chosen by the children.)

In most of the activities in which there is a great proportion of complex behaviour, the child builds or creates something tangible. He has an objective in mind and can judge whether what he is doing will further that objective or not. Of course, he may not have an image in his head of the exact form a painting should take, but he often knows whether he is pleased with the result of adding a strong colour or an additional form. The realization that something has 'come off' implies a standard in the mind, whether conscious or not.

Looked at another way, in the more structured tasks the child knows that he has done 'good work'. For instance he leaves a meccano construction with a sense of accomplishment. A feeling of pride is rarely seen when a child leaves the dough table or the swing. It's not fair to claim that all high yield activities require structured materials, for there is no structure inherent in crates or paint. What there *is* is potential for building or drawing a product. These endeavours call for perseverance for they have a definite end state. The child knows the moment that he has finished. He wouldn't decide 'that's done' unless he had a goal, no matter how unconscious or ill-defined. (Perseverance, goals and creativity may be found in pretend and other moderate yield activities. However, they need not be and often are not.)

We turn now to those activities and materials in which there is only moderate challenge. Here we find pretend, arranging scale version toys, and all manner of manipulation. These sometimes entail commitment to goals and risk of failure, but they need not. Children often use manipulative materials as a 'cover' for observation or just plain rest. And their play with cars, dolls and miniature animals can be quite banal. Children enjoying the activities in the moderate challenge group in Figure 4.1 often lack commitment to a goal. The difference between highly challenging and moderately challenging activities probably lies in the fact that there is a risk that the former may not 'come off'. When they do, there is pride and feelings of accomplishment. Perseverance in the sand trough less often leads to a feeling of accomplishment.

Children no doubt benefit from moderate or low yield activities in ways that are not intellectual. While pretending or splashing in the water, they often seem more relaxed, perhaps chatting amongst themselves. Activities with looser goal structure may provide the ease necessary for conversations and learning about social conventions. As such, they are as beneficial as three Rs work.

The last group of activities, those empty or lacking in complexity, rarely involved goals or planning. One action might lead to another, but the play or the conversation has no inner structure. A complicated conversation, enlarging and elaborating on a topic, would have been judged to be of high challenge. Unfortunately, such conversations rarely occurred. Then, too, games might be complex, with various roles and rules, but these, too, rarely occurred. Much of the play in the low challenge group in Table 4.1 seemed motivated by desire for the pleasure of physical exercise or of repetition. In it, there was little building towards a goal; instead, one action or utterance led to another with very little internal thread to create cohesion.

We argue that the high yield, goal-oriented tasks stretch the mind: that the middle yield tasks encourage social interchange and are therefore beneficial. But too much of the freer, low yield activities must mean diminished opportunity for planning and elaborating. The activities in the lowest yield group seem to evolve spontaneously, with no opportunity for planning, feedback or correction.

There is another way of examining environmental effects on the quality of play; instead of looking at its complexity we can measure its duration. Jerome Bruner (1980) has called this a sign of children's 'commitment' or 'quantitive concentration'. At preschool, we would like to see children develop the capacity for sustained commitment to something they have chosen. This ability to manage one's own attention is prerequisite to effective and satisfying social relations. And, of course, the ability to concentrate is crucial to later school work. Some tasks at preschool appear to nurture or teach it.

To look at the tasks that encourage concentration, we now examine the 'play bouts' described in the previous chapter. These are sequences of activity joined together by a coherent thread, be it dramatic or artistic, or a thread of sheer physical exuberance. The analysis in Table 4.1 was based on judgements of cognitive complexity made on half-minute segments; here we look instead at the sequence of activity over time. Bouts have been given names identical to the codes used for activities. In other words, the half-minute blocks are coded according to the activity list and these same names were used for the longer bouts.

In Table 4.2 we have grouped together those activities whose duration is usually determined by an adult and those in which the concentration span is under the child's own control. Two of the three activities with 'excellent' concentration are of the high goal structure recently discussed, as are four of the six with 'good' concentration. Since two thirds of the activities with long spells of concentration contain clear goal structure, we conclude that children stick at activities that challenge the mind.

But what about pretend, an activity associated with only moderate complexity but possessing an impressive record for concentration? It seems to us that children are committed to two kinds of activities, those with clear goals and those with dramatic force. Pretend contains the latter, as do stories in 'circle time'. We do not wish to over-sell structured materials at the expense of all else, especially at the expense of drama. Some of the make-believe in our sample was not considered complex because it was ritualized, even stereotyped pretence. Although dramatic ritual does not challenge the mind as a puzzle, it rivets children's attention. Pretend play is almost always sociable and we know that children stick longer at play episodes if they participate with others. Since there are two powerful reasons why pretend play compels, we cannot say for certain whether it is the social participation or the drama which keeps the children at it. No matter the cause, pretend, with its long bouts and moderate-to-high levels of complexity, is desirable on intellectual grounds. But naturally a sociable activity such as this is worthwhile on other grounds as well.

Tizard *et al.* (1975) observed children of similar ages in London and found that play activities, on average, lasted about five minutes. They did not make fine distinctions between the kinds of play, nor did they include non-play categories; still their calculation of concentration span is not unlike ours. But they were disappointed with the play of the 109 children they observed and concluded sadly:

> Our findings suggest, in fact, that in preschool centres much play is at a rather low level; it may indeed often be the case that symbolic play and complex games occur more often in the home or the street. We found that in the preschool centres games tended to be brief and simple; on the average, children remained with one play activity for less than five minutes; they appeared to be constantly running from one activity to another. Children of three and four are, of course, capable of considerably greater persistence, but certain factors in the free-play nursery setting probably militate against a longer attention span, notably the great range of alternative play materials present, the lack of pressure to persist by the staff, and the distraction offered by large numbers of other children. Thus, although it is often argued by educationalists that the intrinsic motivation of self-initiated play leads to the kind of serious absorption which is the best guarantor of learning, in practice other

Activities whose duration is usually determined by an adult		Activities whose duration is usually determined by the child		
Adult-led group activities (such as singing or story)	6·4	Art	6·3	excellent concentration
		Small scale construction	5·1	
		Pretend	5·0	
Adult-directed art and manipulation skills	4·5	Manipulation	4·5	good concentration
		Structured materials	3·9	
Group routine (like tidy-up)	4·4	Three Rs	3·9	
		Examination	3·8	
		Scale version toys	3·8	
		Large scale construction	3·5	
Waiting	3·1	Watching staff	3·1	Moderate or poor concentration
		Gross motor play	2·7	
		Informal games	2·6	
		Rough-and-tumble	2·5	
		Individual physical needs	2·5	
		Social play with spontaneous rules	2·2	
		Non-playful interaction	2·1	
		Watching events	2·0	
		Watching peers	1·9	
		Purposeful movement	1·9	
		Aimless standing around, wandering or gazing	1·5	
		Cruising	1·3	

Table 4.2 *Mean 'bout length' of activities, in minutes*

aspects of the free-play situation tend to prevent such absorption.

We take a rosier view, at least of concentration. A mean bout length, as in the case of *art* at six minutes, includes many long spells of play, although the aborted attempts at drawing or easel painting depress the mean. (Note that we do not include in concentration analyses bouts that occur at the beginning or end of observations.) Further, when we computed average length of play spells in individual centres we found that some were regularly host to bouts of ten minutes or more. No mean feat for young children playing together in cramped, noisy spaces.

A measure of how absorbed children are in their actions may be seen in their resistance to distraction. Montessori teachers are fond of telling how young children in the Italian classrooms of their founder astounded the Inspector by failing to look up from their 'work' when he entered the room. In our sample we looked for the same kind of concentration and measured it as the incidence of activity 'embeddings'.

Table 4.3 shows the frequency in each behavioural category of another task being inserted within it or running concurrently. One activity embedded inside another may indicate lack of concentration on the primary task.

Activity	Percentage of half minutes within each category in which there was an embedded behaviour	
	No embedding	Embedding
Structured materials	98	2
Pretend	94	6
Small scale construction	93	7
Art	93	7
Large scale construction	92	8
Three Rs	91	9
Manipulation	89	11
Gross motor play	87	13
Non-playful interaction	87	13
Informal games	86	14
Adult-directed activities:		
Adult-led groups, such as singing or story	98	2
Adult-directed art or manipulation	82	18

Table 4.3 *Presence of embedded behaviour within common activities*

We do not claim that a child who temporarily leaves a puzzle to look out the window is acting in a way that is intellectually impoverished. Indeed the child who leaves a tricycle to chat with a friend or adult may be heading towards some more fruitful activity. The argument here is that those tasks which are resistant to distraction provide evidence for concentration and commitment.

Three kinds of evidence have been put forward to show that it is activities with clear goal structure that best foster complex play. First, a higher proportion of half-minutes (and also bouts) within these categories were scored as challenging. Second, they have longer spans of concentration. Lastly, they are less likely to have another activity embedded within or alongside them.

Many of the findings here and in subsequent chapters centre on the distinction between complex and ordinary. Recall that it was devised according to the intuitions of teachers, playleaders and teacher trainers. These findings are now given extra weight by the fact that two independent measures (bout length and frequency of embeddings) select the same activities as 'stars'. Although these activities, such as *structured materials, art,* or *construction*, call for large doses of convergent thinking (Hudson, 1966), they often require divergent thought as well. Making a painting, building a den, and exploring the xylophone are so far from prosaic activities that it would be wrong to dismiss our goal-structured categories as anti-imaginative. Although pure chats and gross motor play occasionally scored as complex, the fact remains that the more structured activities have higher proportions of complex play. They may not claim exclusive ownership of intellectual challenge, but are more closely associated with it in the preschool.

Social settings associated with challenging play

Although it's certainly true that the more structured activities are associated with challenging play, the social setting exerts a powerful influence as well. The preschool day is often divided into parts, some of which allow the child free choice of activities or mates and others requiring him to participate in a group or remain parallel to others. If we look at children's social participation insofar as it is associated with cognitive challenge, a complicated picture emerges.

Table 4.4 shows that at both age groups the proportion of complex activity was low amongst children on their own. Further, for both age groups the highest proportion of challenging play occurred while in pairs. It seems that a child's social participation is not only the 'classroom' for acquiring interpersonal skills, it is also the scene of his most complex and creative thought. (We assume that complicated *thought* must lie behind the complex *behaviour* that we observed.)

Many parents think that the major goal of preschool should be, or indeed is, helping the child to get on with his peers (Turner, 1977). It seems that practitioners agree wholeheartedly here as Webb (1974) so boldly states. 'Common practice, as well as passages in most reports and texts, accept opportunities for social development as the very heart of good nursery school provision.' The Oxfordshire study shows dramatically that the fruits of cooperative play are more than social ones – they are intellectual as well. Psychologists and educators interested in the factors associated with intellectual development will do well to leave the laboratory where they study the single child and enter into the nursery. It's not argued that the structure of children's thought is different in the preschool – only its content, and perhaps the motivating factors that affect its form.

Note that in Table 4.4 we have grouped together all instances of challenging play so that we can see in which social settings they most commonly appeared. This makes an important assumption, and one that may not be justified, in that it lumps together very different kinds of activity. For example, the *pair* might be associated with complex play in pretend but not in gross motor play. While we know that the relationship between challenging play and social participation might vary from category to category, we have grouped together the 12 most common kinds of play to provide a

	TC *alone*	*In pair*	*In group*	*Parallel to others*
4½–5½ years				
N	705	1380	1417	1296
Challenging play	26	54	42	43
Ordinary play	74	46	58	57
3½–4½ years				
N	825	1220	923	1832
Challenging play	21	28	23	17
Ordinary play	79	72	77	83

Table 4.4 *Percentage of challenging play in each social category*

rough estimate of the *general* association between social setting and cognitive challenge.

It's a well known fact that certain zoologists are 'lumpers' when categorizing animal species and others are 'splitters'. There's no right answer when deciding whether two groups of animal are the same, or closely related, species, but scientists seem to have scholarly preferences in one direction or the other. People conducting studies of children have somewhat the same dilemma when they must decide whether or not to 'lump' ages, sexes, activities and the like. In most of our analyses we do not look separately at children of the two age groups. If we did, and also included differences between boys and girls, the number of tables in this book would treble. In all instances where the differences between the age-sex groups are small or banal, we have combined information across the groups. However, when discussing the effect of social participation, especially interactions with the adult, we present the findings separately for each age group because they respond differently to social influence.

This is seen clearly in Table 4.5 which describes once more the association between challenging play and social grouping. This analysis, however, separates the social categories in ways that distinguish adults from children. With this separation it becomes apparent that older children achieve their highest levels of play when in the company of adults, whereas younger children have higher proportions of challenging play

	TC alone	Child–child pair	Child group	TC parallel to children	TC with other children, adult near	Adult–child interacting pair	TC in group–adult interacts with TC
4½–5½ years							
N	704	877	889	536	274	429	322
Challenging play	26	49	44	45	40	65	46
Ordinary play	74	51	56	55	60	35	54
3½–4½ years							
N	821	688	621	535	148	459	224
Challenging play	21	33	24	30	13	24	21
Ordinary play	79	67	76	70	87	76	79

Table 4.5 Percentage of challenging play in each social category: adults and children distinguished

when in child-child pairs or parallel to others. Note also that children in both age groups, when in the company of adults, are more likely to engage in complex play when actually interacting with them rather than merely in their presence.

In Tables 4.4 and 4.5 we have shown an association between interacting pairs and the complexity of children's play, especially the adult-child pair in the case of older children. But which came first, the adult or the challenge? One might suppose that adults are attracted to children engaging in rich fantasy or solving complicated problems and so join them at their interesting tasks. In order to explore this further, we analysed sequences of time units, not just associations between social groupings and challenge within the same half-minute interval. Further we confined this analysis to those activities in which we felt confident enough to judge the intellectual level. These are, of course, the 'standard' nursery fare of manipulation, construction, art and physical play, and are the very activities in which teachers attempt to have a positive effect.

To examine sequences of events instead of simultaneous associations, we drew from the data all transitions across time intervals in which a change in cognitive level had occurred. In effect, we examined every case where time 1 and time 2 had been coded for level of challenge and where there had been a shift either upwards or downwards. Next, we examined the social codings that had been assigned to the half minute preceding the change in intellectual level.

Figure 4.1 shows the probability of a shift either up or down in play complexity in terms of the social setting, immediately preceding the change. Children alone rarely shift in either direction, but the child in a pair is the most likely candidate for a shift upwards and the child in the group for a shift down. Again, this is not *causal proof* that the social setting has brought about the shift, but we now know for certain that the 'beneficial' social settings (that is, those associated with positive challenge) precede the change in activity level.

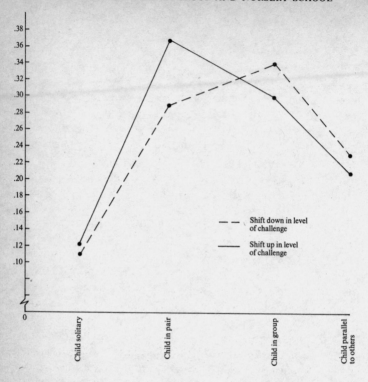

Figure 4.1 *Transitional probabilities of shift in challenge according to prior social participation*

Figure 4.2 is even more interesting for it shows the sequence of events involved in a child's movement up or down a scale of complexity. Although the probability of *any* change in level is rather low, it is clear the interacting adult in the interval before the shift is associated with gains in cognitive complexity while the child on his own is more often associated with a deterioration. Again, as in Figure 4.1, the analysis is made on both age groups combined. The effect is stronger for the older children.

In our sample, the tutorial described so exquisitely by Isaacs and taking place between 'informed' adult and child

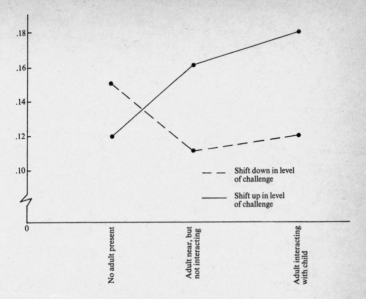

Figure 4.2 *Transitional probabilities of shift in challenge according to prior adult contact*

occurs only with older children. In it the adult deftly expands the child's scope of action or conception, often using the concrete task as take-off point for discussion in a more abstract or imaginary vein. This kind of enabling interaction is what many teachers and playgroup leaders aspire to, and it does indeed take place. Note, however, that it occurs mostly with older children and that, although extremely rich, each child experiences very little of it in a day. Although the adult-child interaction is likely to be associated with challenging play, its infrequent occurrence means that this social setting does not account for a great proportion of the high level play observed in our study. One can ask two questions here. In which social setting is most complex play seen? The answer is the child-child pair. The other question concerns the potential for rich play. One answers this by looking *not at what actually occurs* in the preschool but at the role of the adult in the instances when she is there. In these the child is more likely to engage in challenging play than when she is not. We might say that the 'yield' of half-minutes in which the adult is interacting with TC is higher than those when she is not. But the greatest proportion of high level play in fact took place in child groups, not because this social setting 'produces' the richest play, but because it is the most common form of social group in the preschool.

Should adults interact more with children? And if so, how? Much of adult interaction is of a 'housekeeping' nature; it consists largely of invitations to milk-time, instructions about tidying the room, exhortations to wash hands. This rather domestic chat comprises a great portion of adult talk, probably of necessity. And much of the talk of adults is of a 'one off' nature. 'Stop hitting her,' – or 'That's beautiful, Tracy,' while tying Peter's shoes and finding Darren's hat.

We've shown, at least for older children, that adult interaction helps raise the cognitive level of play. Why isn't there more of it? And does it have to be so 'one-off'? Is it as it is because our teachers and playleaders are poor at managing their time? Or because children's play is so boisterous it needs quick admonition? Or because daily interaction requires small remarks and reassuring chat? These questions will be explored in Chapter 5, but from the data presented here, we can make three recommendations about improving preschool practice:

1 Make the most of materials/activities with clear goal structure. With them, children can progress to complicated schemes in a self-initiated and self-sustaining manner.
2 Encourage children to work in pairs. Teachers do this already because they want children to acquire social skills. They might do it even more, however, as it has been shown to improve the intellectual level of children's play.
3 When staffing permits, encourage the subtle tutorial. This is discussed in the next chapter.

5

Conversations

What must preschoolers know of language?

Every preschool programme has as one of its priorities the fostering of language. The message 'language is important' has filtered recently to parents, paediatricians, health visitors, social workers, and childminders. Teachers, it seems, have always regarded language as central, perhaps because they are members of the profession charged with instructing children to read and write. During the first six decades of this century, nursery teachers were concerned to 'teach' vocabulary and standard pronunciation. These are important still but to them have been added other kinds of linguistic knowledge such as conversational rules (Bruner, 1975a and b), 'elaborated codes' (Bernstein, 1971), and metalinguistic awareness (Cazden, 1975). The new language teaching has stressed the function of speech rather than its form.

It was the philosophers who first turned our attention to rules of conversation. They pointed to the fact that it takes more than knowledge of grammar to be partner in a conversation (Austin, 1962). There are appropriate ways to begin and end, to interrupt, and to remain 'on the topic'. Added to the rules for graceful conduct of dialogue, there are rules about grammatical appropriateness according to context. We say 'get out' to our customers when we notice that the shop is on fire but 'would you kindly come back tomorrow?' when we're tired and eager to lock up. Bruner (1975b) describes how such 'felicity conventions' are learned at home in mother and baby play.

Young children, in fact, have an astonishing command of the complexities of the social aspects of language use. There follow examples showing such skills.

(a) Children as young as four years old are apparently aware that infants do not yet have as much language as they do, for they use the 'baby talk register' when talking to younger children. That is, they talk in sentences that are shorter, simpler, and higher-pitched to younger children than they use to peers or adults (Snow, 1977). Thus, four-year-olds already have a notion of what others are capable of understanding in language and command several means to make themselves understood.

(b) Preschoolers can make a clear distinction between 'playful' talk and talk that is 'serious business', for they readily switch in and out of 'silly voices' and 'well-formed utterances' according to the context in which the talk is occurring. For example, in pretend games 'silly voices' abound, but if during the game a child wants to make a real request of another, he switches into 'ordinary voice', then resuming the 'silly voice' when the request has been fulfilled.

(c) Children show knowledge of different ways of accomplishing goals with language, some of which are extremely indirect. In one of our observations two children, Peter and John, were squabbling over possession of a tricycle, each trying to snatch it from the other. The teacher intervened and said 'it's John's turn on the bike'. When Peter protested, the teacher suggested he come indoors with her. Peter sat at a table indoors with the teacher but constantly kept an eye out of the window on John with the bike. After some minutes the teacher, who was quite aware of Peter's focus on the bike, said he could go out and ask John if he could now have a turn, but added that Peter was 'not to fight over the bike' but was to retire gracefully if John would not concede. Peter rushed outside and announced to John: 'Mrs Shaw (the teacher) wants to talk to you – you've to go inside.' John obediently went indoors, leaving the bike which Peter grabbed.

This four-year-old clearly had a command of how to get things done with words. He could have simply asked John, 'Can I have a go now?' He could have added the teacher's name to give more 'authority', as in 'Mrs Shaw says can I have a turn now.' Either way, he faced the risk of outright refusal, which he had been told to accept. So instead he chose a way that was guaranteed to get him the bike unless John defied the teacher's supposed injunction, which was unlikely. Peter must have known about the conventions of requesting in language yet chose not to use a request form. He 'thought ahead' to the consequences of his utterance to John: 'material' and 'social' consequences – for himself, getting the bike and not getting into trouble for fighting over it; and for John not risking disapproval by defying her supposed request.

There are many other examples of such social, cognitive and linguistic competence. Consider the number of ways in which a child might attract an adult's attention. He might tug at the teacher's sleeve; call her name; go and stand quietly beside her and wait for her to notice him; wave his hand to her; throw a 'tantrum'; launch into what he had to say without regard to whether he was interrupting her, and so on. For most children, preschool is the first experience of being in a large group where one does not have frequent doses of attention from the adult. So each one must now learn: (a) when it is appropriate or not to try and get the teacher's attention; (b) what is the appropriate way, on this particular occasion, of getting her attention. That is, which way will be effective but will not earn 'disapproval', will be 'socially acceptable'.

In addition to conversational conventions, the child entering school should be able to use what Bernstein has called the 'elaborated' code. This means that he can make reference to objects and events not in the immediate surround and, to some extent, take into account the listener's point of view. There have been heated arguments about whether the linguistic abilities inherent in the elaborated code (as opposed to the 'restricted' one) are a consequence of the speaker's syntax or speech style (Labov, 1970). Leaving these aside, we can safely conclude here that children from less advantaged backgrounds are not skilled at talking about things outside the perceptual present nor indeed in using explicit reference to objects they can see. These skills are necessary if the child is to plan a future event or to tell a stranger which of the tins on an out-of-reach shelf holds his felt-tipped pens.

Lastly, the child learning to read must have metalinguistic awareness. This means that he does not merely use language, he is aware of it. Children who construct nonsense rhymes show this awareness, as do children who laugh at riddles. Perhaps language, to the small child, is like water to the fish – something he knows well and uses daily but something *seen right through*. Courtney Cazden argues that the child is not prepared for distinguishing the sounds of words nor even their boundaries unless he sees language as opaque.

There have been a host of studies all showing that children from advantaged backgrounds enter school 'language prepared' and eager to work out the puzzle of sounds, letters and sounds. In fact, a difference between children from privileged and not-so privileged homes appears as young as three (Tough, 1977). Do nursery schools and playgroups compensate for lack of training in the home? Some studies indicate that they do, and others show disappointing results. The programmes shown to foster language skills usually combine special language teaching (often one-to-one tutorials) with parent participation in the child's programme.

The Oxfordshire study

Our study sheds just a little light on the role of preschools and language teaching. None of the centres we studied had special language tutorial schemes, although all concentrated on it obliquely in stories, songs and games. Furthermore, our hand-recorded notes did not always give precise transcription of speech we overheard. Still, we learned quite a lot about language in the preschool, not its intricate detail but rather its ecological surround.

Our analyses focused on several measures of talk at preschool; how much of it there was, who were the participants, and which were the tasks or social settings that fostered it most.

First, we turn to the amount of dialogue in the preschool. Here, dialogue is defined as a three (or more) turn sequence with the following minimal structure: $A \rightarrow B$; $B \rightarrow A$; $A \rightarrow B$; and so forth, where the topic is identical or similar throughout all three turns, and each contribution expands on the previous one. In our study, the children engaged in little conversational exchange. In all half-minutes we analysed (9,600 of them) 80 per cent had no dialogue in them at all.

Children sometimes talk to themselves and often engage in 'one-off remarks', such as 'I need the scissors,' *but they rarely have conversations*. When teachers, playgroup leaders and psychologists conjure up an image of a child at preschool, they imagine him in fantasy play with others, or chatting away to a teacher. According to our observations, the typical child is careering through the garden on a bicycle, blowing bubbles at the water table, or quietly watching another child paint. He is not yet a conversationalist at preschool, even if he is at home.

If the school-age child must know how to begin and end conversations gracefully, to remain relevant to the topic, and indeed to take his turn, then he has little scope in the preschool for such learning. When there *is* some teaching of 'conversational rules', it does not happen in the one-to-one 'tutorial chats', for in these chats the focus is not on the conversation *per se*, but on furthering the task at hand. The occasions in which 'conversational rules' are taught explicitly (rather than learned spontaneously) are small *group* discussions led by an adult, for instance when the children discuss a story they have just heard, or discuss a given topic such as 'outings to the zoo'. At these times the adult ensures, for example, that a child doesn't interrupt another speaker, stays with the subject or a related one, expresses himself so that others can understand, and so on.

Which settings promote conversations?

Barbara Tizard and her colleagues (1979) found that children were five times as likely to address another child as to address an adult. In our study they were three times as likely to – which indicates, once again, that the Oxford preschools were the scene of 'better practice'. In our large sample about 15 per cent of the half minutes contained one or more exchanges with a child; only about 5 per cent contained any dialogue with an adult. If, as observed earlier, children rarely have conversations, it's not because they lack dialogue skill. Clearly, many children are competent at chatting with both peers and adults – even our three-year-olds. The typical preschool does not nurture dialogue, whereas other (see the work of Garvey, 1977) out-of-home settings *do*. Such 'dialogue inducing' settings are small, quiet rooms, with two or three children in them, and furnished like a home rather than a school. In our own observations, some of the richest conversations took place in the home corner, or in 'dens' which two or three children constructed on their own by, for instance, draping curtains over chairs or planks and crawling into the dark, enclosed space inside. Rich dialogue may require quiet intimate settings, and the preschool seems to specialize in their opposite. The following record provides an excellent example.

Activity record	*Language record*
With 2 cs, finishing construction of outdoor den in corner of yard.	TC → C (to take wood from him)
Lifts large sheet of wood over low doorway.	TC → C
Passes wood to C.	TC → C (to stop block about to fall on C
Climbs into den himself.	
Stands over C lying on plank blocks (bed) in corner. C gets up.	TC → C: 'Get up a minute. You're on it, Philip. Look, just move.'
Moves huge wood sheet around; heaves it into place.	TC → C (about making house)

Activity record	*Language record*
Third c brings hat to corner.	TC → c: 'My new fire engine hat.'
Puts on hat.	
Arranging 'house'.	TC → cs: 'Can we buy some food; put it in here.'
	TC → cs: 'We need … We're making a new house.'
Arranging 'house'.	TC → cs
Runs indoors.	TC → cs: 'Hey, make the house.'
Goes to home corner.	TC → c: 'Let's go out.'
Fetches pans and plates (plus c).	
Drops them.	TC: 'Ooh.'
Picks them up.	
Watches his brother at woodwork	
as he passes.	CL → TC: 'Oh, good.'
Carries cups etc. to den.	CL → TC: 'Oh, we don't need that.'
Throws pans into cart.	TC → c: '… in the cart now.'
c offers him a 'lollipop'	TC → c: 'Oh, lollipop.'
made of plastic construction	TC → c: 'Oh, I haven't got a lollipop.'
kit.	TC → c: 'Oh lovely!'
Trundles cart inside den.	TC → cs: 'Open up. Put it back on the hat rack.'
In den with cs.	TC → c: 'Move, or you'll get run over. Come on then.'
Empties cart and puts crockery	
in box 'cupboard'.	TC → c: 'Here you are. You got all the things in here. Don't dump that down on me. I'll show you where to put the ??!'
Fetches pan.	TC → c (about hat)
Pretends to eat.	TC → c: 'Cook something now – bacon.'
Stirs and shakes saucepan.	TC → cs: 'Who wants some food – pancakes – do you want a pancake?'
	cs → TC
Runs across yard to teacher.	TC → c: 'Do you want a taste?'
	TC → s: 'Do you want a taste of food?'
	s → TC

Activity record	Language record
Runs to c. Runs to observer.	TC → c TC → c: 'Do you want a glug of soup?' TC → c: 'Do you want a pancake?'
Goes around yard; offering pancakes to cs and adults. Goes into den and pretends to cook.	TC → cs TC → s TC → c: 'Oh barley.' c → TC (about cooking) TC → c: 'Eeeugh!' (disgust)
Pretending to cook.	TC → c: 'It's burning, turn it off – put some chips in – that made it.' c → TC
Tips up saucepan.	TC → c: 'Do you want some chips? Do you want some for your dinner?'
'Pours' from bottle.	TC → c: 'Do you want some tea?'
Pretend cooking (very active).	TC → c: 'Do you want some milk? Will you give me some egg?'
Calls to girl across yard.	TC → c: 'Sophie, do you want some egg?' c → TC: 'No!'
Pretend cooking.	c → TC: 'Some water on!' TC → cs (about cooking)
Goes across yard and gives Sophie a plate. Pretend fire.	TC → c: 'Here's your dinner. Why are you so late?' c → TC: 'Fire!' TC → c: 'Put water on.' TC → c
From den calls across yard to girl. Goes over to her. Takes lollipop!	TC → cs (about frozen 'lollipops') TC → c: 'Do you want a lollipop?' c → TC: 'No.'
Pushes lollipop in Philip's mouth (back in den). Lies down on floor and 'sleeps'.	TC → c: 'Go on, have a bit.' c sleeps beside him, then 'wakes up'. TC → c: 'Get out of bed.' c → TC: 'I want to sleep here.'
Philip is lying in plank corner and refuses to move.	TC → c: 'Take the plank away. Philip, you're spoiling my game.'

Activity record	Language record
	c→TC (about beds)
Sits beside Philip on plank bed. Wails.	c→TC: 'I'll make myself messy' (if 'sleep' on ground).
	TC→C: 'Get out of this house then. Take your hat off.'
Trying to persuade, then browbeat Philip into cooperating.	TC→C: 'If you don't, I'll tell you to get out – right – right.'
Child enters with hat. Grabs hat.	TC→C: 'Or I'll keep this hat; Philip? Right?'
	TC→C (about hat)
	TC→C: 'You lie on here or I'll…'
Holds hat and talks to Philip who is still lying on 'his' bed.	TC→C: 'I won't be able to have anywhere to sleep and then I might keep this hat, mightn't I, Philip?'
Four cs arguing.	TC→C (about bed and hat)
Rushes onto plank beside Philip and lies down to 'sleep' next to him.	TC→C: 'Let's go to sleep. Night time.'
Gets up again. Goes to cupboard.	TC→C: 'Do you want some milk in here?'
	c→TC: 'Yes.'
Looks at ladder, etc.	TC→C: 'Alright, you can.'
	TC→CS
	TC→C: 'Is that the cupboard? Sleep on the ladder.'

The paucity of conversation is found in both older and younger children. Table 5.1 shows the distribution of dialogue according to age.

Contrary to popular belief, girls do not have more conversations than boys. The young boys talk with their friends more than girls do, perhaps because they are fond of rough-and-tumble play. Young girls engage in quieter activities, often parallel with other girls but not conversing with them. Older girls, however, have more conversations with peers than the boys do. We saw many rising-five boys

	Percentage of time units in which one dialogue or more occurred	
Type of dialogue	Younger children $3\frac{1}{2}$–$4\frac{1}{2}$ years N = 4800	Older children $4\frac{1}{2}$–$5\frac{1}{2}$ years N = 4800
None	81	78
Child-child	13	14
Child-adult	6	8

Table 5.1 *Percentage of dialogue according to age group*

apparently eager to act 'masculine tough' and this involved physical play with one-off shouts rather than connected discourse.

One surprising finding is that the older boys were observed to have twice as many conversational exchanges with adults as the girls had. Many of these were quasi-disciplinary; adults tend to adjudicate, cajole, admonish and entice the boys whom they see as potentially (or in fact) troublesome. Cherry (1974) found similar patterns in American nursery teachers, who talked more to boys in efforts to keep them busy and out of trouble.

	Percentage of time units in which one dialogue or more occurred			
	Younger children		Older children	
Type of dialogue	Boys	Girls	Boys	Girls
None	79	82	78	78
Child-child	15	10	12	16
Child-adult	7	7	10	5

Table 5.2 *Amount of dialogue according to sex*

Imagine for a moment a preschool setting with 20 children and two adults. In one hour, each of the children has three minutes in which some dialogue with an adult occurs. Let's say, for the sake of argument, that each child has three short conversations in that hour with an adult. There are then 60 conversations in the hour 'partnered' by the adults. If each adult has half of them, they have 30 conversations each in the hour. Surely, our adults were heroic conversationalists! We might wish them to make better use of their exchanges, but we can hardly ask them to achieve more output.

Which activities promote conversation?

We know that children must acquire syntactic and conversational skills before entry into school, but we have shown that they have little opportunity in the preschool to practice them – let alone develop them. We turn now to the kinds of settings that give room for children's talk because our study showed that certain activities prompt or support children's conversations more than others.

Activity settings were defined in Chapter 4. These include the most common play tasks seen in preschools, some of which are structured by materials and some not. They have varying influence on talk and here we shall consider all speech, not just connected dialogue. To begin, children talk with adults in certain settings and with children in others. Let's turn first to talk between peers. If we examine all the half minutes in each activity category, we find the highest proportion of child-child exchanges ($A \rightarrow B$ and $B \rightarrow A$) in the following (in rank order):

Informal games
Gross motor and simple social play: swings, trikes, rough-and-tumble, 'horsing around'
Group routine, for instance milk-time
Non-playful social interaction, with an absence of instrumental task
Pretend

It is clear that most child-child exchanges occur in the looser activities, ones where there are no clear intrinsic goals. Because there is no product or end state implicit in the enterprise, as there is in painting, children can negotiate the goal in conversation. 'Let's have dinner now,' 'No I have to do the shopping first.' Most children's talk occurs while they are engaged in common activity. They need the support of joint action to carry along the topic. But certain activities, the ones with high goal structure, require a kind of single-mindedness that precludes chat.

Often, the goal is negotiated by the children as they move along, as in the case of pretend play. The case is different when children talk with adults. Exchanges between adults and children occur in the following settings, in rank order:

Three Rs school-readiness activities
Non-playful social interaction
Structured materials (such as puzzles, dominoes)
Art, when directed by an adult

It seems puzzling at first that children can carry off a conversation while concentrating hard on something else – provided their partner is an adult. Perhaps the greater conversational skills of the adult help keep the chat going. We wondered whether adults did all the initiating of these conversations, but – to our surprise – found that children initiated as well. Some of child-initiated exchanges in art are requests for assistance or approval, not linguistically rich but an opportunity to develop communication skills while working towards a goal. The preponderance of child-adult exchanges during structured activities is clearly not an instance of an adult 'on the child's back'. Both speakers see this as an opportunity for dialogue across the generations and we call it the 'tutorial chat'.

A tutorial chat in the context of an activity with clear goal potential usually involves the adult's trying to encourage the child towards elaboration of his task.

ADULT: 'What does that make now?'
CHILD: 'It's a house and there are the windows.'

Activity	Percentage of observations with no speech	Percentage of observations with child-child exchanges	Percentage of observations with child-adult exchanges	Percentage of observations with one-off speech or speech to self	N
Non-playful interaction	8	14	7	71	668
Group routine	9	18	0	53	410
Pretend	14	10	1	75	997
Informal games	17	29	3	51	79
Three Rs	29	4	16	51	55
Manipulation	32	6	0	62	1156
Rough-and-tumble	37	20	0	43	298
Gross motor play	40	10	1	49	940
Structured materials	43	3	6	48	432
Small scale construction	48	4	1	47	416
Adult-directed art and manipulation	47	0	5	48	62

Table 5.3 Activities that foster dialogue

ADULT: 'How do you get in?'

CHILD: 'Oh, you have a door' (adds a door to his construction while making the utterance).

ADULT: 'A pretty red door to match the windows...'

CHILD: (adds more to construction) 'And there's the path...'

In this example, the child complies with the conversation because it makes his task more exciting and because it's not polite to ignore grown-ups. The adult enters the child's construction task with related conversation, which is what another child cannot do. The adult intends to expand the scope of the child's task and often succeeds. At worst she bores the child or saps his confidence. ('What colour is that?' 'Red.' 'No, dear.') But children are very patient with adults and forgive sequences such as these. Most tutorial chats are situations in which the child knows that the adult knows that the child knows the answer. When the child concentrates intently on a goal, especially if it is self-chosen, only an adult has the ability to maintain a dialogue and extend his scope. However, she must be extraordinarily deft, as Ziven (1974) has shown in a lovely experiment. When children were bored with a given toy, the adult's extolling its virtues was less effective in re-kindling their interest than merely letting it lie.

While investigating the settings high in exchange and dialogue, rather surprisingly we found many more conversations in nursery classes, compared with playgroups or nursery schools. This was due to the greater chattiness of the children among themselves and not to more talk with adults. Although children from nursery school, nursery class, and playgroup were represented equally in our sample, twice as many child-child exchanges took place in nursery class as in nursery schools or playgroups. This is interesting because playgroups had more adults per child and more total *talk*. However, it tended to be of the one-off variety instead of dialogue, perhaps because playgroup staff avoid 'intervention' or because children are not well acquainted.

In the following chapter we look closely at differences

	Percentage of total minutes in each kind of centre that included dialogue		
Type of dialogue	Nursery school N = 3200	Nursery class N = 3200	Playgroup N = 3200
None	82	72	84
Child-child	9	21	10
Child-staff member	8 } 9	6 } 7	4 } 6
Child-non-staff member	1	1	2

Table 5.4 *Dialogue by kind of centre*

between nursery schools, classes and playgroups. One of our findings is the relative popularity in the nursery class of manipulation and pretend. These activities are often associated with the child-child pair – just the right social setting for a dialogue.

Incidentally, Table 5.4 shows clearly that we found few dialogues between children and adults who are not members of staff. We counted as 'staff' both student teachers and regular mother-aides and found almost no chat between children and adults who were not in the staff category. In other words, even in voluntary playgroups we saw few instances of the parent not on the rota who stays occasionally to chat with the children. From our observations, the 'casually present' parent felt more comfortable mixing paint or chatting with the supervisor – rather than mucking in with the children.

Do preschools teach conversational skills?

The preschools we studied appeared at first glance to be alive with talk. The adults bustled here and there, tossing off a reproof in one direction and a bit of praise in the other. They managed to talk to each of their charges at least once in a session, but often this was fleeting and sometimes it occurred in a large group scene such as story-time. The children too seemed talkative. They aped the adults in the way they tossed 'one-off' utterances freely towards their mates and occasionally towards an adult, as is clearly revealed in Table 5.3. What they rarely conduct are connected exchanges about a single topic, even brief ones of three turns.

We know that language skills are crucial for getting on later in life in classroom or playground. Although this study made no attempts at analysis of syntactic speech, it looked quite closely at dialogue to measure its occurrence and find clues about its support. Its findings suggest that the preschool is not an ideal environment for teaching children the many skills of conversation, since coherent conversations are few and far between. Life ahead will require more than the odd utterance called out across the sand table. A recent study by Barbara Tizard (1979) has shown children's speech at home to be richer than at day nursery. This effect was even more marked in children from disadvantaged backgrounds. How might preschools change programme or materials to allow children more opportunity to be partners in dialogue? We might ask their teachers and play leaders to make more elaborate use of their exchanges, if we can't ask them to talk a lot *more*. If dialogue is a desirable goal, then preschool teachers/leaders might consider the following:

1 Arrange the programme and materials so as to encourage more child-child dialogue. This might mean a more enticing scene for pretend, which is rich in conversation and yet still relatively high in cognitive complexity.

2 Evaluate the content of adult-child dialogue in light of its (of necessity) paucity and its potential for nurturing the child's developing intellectual and social competence. Is it too much devoted to 'management' and not enough to 'elaboration' or to 'play'? (Wood, McMahon and Cranstoun, in preparation).

3 Consider other 'distribution systems' for talk, perhaps aim towards fewer, but longer, chats with individual children.

4 Recruit additional adults into the preschool by inviting parents to serve on regular book-corner rota, etc. If this does not suit them, ask them to mix paint and thereby free regular staff for talk.

When parents send their children off to playgroup or nursery school their expressed reason usually has to do with providing opportunity to play with other children (Turner, 1977). Most do *not* mention the acquisition of cognitive or linguistic (in the syntactic sense) skills for they believe these to be the province of formal schooling. This bias towards the social side of preschool experience is shared by many practitioners, some of whom think that social and intellectual growth may be at odds, or, more particularly, that the decision to focus on one rather than the other dictates materials and activities. They may be right. Some activities stretch the mind, as for example art and puzzles, while others provide 'room' for social interaction, as in the case of rough-and-tumble play. Boisterous play, with one-off utterances tossed into the fray, may indeed be stretching for children. But if it is (and we have no evidence either way) it's a different kind of stretch from that described in Chapter 4.

There are two kinds of social interaction that we have identified as stretching and these are dialogue and game-like play. Both require skills of social exchange (when to take a turn, how to be relevant, how to expand on the last move). We began the chapter by describing how spoken language enables its user to transcend the present, to plan the future, and to be 'ready' for reading. By language skill we mean its effective use in conversation and not merely knowledge of its grammatical rules. The chapter has not demonstrated the importance of language skills, for others have done this before us. Instead it looked at the opportunity for conversation in the preschool environment.

All of us would be horrified upon visiting a preschool to find the children engaged continuously at challenging activities while silent and alone. Good preschools encourage social interaction and talk between the generations as well as within them. We stress the value of conversation for its intellectual side as well as its social nature.

We, like parents, would wish children to be skilled at conversation so that they can express their desires, make cooperative plans, and assert their rights by language and not by physical force. And added to these 'bonuses' of conversation skills are the sheer pleasure of language play and the feelings of warmth and acceptance one gets from a convivial chat.

6

State and voluntary provision

In our year of observing in Oxford's preschool centres we found not one instance of horrific practice; there were no programmes so rigid as to force children to remain in chairs all day, and none so relaxed that children were allowed to victimize one another. In the main, children seemed happy at preschool, spending their time in productive play and getting along well with their neighbours.

However, despite the rosy picture painted above, *some* children spent empty days 'cruising' round the centre, getting into squabbles, or staring blankly at people or events. Other children, almost as worrisome, stolidly took part in the traditional fare of sand or dough but showed no sign of challenge or commitment. Children such as these, visibly under-stretched or making trouble, were not scattered randomly across the centres but seemed to cluster in some places rather than in others. We argue here that not all of the aimless activity we observed was a consequence of children's dullness or 'deprived backgrounds'; it was brought about by certain kinds of regime.

This brings us squarely to consideration of differences between centres. First we sorted the centres into the statutory divisions of *school, class, playgroup*. Next we looked to see whether there were differences between the groups; did children act differently in the three types of provision?

Three different types of preschool

To begin, a great deal of rhetoric – although not many facts – has been amassed concerning the advantages of nursery schools, classes, or playgroups. We observed differences within each statutory category but also found surprising commonalties. Corinne Hutt and her colleagues (1977) found that the behaviour of children and staff varied according to a variety of institutional constraints. Our own findings echo theirs, though they observed in Staffordshire and we in Oxford.

There follows a detailed description of three very different preschool centres. Morris Road Nursery, Poplar Hill Class, and St James's Playgroup are not pseudonyms for actual centres but are composite pictures drawn to highlight features important in the empirical analyses that follow.

Morris Road Nursery School

The Morris Road Nursery School, situated in an old industrial area, is a self-contained, custom-built unit in spacious grounds. On one side a stout fence cuts it off from a busy road and the rest of the grounds are surrounded by a high brick wall, making a secluded garden.

The front door leads into an open area flanked with rows of pegs for the children's outdoor clothing. On one side is a large play room and at the other side two smaller play rooms adjoining each other; the doors of these rooms are rarely closed. The open area gives onto other rooms too: a large washroom with rows of child-sized toilets and wash-basins, and pegs for each child's washing things; the office and staff room; and a large kitchen. A glance around gives the impression of space and bustle.

We look at the outdoor area first. A concrete path surrounds the building, leading, in the back, to a playground: first a tarmac hard-surface area, and beyond that a grassed area with trees and a shed housing the outdoor equipment. Permanently stationed are two different climbing frames, one incorporating a slide. A rocker, tressles and car tyres are always out but may be moved around. Other apparatus is stored in the shed during bad weather and brought out as required: planks, small ladders, large hollow blocks and crates, a barrel, footballs, and wheeled vehicles – large and small carts, pram frames, and so forth. On the grassy area is a small garden plot with shrubs and flowers, and a rabbit hutch.

Indoors, in the three play rooms, a wide range of materials is permanently laid out or readily accessible: two water troughs, a sand trough, a dough table, two painting easels and a blackboard easel, a home corner with cots, crockery, dolls, model sink, ironing board, toy first-aid kit, and so on, a large art table with a selection of drawing and decorating implements, a woodwork table, a construction table with lego, connector rods and mosaics, a nature table, rows of pegs for dressing-up clothes and aprons, a music corner with a piano, record-player and small instruments, a book corner, a 'crane' (two basins of bottle-tops and a pulley and hook to which a bucket can be attached for moving bottle-tops) and a cage with a hamster. The rooms are surrounded by open shelves containing jigsaws and other puzzles or games such as picture-lotto, dominoes, building block sheets of coloured paper, a model zoo set, transport toys including a garage set and train-track sections, boxes of beads and thread, and an assortment of other materials such as pegboards, a shape-posting box, and a music box. Materials may be taken from the shelves to tables or used on the floor. The walls are decorated with paintings, tapestries and collages done by the children.

One of the smaller rooms is designated the 'quiet' room, containing the book corner, nature table, and table top activities (such as puzzles and crayoning). The other small room contains a few tables around the sides and some easily-cleared-up materials on the floor, but the space is kept fairly free for dressing-up games and physical-movement activities. This room is also used for 'large group' times such as story or music-and-movement. It contains the music corner.

Although most of the materials are available most of the time, there are some day-to-day variations. The contents of the water and sand troughs, for example, are changed, the nature table varies with the seasons, and 'unusual' materials – such as trays of sugar, salt and flour for the children to examine – may be put out occasionally. Children help themselves to what is available on tables and shelves, with a few restrictions. Water isn't permitted in the home corner, and things from the home corner may not be taken out of it; books remain in the book corner; permission has to be requested before adding water to the sand trough.

Temporal restrictions, too, are minimal. Weather permitting, there is usually free access to the outdoor area. Various adult-led activities are offered in each session – a group may go to the kitchen to make rolls, small groups or individuals may be led in 'arts and crafts' such as collage work or sewing. Large group activities such as story, singing, music-and-movement, listening to a radio programme, are offered at least once per session. None of these is 'compulsory' though all children are invited to join, and no rigid time-schedule is followed – children who elect not to join in go to another room or outdoors. Milk- or snack-time occurs at a fixed hour but is 'staggered' in small groups, so that a child may come to a later group if she wants to finish some task first. Some routine is of course inevitable, at the ends of sessions, for instance. At the end of the morning, all children have to help in tidying up, then to line up to go to the toilet and wash, returning to a large group activity such as action-songs, until it is time to go home or to lunch. The entire group of children participates with one adult (allowing other adults to complete tidying up and lunch preparations), though if a single child preferred to go off to the book corner he would not be forced to join the singing group.

Fifty children, mostly from the local lower-middle and working-class families (including a few immigrants) are enrolled per session. At the moment, eight of them are 'social services referrals' – children with special needs (arising from, say, physical handicap or home problems) assigned to Morris Road by the local authorities. The age range is from three years eight months to five years four months, with more older than younger. All come for five days a week; in their last two terms before moving up to first school, most of the children attend for the full day (9 to 3.30, staying for lunch), while the others attend either only morning or only afternoon sessions. Children are nominally assigned on an age-basis to one room and to a teacher in charge of that room, but all that this entails in practice is that the child goes to his room and teacher at the start of a session, after which he is free to roam where he will.

The Morris Road School is quite well-off for staff. It has five permanent, professionally-trained staff – three teachers (one the head teacher) and two nursery nurses, and in addition two students serving part of their training for the Nursery Nurse Education Board qualification on placement in the school. One of the mothers comes in one day a week to sit with the children in the 'quiet' room. Although ultimately answerable to the local education authority, the head teacher is clearly in charge of everything that happens in the school. There are informal staff discussions, but it is the head who takes final decisions and has final responsibility for daily and long-term management and policy. Within that framework, each staff member has a considerable degree of freedom to specialize in activities of her choice. Thus one takes the music-and-movement groups while another prefers to do art work. Who does what is quite flexible, with the proviso that there is at least one adult in each area – room or playground – at all times.

Not only the staff but also the parents look to the head for counsel, inquiring about their children's progress, seeking advice, reassurance or even 'someone to talk to' about family matters. Parents are encouraged to stay with the child at the start of the session to take off his outdoor clothes and settle him in the room, and to come into the room to fetch him at the end of sessions. The head makes a point of exchanging at least a few words with each parent at these times. The parent of a new child is urged to stay with him in the school during the days or weeks of his 'settling in' period. With the exception of the single regular mother-helper, however, parents do not participate in the daily activities; there is a feeling that the staff are professionally trained to look after the children and that parents do not become involved. Although a termly 'open' staff meeting is held to which parents are welcomed, few – always the same few – ever attend.

What of the less tangible characteristics of the school? Morris Road views itself as a half-way house between the small family unit and the wide world of the first school. The focus is on the social and emotional security of the child as well as on the development of his cognitive skills, and there is at least as much emphasis on 'unstructured' activities (body movement, pretending, sand/water/dough manipulation, exploring) as on 'educational', structured ones (shape-matching tasks, letters and numbers, and so on).

The children are never regimented in traditional classroom fashion. There is a notion of not forcing the child, of letting him decide on his own capabilities and interests and of allowing his skills to develop 'naturally'. Although adult-led group activities are offered overt *direction* by the adult is kept to a minimum. This is not to say that staff keep out of the way; rather, instead of choosing what the child does and how he does it, the adult tends to hover, monitoring what is going on in the room and waiting until a child settles at a particular activity before coming over to him. In these situations, the 'tutorial chat' is common. The adult works with a single child or a small group, in a role not of leading but of helping the children to elaborate the talk or task themselves. The task with which a child has settled provides a 'here and now' basis for discussion with a topic shared by both child and adult, and the conversation may develop around the present materials and activity or may take off to a more abstract level, to talk about general concepts (like the relationships between the size and the weight of objects) or about other times and places (typical child-initiations being, 'We've got one of those at home,' or, 'I saw one like that last week. We went to see my uncle's farm...'). Rarely, on the other hand, do the children spontaneously approach a free adult for a chat; for one thing, free adults are scarce, and for another, children's initiations are likely to be about arbitration and services 'I can't tie my apron,' 'Stephen's just taken the paint and it's *my* turn,' 'Can we have a story?'). Much of the adult's time is in fact devoted to such management tasks – getting the milk ready, rounding up children for a story, taking a child to the toilet, comforting another who has fallen off the slide. And there are certain activities that the adults rarely join in unless asked – pretending, free art, free outdoor play; adult involvement in these is generally regarded (by the adults) as interference.

In general, then, the children have considerable freedom of choice and much to choose from among the material, adult and peer resources. On any day in Morris Road Nursery School, there is a hubbub of activity and children in every corner; a group listening to the teacher reading a story; a few noisily playing firemen outside; two playing in the sand while listening to music; two more experimenting with soap bubbles in the washroom; a quiet group at the construction table; a 'hospital' scene enacted in the home corner....

St James's Playgroup

St James's Church lies in a modern, middle-class housing estate on the town outskirts. It is a quiet area, populated mainly by young families, fathers commute to neighbouring towns to jobs in the professions, while mothers are rarely in paid employment.

Adjoining St James's is the church hall, which serves as a kind of community centre. Several meetings take place there each week: boy scouts, girl guides, a men's club, a women's guild, coffee mornings and jumble sales, a mother-toddler group, a church choir, a dramatic society – and the local playgroup. On each occasion, the users have to adapt the hall for their own requirements – setting out or clearing up furniture, for example. The multi-purpose nature of the hall, where nothing is custom-built, poses certain problems for each set of users; but before examining how this affects the running of the playgroup, we look first at the permanent structure of the premises.

A low wall separates the site from the road. There is no gate across the entrance; an open concrete path leads round the side of the church to the hall behind it, terminating in a small, paved 'patio' by the hall door. The rest of the grounds are surfaced with gravel or grass-plus-flowers.

Going indoors, one enters a gloomy hallway with a few coat-hooks. To one side is a small kitchen with rather antiquated but adequate facilities, and in an alcove next to it a large, old-fashioned sink, while the toilet is across the yard.

Off the other side of the hallway is a closed door leading to the hall itself – a large rectangular room with a permanent stage (curtained off when not in use) at one end. Wooden benches are aligned against the walls all round the room; there is a piano in one corner and a cupboard in another. The rest of the furniture and equipment of all the hall users is stored either under the stage or outside in the alcove with the sink – a collapsible tressle and card tables, stacking chairs, stage props... and all the playgroup equipment.

What are the implications of these permanent physical characteristics for the playgroup? Most important, since the premises were not designed with childcare in mind, is that none of the structural features are child-sized or proofed. Because there is no barrier at the front entrance, children outdoors have to stay at the back of the hall under close surveillance to ensure they don't stray out onto the road. They are restricted, further, to the tiny paved area – the rest of the grounds, gravel and grass, are out-of-bounds lest the children either damage themselves on the gravel or damage the vegetation. For similar reasons, the door to the building remains locked during sessions, and since it locks from the inside, visitors or parents calling in the middle of a session (for instance to bring a child in late, to talk to the supervisor) must knock for entry rather than just walking in. At the start and end of sessions, the door is open for a while with an adult on duty. A visitor into the hallway at these times, start and end of session, would encounter a chaos of bodies. Since the pegs are so closely parked, coats are crammed together and there is a scramble as adults and children, cramped in the narrow, dimly-lit space, search for gloves, shoes, aprons, lost drawings. At the sink, the taps are too high for a preschool-size child to reach. The light switches for the stairs and toilet are also too high, as is the lavatory itself; so an adult has to be on hand to help whenever a child needs these facilities.

Yet, far from the spirit of 'making do' and disorganization that one might expect, everything runs in smooth and orderly fashion as a result of thoughtful management. The same is true of the setting up, clearing away and arranging of furniture and equipment in the hall itself, to which we turn in a moment. Before that, however, we deal with the financial side.

Whereas nursery schools and classes are state-supported, playgroups operate largely on a voluntary basis. Though they do receive some government aid (it varies from county to county but a £50 per annum grant from Social Services is not unusual) the playgroups must seek much of their funds elsewhere. One source is the small fee paid for each child per session, and thanks also to fund-raising efforts and to goods and services donated by parents and community, St James's is by no means impoverished. Of course they keep a strict eye on the budget and save where possible. Regular essential expenses drawing on these government and privately raised funds are: rent of hall (a nominal sum to cover share of maintenance and energy costs only); the 'salary' of the permanent staff – supervisor and assistant, other helpers being unpaid; and biscuits for children's mid-morning break (adults contribute separately for their own refreshments). What is left over goes towards equipment and materials.

Some of the standard furniture – tables, chairs, piano – is owned by the church and is for general use. Some other basic items had to be bought new by the playgroup: small children's chairs and tables, a collapsible wooden slide with adjustable climbing bars, beakers for milk-time, jigsaw puzzles, lego, large building blocks, two painting easels and supplies of paint, and so forth. But as much as possible is obtained second-hand, donated, or contributed by parents. Paper for painting is used computer print-out begged from a nearby college. Mothers provide dough for manipulation activities – flour and water mixture that is carefully collected after each session and stored in refrigeration so that it can be re-used several times; paste for glueing is similarly home-made. One of the fathers built a collapsible hardboard wendy house and others donated its contents, cushions, blankets, cot, pots and pans, crockery, dolls. Parents collect news-papers, cardboard boxes, toilet-roll tubes, bottle tops, but-tons, sawdust, scraps of cloth and wool, egg-cartons, silver paper, bits of wood, nails, old paintbrushes and other tools for art work, junk modelling, paper and woodwork construc-tions. An old plastic baby bath on the floor serves for water-play. Hand washing bowls are set out on chairs.

Old clothes go into the dressing-up box. Parents from past years give games, puzzles, building bricks, toy cars, train sets, books and occasional larger items such as light tricycles, dolls' prams. Repairs, too, are often carried out by parents and friends.

Not all the equipment, however, is available to the chil-dren all of the time, owing in part to the physical structure of the premises and in part to the temporary nature of its occupation. Because nothing can be permanently stationed, both geographical and temporal restrictions are imposed and careful planning is required to ensure that everything runs smoothly with minimal disruption. Either for these reasons, or simply from preference, St James's follows a rather structured schedule: a typical daily programme would be: *9 a.m.* The staff arrive and set out the equipment. Benches are arranged to mark off a book corner, a dressing-up corner, and so on. The wendy house and slide are erected. Tables go at one end of the room for 'quiet' play, the activities being varied from a selection of puzzles, and construction toys, to dough, beads, drawing materials, and so on. Climbing apparatus goes at the other end where areas are left free for physical movement with carts and tricycles, or just running and jumping.

9.15–9.30 a.m. Children trickle in as adults finish setting up the room. Some parents stay for a short while to settle a child at a table, though many of the children head for the climbing/open area to let off steam.

9.30–10.30 a.m. Free play, the children choosing as they wish from the range available. During this period at least one adult-directed project is offered; sometimes a single project spans over several days. Most of them have to do with 'arts and crafts': junk modelling, collage, making Christmas decorations, Easter cards or woodwork. Children are taken a few at a time to work with the adult; almost all children have a turn and are eager to participate, though the odd one who refuses is not forced. The adult's role may be supervisory, standing by until asked for help or comment; or, depending on the nature of the project (and her own attitude), the adult may be very much in evidence, explaining just what to do and how, helping with cutting and pasting, and closely involved with every step of the child's task. Adults not engaged in such projects are scattered about the room, perhaps sitting at a table discussing puzzles with a group, perhaps helping children on the climbing frame, changing paper and chatting about painting at the easels, or joining in a pretend tea party. Towards the end of the period, one or two go to the kitchen to prepare for milk-time, and children are called to wash their hands.

10.30–10.50 a.m. Milk-time. All the children and adults gather in a large group at the same time, bringing chairs to a circle in the middle of the room. Although the staff try to arrange things to avoid it, occasionally children have to abandon a task in the middle to go to milk. Yet the children seem not to mind, accepting it as part of the daily routine. A few children are appointed to hand out beakers of milk and biscuits. During their rapid consumption, children are urged to remain seated, but there follows an open discussion on any topic of interest. The supervisor may ask someone to tell the group about a holiday trip; a child may initiate talk about a visit to the doctor. Often a child or adult brings something to show – a new toy, photographs, a collection of pebbles.

10.50–11.00 a.m. All the children stay in the circle and one or two adults lead them in group activities – story, song, circle games. Exceptionally, the entire group may go outdoors to the small paved area for organized games, such as 'stepping stones' on a tiled floor. These are the only occasions – few and far between – on which children have access to the outdoor area. During this period, other adults are busy tidying up the milk things, and clearing away or rearranging equipment. In particular, large-scale apparatus or 'messy' activities that take time to put away and clean up are dealt with. The climbing frame, slide, and wendy house are dismantled and stored, dough and paints are removed and utensils used for them cleaned. Tables are rearranged and some fresh materials put out. The children are strongly encouraged to stay with the concurrent group activity to allow clearing up to progress unhindered.

11.10–11.45 a.m. Free play, conducted as in the earlier spell though now mostly with table-top materials, and adults joining groups or individuals.

11.45 a.m.–12.15 p.m. The entire group, children as well as adults, tidies up. Children are allowed a few extra minutes to finish what they are doing, but most stop promptly when called. Hands, dirty toys and spills on floor or tables are washed, paintings or other products laid out on a bench ready for taking home, toys stacked in boxes and taken to the cupboard, dressing-up clothes retrieved, and furniture collapsed and stacked. Children are free to choose their task, though a child standing at a loose end is assigned a chore. As soon as a child finishes his duties, he joins a group forming around the piano for adult-led singing games while storing of furniture and equipment is completed. The singing continues until the children are collected, but a few don't join in, preferring instead to run around the now vacant floor, climb on the benches, examine each other's paintings, or watch from the sidelines. The door of the hall is unlocked at noon and parents enter during the next 15 minutes. At this time, the regular supervisor or assistant are always available for chat. The staff tend not to make the first approach unless there is something specific they wish to discuss with a parent.

Currently, 22 children attend, two of them social services referrals whom the playgroup accepted although they were not obliged to. Almost all come from the neighbouring houses, with one or two from a nearby poorer estate. The youngest child is just three years and the oldest five years two months. Occasionally unenrolled siblings are present, accompanying parent-helpers. Unlike the state nurseries, the balance is towards the younger end of the scale, the majority being between three and a half and four and a half years old. Two factors account for this. One is that the nurseries, with longer waiting lists and more selective intake, allot places to older children to give them preschool experience before first school. The second is that many children attending the playgroup initially switch to the nursery when a place becomes available.

St James's operates on only three days a week (Mondays, Wednesdays and Fridays) for morning sessions only. Parents are discouraged from sending a child to another centre for afternoons or on intervening days as it is felt that it is difficult for younger children to adjust to *two* sets of children, and *two* different regimes.

There are two 'permanent' members of staff at St James's, the supervisor and her assistant. Though no formal qualifications are required, the centre is affiliated to the Pre-school Playgroups Association, and both staff members have undergone PPA training courses. The supervisor, moreover, is a formally trained primary school teacher who gave up practice when she started a family. Leadership is passed on when the supervisor's children leave the centre, if she gets another job, or moves. St James's, then, changes hands every few years. For the same reason, members of the parent committee also change frequently. Whereas the supervisor and assistant handle daily running of the group, they are responsible to this committee, elected from the parents, which governs financial matters and takes decisions about long-term policy.

In addition to the permanent staff, at least two other adults are present daily. It is expected that parents assist, and at the start of term a rota is drawn up. There is one helper in attendance for many mornings of the playgroup week; a turn comes round about once or twice a term, and children get to know the various adults. St James's is perhaps unusual in the customarily female-dominated preschool world in having two father-helpers whose jobs permit flexible hours. Helpers assist in the domestic chores, setting up and clearing away equipment, preparing for milk-time, mopping up, but whether or not they involve themselves with the children's play is up to them. The supervisor does not offer directions unless helpers ask for them or make suggestions. Some do actively participate, taking story or music-periods, joining groups at tables, and so on. Others, perhaps in awe of the large body of children, prefer to stay with the domestic duties or sit passively alongside children engaged in some activity on their own. The parent-on-rota and occasional parent present while a new child 'settles in' make a liberal sprinkling of non-staff adults among the children.

How does this regime affect the children's activities? For one thing, obviously, the relative lack of space and stricter temporal and geographical arrangements mean fewer physical movement activities, more adult-led large group ones, and fewer children engaged in solitary pastimes. In the playgroup moreover, the children spend a smaller proportion of their time examining materials or cruising through the environment; and they switch tasks less often. Does the child engage busily with his task while he can, knowing that those materials are available for only a while?

The concomitants of the playgroup's structural limitations are counterbalanced by great flexibility in other ways, for example in freedom to combine materials. Children can and do take dough, implements and dressing-up clothes into the wendy house for a pretend birthday party, rearrange furniture to create a den, or take blankets, cushions, dolls, out of the wendy house and set them up elsewhere in the room. Far from being hampered by the relative lack of custom-built preschool equipment the children make the most of what is available; witness the incidence of creative art, construction and junk modelling activities using left-over scraps brought from home. An old cardboard box serves many functions; it can be jumped on and smashed; turned into a cart to be pulled along the floor for transporting toys or a friend; it can be added to others to build a wall; it can be used in a game of 'see who can throw the brick into the box'; or it can be turned into a garage for cars. . .

Adults appear in a role of 'family friend' as much as of 'tutor' or 'manager', and this is reflected in the children's interactions with them, for they spontaneously approach adults, even comparative strangers, not just for service ('I want to go to the toilet') but for an informal chat ('It's my birthday today and see my new dress, and we're going to have a party').

Poplar Hill First School nursery class

Not far from St James's Church is Poplar Hill First School. Still in the suburban housing area, it serves two neighbourhoods, that of the middle-class professional families, some of whom are involved at St James's, and the adjacent council estate.

The school, which takes children up to 11 years old, spreads over a large site. Modern, purpose-built classrooms of open-plan design are housed in several buildings surrounded by spacious tarmac playground. As enrolment began to dwindle in response to the falling birthrate, one of the rooms was converted into a unit for preschool children, so the nursery class is a recent addition at Poplar Hill.

The unit was allocated a room in one of the inner buildings of the complex, together with its own private section of playground. Older children may not enter this area, and for safety the preschoolers are not allowed outside it on their own. Parents are advised to accompany them to and from class, for the route from the school gate to it is circuitous.

The nursery playground is cut off from the rest of the

grounds, bordered on three sides by the nursery and other classrooms, with the fourth side and gaps between barred by old benches, permanently stationed except when moved for passage at the start and end of sessions. Few parents do enter, however, rather than deposit and collect their children at the bench-barrier.

One half of the playground is crammed with fixed equipment: a row of three swings, a climbing frame with slide, and a pyramid constructed from large wooden logs stepped up to a peak. The other half is open for free physical activity or moveable equipment which is otherwise stored under large eaves overhanging the side of the building – two tricycles and pedal cars, a scooter, sand and water troughs, a set of large building blocks, tressles and planks, foam rubber mats, hoops and balls. Also under the eave is a large permanent sandpit sheltered when not in use by a tarpaulin weighted down with old tyres.

From the playground one enters the nursery through a door kept locked on the inside when all children are indoors. Off one side of the classroom runs a corridor giving onto staffroom, storage alcoves (one containing deep sinks and refrigerator), and a spacious cloakroom with children's toilets and washbasins as well as rows of coat-hooks for outdoor clothing and overalls. At the far end of the nursery, at a boundary marked off by a row of tables, a few steps lead up to an openly adjoining room occasionally occupied by older classes.

The large nursery classroom itself is divided by shelves or benches into smaller areas. Though some of the activities within areas are varied, the physical lay-out of the room is fixed. Near the neighbouring classroom is a 'free play area'. To one side of a central open space are tables and chairs in alcoves formed by shelves containing materials such as jigsaws, picture lotto, dominoes, lego and other small-scale construction sets, beads and thread, paper, pens and crayons. On the other side are a well-equipped home corner, pegs with dressing-up clothes, a set of large building blocks, and a music ledge with a few small instruments – a xylophone, percussion instruments, a music box. Sometimes in winter the water trough is brought indoors to the free play area. Towards the other end, the room is devoted to more 'serious business'. Partitions again mark off side areas: the nature table, a secluded book corner with piles of bright cushions on the floor, a further table of 'structured' puzzles and games, another home corner (this one given over mostly to toy shop equipment) a cash register with coloured counters and a coin-box telephone as well as stocks of tins and packets and a 'dymograph' for marking prices. The walls above these are covered with coloured pinboard for displaying children's work. Free-standing tables occupy the central floor space here, with materials varied daily from a range including miniature zoo and fort sets, plasticine, mosaics, numbered bricks, and several art activities – printing, collage, drawing, papier mâché, finger- or string-painting, stencils, and so on. This end of the room also contains storage cupboards and another deep sink.

In fact, much the same sorts of materials are in evidence here as at other State-run centres, though, lacking Morris Road's space, the class has restricted its range slightly and materials for certain activities have to be laid out at special times. At the free play end, equipment is permanently available and children help themselves at will. Only things from home- or block-corners may be used on the floor, however; table-top materials are confined to designated tables and must be returned to the appropriate shelf when finished, a rule which holds for books and musical instruments as well.

There is a clear distinction between the 'free play' and 'educational' sections of the room, for adults are noticeably in charge in the latter area. Not only do they control the activities set out, rotating them daily from cupboards inaccessible to the children, but they spend most of their time here supervising children's projects and rarely venture into free play activities either indoor or out; in this respect they resemble Morris Road. Despite the designation of 'work' and 'play' areas, however, the distinction lies more in the eyes of the staff than the children, who have considerable freedom. It means simply that the range from which the children may choose always includes at least one adult-led activity, the adult working with small groups of individuals. Normally the adult waits for children to request a turn, though if a particular child has not joined in for a while he is strongly encouraged to 'make something to go on the wall' or 'to take home'; but most children eagerly await a turn, showing great interest especially in the 'messy' or unusual art activities. Sometimes the child has freedom to do what he pleases at these tables, or sometimes the adult directs step by step towards a specific end product, taking the opportunity to discuss task and materials in the kind of 'tutorial chat' we heard at the nursery school.

Unlike Morris Road, however, with its roomy self-contained premises and freedom of access throughout, the nursery class has a special set of time-and-space restrictions arising from its location within the main school. Its own playground is not used when older classes either are working in the adjacent buildings (lest the preschoolers' noisy outdoor play be distracting) or are occupying surrounding playgrounds (when it is they who distract the younger children). This means that on most days outdoor access is limited to a forty-minute period in the morning and again in the afternoon, further cuts being imposed by bad weather. When the playground is available, there is a rush outdoors. At these times, the staff remain with the few children who elect for indoor activities, looking out occasionally but rarely becoming involved unless to set up the sandpit or to arbitrate in a dispute over the scarce resources of wheeled vehicles or swings. Although most children do head for these or for the climbing apparatus, there are always quiet spots for water play or construction.

Indoors some restrictions are in force too, again imposed by the proximity of older children on the occasions when the adjoining classroom is occupied. Then not only are the preschoolers kept away from the free play space nearest the other class, but quiet activities have to be found for them, either compulsory story-time for the whole group or work at the art and puzzle tables. The unit does, however, benefit from its place within the school in being able at prearranged hours to use the school gymnasium (particularly helpful in winter when outdoor physical activity is impossible) and television or radio. In fact, the short daily programme *Play-school* proved so popular with the children that the entire group is taken into the main school regularly to watch it.

Temporal scheduling outside of that imposed by the unit's setting is minimal. Milk- or snack-time is held at a fixed hour in each session. Two children first help with preparations (inserting straws in bottles, for instance), then summon the rest – the entire group assembles at once in the book corner, though occasionally a child asks to be a few minutes late in order to finish some task. While the group is assembled, an adult-led activity proceeds – singing, story, music. These are offered at other times too, again for the entire group all of whom are expected to attend, though it is not unknown for the children to vote *en masse* not to participate and, rather than compelling them, the activity is abandoned!

At start and end of sessions, outdoor play time, and in preparation for milk, children routinely go to the cloakroom to change clothes or wash. As this entails marching through the quiet work area to reach the corridor to the cloakroom, to avoid disruption of activities children are lined up to go all at once. Parents are urged to bring their children promptly at the start of the session, and all leave together, so that stragglers don't interrupt at other times. In the cloakroom, each child has his own peg labelled with a name and picture of a creature or flower, the symbol appearing also on his overall. As each quickly learns his own symbol, finding the right peg or clothes is easy and accomplished by the children themselves without supervision. Perhaps this exemplifies the idea evident in the class of instilling self-discipline and independence in the children, who are encouraged to decide what to do and get on with it themselves. The symbols occasionally crop up too in group games or music-and-movement, as in, 'All the animals crouch down and all the flowers stand up tall; those children with wings fly to the other side . . .'.

Who are the children? Twenty-six are enrolled for morning sessions and a further twenty-six for afternoons. Although the unit originally had the option of taking full-timers with lunch available in the main school, it was decided to have half-day attendance to provide opportunity for preschool for the maximum number. The children, all at this moment over four years old, come equally from the two adjacent neighbourhoods and include several from immigrant families who are initially non-English speakers.

As in Morris Road Nursery School, the staff are professionally qualified and the unit run by a head teacher who decides how the class operates, is consulted by parents and staff, and has the ultimate authority. Very different from the nursery school, on the other hand, the head takes little part in daily events in the unit, for he is also the head of the entire school and his office and duties are centred away from the preschool area. Day to day administration and activities are handled equally by two full-time staff, one an infant teacher from the school who transferred to the nursery when it opened, the other a nursery nurse. Two part-time staff complete the adult quota – another nurse for afternoons and an experienced but untrained assistant for mornings. Staff share all duties, both the domestic ones and those involving work directly with the children, and all are equally responsible to the 'external' head.

Parents enter the classroom rarely – except on Thursdays, when in the second half of sessions parents are invited in. The staffroom is set aside for them to meet over coffee and chat together or with staff who take turns on duty at these times. Towards the end of these sessions, parents may go into the classroom to watch or to sit with children and join in their play and talk. This arrangement has proved very popular, and many of the mothers and several fathers attend the coffee meetings; fewer, though, actually go into the classroom, which, as at Morris Road, is felt to be the province of the professionals.

On other days, the nursery staffroom is rarely used, for the adults take breaks and meals in the main school, where they also participate in staff meetings. In many ways, in fact, the nursery unit functions much as any class in the school and carries much more of an air of 'preparing for school' than do other centres. Unless they choose an activity where an adult is already stationed, the children are left much to their own devices. Because of the numbers of children present and relative lack of space, there is little opportunity for solo or indoor physical activity. In the free play area away from the adults, children play together calmly, sometimes silently side by side, sometimes chatting over the puzzles, the water, or in a retreat they have built from blocks and home corner equipment. At the 'work' end of the room, the emphasis is on 'getting something done'. Here the children busily engage, a few at free drawing, a couple listening to a story, one learning with an adult how to make a cut-out paper doll chain, a group laying dominoes with adult help. The talk at this end, as well as the discussions taking off from tasks and materials, is mostly the language of instruction and management. The attachment to the school is further accentuated by the fact that most of the children will subsequently continue in the same school – several at present have siblings in the older classes – and termly excursions are made into the reception class that they will enter when they outgrow the nursery.

How the types of preschool differ

There follows discussion of the organizational differences in the three types of preschool we studied in Oxford. Preschool practice varies throughout Britain and the characteristics of nursery schools, for instance, will vary from county to county. In Hutt's Staffordshire study, nursery schools tended to be staffed by nursery nurses (NNEBs) whereas nursery classes had teachers in them. This was certainly not the case in Oxfordshire where heads of nursery schools were invariably trained teachers and nursery classes had at least one teacher on the staff. Therefore, differences between statutory type should not be generalized literally to the rest of the UK. Instead, the reader should examine ways that differing organizational patterns (no matter what their official names) are associated with differences in children's activities.

Our findings in this and subsequent chapters are based on three kinds of data: information in the twenty-minute observational records, observations made in the preschools but not actually part of the observation instrument, and interviews with staff members. Obviously these sources yield different kinds of information and we will attempt to be explicit as to the nature of the data on which the various claims are made.

Because potentially dangerous generalizations will be made about 'typical' nursery schools or playgroups in Oxfordshire, keep in mind that centres do vary considerably. Despite this, our researchers were often heard to say, 'That playgroup is run like a nursery school,' or 'Compared to other nursery classes, this one has a remarkable array of outdoor equipment.' Statements like these show a loose group of characteristics to be associated with the statutory title *nursery school, nursery class,* and *playgroup* – at least in Oxfordshire (Table 6.1). We now turn to an examination of differences in the overall organization of the three kinds of centre.

Physical premises

On this dimension the state sector clearly shines. Most important is the fact that nursery schools and classes are housed in stationary quarters with rather permanent equipment, so that there is no need to store things away at the end of the day. In general, both schools and classes have plenty of outdoor space, although it is not always available to the nursery class who usually share it with the rest of the infant school. The indoor area of the nursery class is usually smaller than that of the nursery school and often has about it an air of a classroom rather than of a home. In it, children work and play quite close to one another.

Morris Road Nursery School	Poplar Hill First School Nursery Class	St James's Playgroup
Permanent, self-contained premises	Permanent premises located within main school	'Temporary' shared premises in church hall
Three indoor playrooms plus other facilities; hard- and soft-surface outdoor areas; free access throughout	One large room plus other facilities; small hard-surface playground; restricted access to playground	One large room; limited facilities; no outdoor space to speak of (only a concrete path)
Full range of materials/equipment always available; permanent geography	Wide range of materials and equipment, not all available at once; fairly permanent geography	Fair range of materials/equipment not all available at once; flexible geography
Hours 9.00–11.45 a.m. and 1.00–3.15 p.m. five days per week; some children full-day, others half-day session only	Hours 9.10 a.m.–12 noon and 12.50–3.20 p.m. five days per week; children attend half-time, either mornings only or afternoons only	Hours 9.15 a.m.–12.15 p.m. three days per week
Temporal schedule very flexible	Temporal schedule fairly flexible but with some routine	Temporal schedule rather inflexible; routine activities occurring daily at the same hour, some of them compulsory
Very little 'compulsory' activity	A few compulsory activities	
Enrolment 50 children per session; adult-child ratio 1:7	Enrolment 26 children per session; Adult-child ratio 1:9	Enrolment 22 children; Adult-child ratio 1:5/1:6
Run by autonomous teacher within the unit	Run by 'external' head teacher of main school	Run by playleader responsible to parent committee
Little parent participation	No parent participation	Rota of parent helpers in the group plus parent participation in fund-raising, equipment-repairing activities, in addition to parent committee

Table 6.1 Summary of characteristics

Playgroups vary widely in terms of physical environment and there is no such thing as typical playgroup premises. But it can be concluded that playgroups have less equipment than the state-maintained classrooms and are often short of outdoor playspace. They are forced to move things about frequently and to use every bit of space for a variety of purposes. In a small study carried out in Oxfordshire on 20 randomly selected playgroups (Bradley, 1976) 16 of them occupied shared premises and had to put away equipment after each session.

Spatial lay-out

Here we look at arrangement of rooms, furniture and equipment. Playgroups, because of their cramped and often temporary quarters, do not have fixed equipment. This perforce leads to multi-purpose, flexible floor arrangements. The part of the room that houses the sand table at 9.00 may be the site of the lego set at 11.00, because the sand table has to fit in first into the storage space. By way of contrast, nursery schools and classes have permanent quarters and more fixed equipment, giving them a more stable geography.

Temporal schedule

Perhaps the counterpart to spatial fixedness is what might be called temporal rigidity. In this, there is a fixed schedule for each session and activities and materials are highly predictable. Sometimes the fixed activities are mandatory, as is often the case in playgroups with makeshift premises. Here, a child might be called to story so that the adults can prepare milk-time at the table he occupies. In our sample, more voluntary preschools had fixed schedules, probably due to spatial constraints that did not hold for the state sector. The situation, the Hutt *et al.* study tells us, is very different in Staffordshire, where nursery schools were most structured in daily schedule and nursery classes and playgroups were more free.

Professional status

This is the greatest difference between the state-maintained centres and the voluntary ones. Playgroup staff are 'non-professionals' working for an extremely low wage. They require no formal credentials, such as a teaching certificate (though they have perhaps a PPA foundation course), and have no tenure, nor paid holidays, nor sick-leave. But Oxfordshire like other counties is amply provided with playgroup staff who are highly trained for children's work. Seven of the nine playgroup supervisors in our sample had formal credentials in work with young children, such as a teaching certificate, an NNEB qualification, or an advanced PPA training. Thus, we observed highly skilled playgroup staff in jobs that were 'officially' open to 'ordinary mums'. Some methods of training playgroup staff are discussed in Appendix B but in general one might conclude that PPA training is flexible and de-emphasizes formal credentials. There is a mood of improvisation and experiment within the playgroup movement.

By way of contrast, all nursery schools and nursery classes employ staff with formal credentials for the work and their terms of employment are similar to those of other highly-skilled, professional workers.

Locus of responsibility

Each nursery school in Oxford is led firmly by its head teacher. She (and heads were invariably female) is responsible for all that transpires in the school. Heads possess a great measure of independence in running the school – there is no one on the premises with more authority – and, in times of difficulty both parents and other teachers look to her for guidance.

It is otherwise for the nursery class, where ultimate responsibility lies with the head of the entire first school, of which the nursery class is but one unit. Thus the person with ultimate responsibility is distant from the class itself. That can lead to a more democratic atmosphere since all those 'on the shop floor', so to speak, are workers under the supervision of an outside person and they often feel more free to experiment or 'do their own thing'. Naturally heads of nursery and first schools share ultimate authority and responsibility with the Boards of Managers. We are concerned here, however, with the face-to-fact lines of authority during the preschool day.

Playgroups are different again, but certainly the staff hardly think of the centre as under their sole authority. In fact the common arrangement is that the parents choose the supervisor and keep close tabs on her. She is, in fact, their employee. Thus, responsibility is divided between inside and outside sources. Furthermore, staff often retire a year or two after their own children have left playgroup, usually bringing turnover every three years. Again, a contrast to the state sector where staff may remain for years.

Relations to School and Home

The ethos of a centre is difficult to describe but easily felt on visiting. For each statutory category we shall attempt a composite picture of the views held by staff members concerning the children and the larger network of which the centre is a part.

Both the nursery school and the playgroup operate as independent units whereas the nursery class is formally an adjunct of the first school. Nursery schools and playgroups emphasize a caring relationship between adults and children and staff spend more time with them. Children sometimes call playgroup staff by Christian names – as they might a family friend. By way of contrast, staff in nursery classes perceive the child as a rather sturdy being able to manage on his own. (The notion of *adult as tutor* contrasted with adult as manager is discussed by Wood *et al.*) Both nursery schools and playgroups are removed from the first school and see themselves as part of the community, midway between home and school. In contrast, the nursery class sees itself as part of schooling and the child in it as a sturdy being fully 'ready for school'.

Perhaps the most important characteristic of a preschool centre is the attitude towards it of the parents. This influences the staff and certainly children respond to it as well. Playgroups are exceptional here as parents usually know that the finances, equipment and over-all policies of the playgroup are their responsibility. If the debt isn't made good, there will be a CLOSED sign on the door. If burst pipes ruin the toys, parents must raise funds to renew them.

How children's behaviour varies

We turn now to differences in ways the children behaved within the three categories. Remember that we studied only six nursery schools, six classes, and seven playgroups. There were, however, 80 observations in each kind of setting, at random throughout the sessions. We begin now by looking at the kinds of activities children engaged in throughout the day.

Activities

Children in nursery classes concentrated very heavily on pretend play and manipulating of 'plastic' materials such as sand, dough and water. They also went in for a great deal of sociable rough-and-tumble play, and informal games such as giggling-in-turn. They were lowest on constructional activities and also on watching others. In short, these children were the most sociable and 'productively busy' of our sample. Why? Their classrooms were usually smaller in size than the nursery schools and, being newer on the scene in Oxfordshire, were not so well endowed with outdoor equipment or specially constructed furniture. There was an atmosphere of orderliness, camaraderie and calm cheerfulness but not much room for gross motor play.

By way of contrast, nursery school children played rather little at pretend and manipulation, specializing instead in school readiness activities and gross motor play. The reasons for this, at least in Oxfordshire, are obvious, as the nursery schools have large and well-equipped gardens and they tend to allow children free access to the outdoors. But the children's fondness for gross motor play is even noticeable indoors, since these schools tend to have more open space for running and jumping about. Nursery school children were less social; when they were not engaged in muscular play they spent considerable time alone at structured materials, three Rs activities, or solving intellectual problems. Unfortunately, they also devoted quite a bit of time to wandering about the room, washing and dressing. It seems that the nursery schools in our study encouraged play with structured materials but also quite a bit of horsing around and 'empty' behaviour. The ethos of the schools, very well established, was one of providing stimulating materials but then giving a minimum of direction.

We come now to the voluntary sector. Here the children were most frequently seen participating in an adult-led group. It might be story circle, singing or dancing, or even organized games. Or the group might be small – but still led by an adult, often demonstrating an art skill. Manipulation and pretend were also popular in playgroups but not to the same extent as in the nursery class. Playgroup children were also sociable in their activities but the sociability was more often supervised or led by an adult. It has been pointed out earlier that playgroups were the most cramped for space and also had to share premises and tolerate the consequent clearing away. One response to these constraints is adult-led activities: one adult keeps the children busy while the others perform a caretaking task.

Task	Percentage of all observations in each category seen in each kind of centre (N = 80 observations in each case)			
	Nursery school	Nursery class	Playgroup	N
Three Rs and problem solving	92	1	7	78
Gross motor play	45	24	32	942
Structured materials	40	28	32	173
Aimless standing around, wandering or gazing	42	31	28	232
Manipulation	23	47	30	1156
Pretend	20	48	32	997
Adult-led group activities	26	20	54	742
Organized games with rules	25	21	52	87

Table 6.2 *Distribution of activity type across three institutional settings (Statistical test: Chi squared = 588·65)**

Conversation

It has been pointed out that children in nursery classes chose the more peer-sociable activities. Another way of investigating this claim is to look at the amount of dialogue seen in each category of centre. Table 6.3 shows very clearly that the 'sociable' child of the nursery class engages in child-child talk twice as frequently as his peers in either nursery school or playgroup. It also shows that playgroup staff, despite their greater numbers, do not have many conversations with children. Why? They engage in one-off remarks, or lead group activities.

---

* Chi square tests on the raw data are reported here and in subsequent tables as conventional indicators of significance. Like other classical tests of significance, they are not entirely appropriate to sequential, multi-stage sample data.

	Nursery school	Nursery class	Playgroup
Child-child	9	21	10
Child-staff member	8⎫	6⎫	4⎫
	⎬ 9	⎬ 7	⎬ 6
Child-non-staff member	1⎭	1⎭	2⎭
No dialogue	82	72	84

Table 6.3 *Percentage of time in which there was dialogue in three institutional settings (Chi squared = 271·65)*

Social groupings

Further confirmation of this finding is provided by Table 6.4 which looks at the relative frequency of various social groupings found in the three kinds of centre. Examining the most common groupings, it is clear that interaction between pairs of children prevails in nursery class, and the parallel pair in nursery school, and the playgroup divides its preference between the parallel pair and the group. These data nicely match the earlier findings on 'favourite' activities. The children in nursery classes choose the sociable activities (such as pretend); the children in playgroup participate often in groups led by adults; nursery schools have the highest percentage of children who pursue solo activities (concentrating for instance on three Rs activities).

	Nursery school	Nursery class	Playgroup
Alone	19	16	13
Parallel to another	38	27	33
Interacting in a child-child pair	24	33	24
Interacting in a group	19	24	30

Table 6.4 *Percentage of time children spend in social groups in three institutional settings (Chi squared = 212·81)*

Lastly, it has been noted that the most generous staff ratios are in playgroups. This should be reflected in the amount of time children in them are to be found in the company of adults. Table 6.5 shows that children in playgroups spend the

	Nursery school	Nursery class	Playgroup
No contact with adult	56	63	50
Some contact with adult	44	37	50
Child interacts with adult	23	20	23
Adult passive in child's company	21	16	27

Table 6.5 *Percentage of time children spend in contact with adults in three institutional settings (Chi squared = 147·6)*

most amount of time with adults, and children in nursery classes the least. Note however, that the greater contact between children and adults in the playgroups is a result of more instances of children in the *presence of adults*; nursery schools have as many instances of adults *actually interacting* with the children.

What lies behind the differences?

We have discussed differences in organization of the three kinds of preschool and also differences in the behaviour of children they serve. Are we certain of a causal relationship? Probably not. Some of the findings are obvious; children in nursery class and playgroup cannot run and jump and climb as frequently as those in nursery schools as their centres do not have access to much garden space or equipment. But why so much pretend and manipulation in the nursery class? One is tempted to say that these activities are fostered by the intimate setting. Recall that nursery classes are smaller in enrolment and also physical size. But the playgroup is also small in enrolment yet it had lower amounts of pretend and manipulation. Perhaps the greater need for quiet in the infant school led children to busy-but-not-boisterous pursuits. And maybe the children in playgroup would have engaged in more pretend if they weren't organized so often into group activities led by adults.

Speculation of this kind can be endless. Why are children in nursery class so sociable amongst themselves? This fact cannot be attributed solely to the lower enrolment as many playgroups are even smaller. But nursery attendance is five days each week whereas children often attend playgroup sessions less than that. Perhaps playgroup children do not know each other as well? Or again, perhaps they don't chat together so much because of the frequency of organized groups?

Hypothesis after hypothesis can be found. What did our observers think? It was their strong impression that the organization and ethos of the various types of centre affected the children. Teachers in nursery classes expected their young charges to plan their own activities and then *get on with them*. There were the usual rules about fragile toys and the occasional mandatory activity, but the children were assumed to be able to fend for themselves – which they did quite admirably. When discussing observed differences between the three preschool types, we are on strong empirical grounds. When discussing reasons for these differences, we admit to informed speculation. One speculation concerns the possibility of different populations of children.

Whereas nursery classes and schools drew children from roughly similar communities, many of our playgroups drew mainly from families where the parents were engaged in managerial and professional employment. Luckily some playgroups had more mixed intake, and one definitely catered to children from 'underprivileged' backgrounds. But on the whole, playgroups in Oxfordshire are like those elsewhere in serving a predominantly middle class child (Armstrong, 1977). It is possible that differences amongst playgroups and the state schools may be attributed, at least in part, to differential intake.

It would be unwise, however, to assume that *all* differences between the groups can be attributed to differential intake since the children in the playgroup who came from blue-collar families tended to act more 'playgroup' than 'nursery'.

Of course one working-class playgroup cannot prove the point. Another more telling argument against the 'differential intake' hypothesis is the fact that it cannot explain differences between the two kinds of state preschools. Recall that in our sample, nursery schools and classes served similar communities and had roughly equal proportions of children admitted off the priority waiting list. Because of this it seems more likely that differences in the two kinds of centre should be attributed to their contrasting organization patterns and ethos.

We know that this argument is weakened by the lack of precise information concerning backgrounds of observed children as well as others on the register. Because our study was not designed to investigate social class differences as, for example, was the study of Tough (1978), we contented ourselves with informal measures of family background. This was obtained by the following means. First, we asked heads and staff members about the kinds of families their centres served. Added to these informal but very informed judgements was information about local catchment areas provided by Oxfordshire's Primary Adviser as well as county officials of the PPA. Lastly, for many years one of the authors supervised the practice teaching placements of students at the local teacher training college and has first hand knowledge of local preschools.

We believe that differences between children's behaviour at nursery school and class is not a consequence of differing intake but leave it to others to conduct studies designed to demonstrate this point. Whatever the underlying cause, the fact remains that children seem to behave 'nursery school' or 'nursery class' or 'playgroup', and these differences, though not demonstrably caused by the different organizations, are at least compatible with them. We conclude with a profile of the behaviour of their children and some recommendations.

Nursery school

Children in the nursery schools show higher proportions of school-readiness work, gross motor play, and social 'horsing around'. Relative to others, they also show a generous amount of talk with adults. These children play most often in parallel with one another (instead of interacting) or to remain solitary. Perhaps nursery schools would be wise to encourage more cooperative play and cut down on the 'total expression' tolerated in the playground.

Nursery class

These children play at pretend and manipulation the most. There is more child-child dialogue but less adult-child contact and they appear to compensate for this by spending more of their time with peers. Nursery classes might experiment with more structured materials as a complement to their more open-structure play.

Playgroups

These show the highest amount of adult-led group activity. They are equal to nursery schools in adult-child interaction (both relatively high on this); some of these interactions were with parents who were not on rota and many were one-off. Children in playgroups tend to play parallel to one another or in large groups. Playgroups might be wise to evaluate their adult-led groups; many of them are well planned and popular with children but more one-to-one with adults would be a boon, especially as there are more adults around. They might also encourage more child-child pairs, but more regular attendance may be a necessary factor for this.

In the end we must conclude that the three kinds of centre provide competent, often imaginative, education and care. Playgroups do this on a financial shoestring, but it may be that this organization can only 'work' in a middle-class setting. The State centres are expensive, to be sure, but cost is usually calculated *per child* and not *per service*. During our three-year study in Oxfordshire, we noted three services performed by the State sector that were largely unique to it. How do we measure their worth?

First, the state centres were more likely to serve children from less advantaged families. This was not always the case (and the exceptional playgroup was mentioned earlier) but it was more often true than not. Could playgroups have managed in these more disadvantaged communities?

Next, there were many more 'priority' children (referred by medical or social service workers) in the state centres. Their more highly trained staff, plus the permanence of the institution, were able to cope very well with problem children.

Lastly, the State schools and classes engaged in continuous training of preschool workers. These included students on courses for nursery nurses, teachers, and playgroup leaders. Can hard-pressed, cash-pressed, playgroups do this as well?

In *Under Five in Britain* (1980) Bruner argues that the greater expense of State preschools must be justified by their performing a more specialized service. Surely the three described above would qualify as such.

Structure is more than routine

It has been shown that the nature of an institution has a direct impact on the behaviour of children inside it. This not surprising fact is confirmed by the investigation made by Caroline Garland and Stephanie White, as part of our own Oxford Preschool Project, into London day nurseries. They found that children's behaviour closely mirrored the organization of the centre. Thus, children in a factory crèche were organized into almost 'production line' routines, while children in the crèche of a hospital were sometimes treated like young patients rather than healthy children. In like manner, we found that playgroups operated a little like extensions of the home, especially when the rota-mum had brought her toddler; that nursery classes operated much the same as 'proper' schools with productive peer-play and work; and that nursery schools fell somewhere between home and school. We were, however, still disappointed with our analysis for it seemed to us that looking at statutory groups obscured the effects of important variables such as those of materials and daily routine.

Having examined differences between centres in three statutory categories we turn to a method of data analysis that ignores the official or statutory categories and focuses instead on daily regime. In other words, we will group together the centres with similar programmes despite the fact that, for instance, playgroups and nurseries may sometimes find themselves in the same set.

From the beginning of our investigations we were keen to study the effects of structure, yet we were baffled when we tried to formulate an operational definition of it. Does a fixed, daily routine constitute structure? Or is structure inherent in the way adults interact with children, supervising and suggesting rather than standing by as resource? Or, is structure to be found in the materials on offer? We devised numerous definitions and found that most were too vague to allow us to discriminate between the centres without disagreement. Finally, we decided on two ways of looking at structure, the one focusing on the nature of the *tasks* given to children and the other on the *regularity* of the daily programme. They will be discussed separately.

Task structure

All preschool centres have some bit of required programme; often it is milk-cum-story and sometimes it is a compulsory bit of outdoor play. To qualify as 'high' on task structure, a centre had to conduct two or more prescribed tasks during each session. Although one might be milk-story, the other had to be more 'school-like' in nature. In these tasks, there was a strong expectation that a group of children would participate together in an activity. Of course no child was brutally brought to the group – kicking and screaming – but everyone knew that a large number of children had to engage for a fixed period of time in some bit of 'work'. We use the word 'work' with caution here for in most instances the children and indeed the staff thought of it as play. The important point is that the activity and materials were not chosen freely by the child but instead were imposed by the adults. Note that no mandatory task had to be common to all children at the same time. For example, the rising-fives might have a specially planned activity at a regular time while the younger children were free to play on their own and then the prescribed activity for the younger group might take place at another time.

We classified a centre as high on task structure if most of its children were required to participate in at least two compulsory 'educational' activities per session. We need a note of explanation about this description since it is easily misinterpreted. When we call a centre 'high' on task structure we *do not mean* that the centre regimented the children throughout each session, requiring them to sit at tables all morning, then militarily marching them outdoors at noon. In fact all of the centres allowed free play for the greater part of the session and children were *invited* to participate by the attractive layout of materials. However, sometime during each session they were expected to take part in a compulsory, structured activity, often lasting no more than 10 or 20 minutes. It should be stressed that centres high on task structure provided a steady diet of free play 'seasoned' with a few mandatory tasks. The general atmosphere was one of freedom and choice; however, a normal session of two and a half or three hours was punctuated at least twice by mandatory activities chosen and planned by adults. For simplicity of labelling, we call these 'high' centres 'structured programme' and their opposites 'free programme'.

To begin, we examine whether children act differently in 'structured programme centres', with several prescribed tasks, when compared to 'free programme centres', with one or none. First let's look at the most frequently observed activities in the two types of centre.

Table 7.1 shows the different kinds of activities seen in structured and free programme centres. Note that we have included only those activities where there were significant

	Adult-led group activities	Manipulation	Pretend	Structured materials
Young children				
Structured programme	9	19	6	5
Free programme	13	10	10	3
Older children				
Structured programme	1	13	2	13
Free programme	4	7	13	4

Table 7.1 *Activities most frequently seen in centres high and low on task structure (percentage of all time devoted to selected activities)*

differences between the two types of centre. Looking first at older children, we see that structured programme centres have three times as much play with structured materials. Recall that this is an activity rich in intellectual challenge. Conversely, their children engage less in pretend and manipulation, both of which are only moderately demanding of complex thought. This finding may seem obvious at first. Naturally children at centres with required 'educational' activities will play more with structured materials. However, bear in mind that the actual amount of time devoted to compulsory activity was quite small, sometimes less than 25 minutes per session. When we subtract those minutes which were mandatory, we still find more play with structured materials in these centres with compulsory activities. In other words, in centres where children are required to engage in structured work for short periods they tend to choose similar activities when free to do as they please. Being required to perform structured tasks does not 'turn them off' educational activity when they're on their own.

We find further proof that the structured programme centres do not keep the children at table-work all day when we look at adult-led activity. Structured programme centres are lower on total number of minutes spent in adult-led tasks. The picture that emerges from our observations in centres with task structure shows a daily programme of one or two *brief but mandatory* structured activities. In these centres, there is actually less adult-led groupwork but when it does occur, it is well-planned and challenging. Further, when children are free to pursue their own interests, they often continue the work of the mandatory session or else choose an activity similar in nature. It may be that they build confidence during the supervised session and continue afterwards out of sheer curiosity. At the end of this chapter there is a case study showing how one of the Oxfordshire preschools implemented a programme with specially planned tasks for each age group.

Having established a difference in kinds of activity, we turn now to the cognitive complexity with which play is pursued. Both younger and older children show more challenging play in structured programme centres. Table 7.2 shows that, at both ages, a greater proportion of time is spent in complex behaviour at the structured centres. Keep in mind

	Percentage of high cognitive challenge	Percentage of low cognitive challenge	N
Young children			
Structured programme	42	58	715
Free programme	34	66	2195
Older children			
Structured programme	66	34	541
Free programme	59	41	2949

Table 7.2 *Proportion of time spent in cognitive challenge according to amount of programme structure (Chi squared, young = 14·21; Chi squared, old = 10·05)*

that we confined our analysis to those categories of behaviour that can be judged as high or low in challenge. When children are engaged in either passive or domestic behaviour, such as watching television, drinking milk or resting, we cannot know whether their thoughts are complex. This kind of behaviour is considered 'inscrutable' and its cognitive level cannot be judged. This is important in the analyses that follow which include only those minutes devoted to the kinds of play tasks that could be reliably judged as 'high' or 'low' in intellectual complexity. Centres with more meal time (perhaps caused by a large proportion of full-timers) or with large amounts of walking (centres with long distances between rooms) are not penalized for necessary 'inscrutable' behaviour.

Turning now to social behaviour, once again we see that there are important differences in the behaviour of children in structured and free programmes. For younger children, the structured programmes encourage interaction with other children, as opposed to parallel play. For older children, there is more contact with adults. Table 7.3 shows these results.

We conclude our examination of the effects of task structure with a profile of children's behaviour at *free* and *structured* preschools. Beginning with older children, we find in structured programmes that they devote more time to 'educational' materials and less to manipulation and pretend. They use these materials both when they are required to, *and* when they are free to follow their own wishes. Their play is cognitively complex and they are more likely to talk with, or pay attention to, an adult.

For younger children the picture is remarkably similar. In centres with more structured programmes, the children more often engage in activities that are complex, such as work with structured materials. They also spend more time interacting with other children – although, interestingly, not with adults.

Benefits of structured programme

We have gone to some pains to look closely at how children respond to structure in the programme. On balance they appear to prosper. Can we be sure that structure *is* the reason? Another candidate would seem to be the children's home backgrounds. Were the prospering children in general from more privileged homes? In fact not; demographic details reveal that the centres with the structured programmes, and excellent results, were not usually in the more privileged neighbourhoods, but catered for children of very mixed background.

If it is not the intake that gave structured centres an edge over freer ones, which other factors might explain their greater intellectual achievement? Interaction with others is one likely candidate, and in structured programmes we see some of it between adults and older children.

By examining our records more closely, we find clues to the beneficial nature of the prescribed tasks. To begin, they provide a shared experience for both staff and children.

	Alone	Interacting with other children	Parallel to other children	Interacting with adult	Near an adult but not interacting	N
Young children						
Structured programme	12	34	8	19	27	1200
free programme	15	25	12	23	25	3600
Older children						
Structured programme	12	31	7	27	22	800
Free programme	12	38	12	22	16	3998

Table 7.3 *Most frequent social groupings seen in structured and free programmes (Chi squared, old = 82·85; Chi squared, young = 58·65)*

Although they consume only a small proportion of each session, they create 'shared knowledge' for later discussion in twos and threes. The teacher *knows* that Samantha or Mark can perform a certain task or, more importantly, has enjoyed making a picture in his private notebook on the day's theme of railways. Good conversation requires shared knowledge or experience and, unfortunately, these are easier to come by at home than in school. (See Barbara Tizard's (1979) description of the elaborate talk at home when compared to that of school.) When chatting with a child near mid-day, the teacher knows a lot about the child's life that morning – or indeed yesterday – if they played counting games together and laughed at a silly joke. Shared experience is the fabric of intimate talk and it is a natural outgrowth of a well-planned prescribed task. Children at preschool are budding conversationalists, able to discuss the task at hand but still finding it hard to talk about the past or the future. A programme of structured tasks helps here for the child knows that the teacher knows what he did earlier in the day. And together *they* can plan what to do tomorrow in the 'special activity' time-slot. Happily throughout it the adults can concentrate on children's talk and work for they are not obliged to search for lost shoes nor mop up spilt milk.

Of course it might be argued that centres with free programme but caring adults encourage shared events and so allow adults to chat with children about common experiences. No one denies this. We state here only that a structured programme *guarantees* it. In a free programme, children who are anti-adult might escape the notice of the teacher, as might also children who are withdrawn but not troublesome.

It's tempting to ask why preschools don't devote the major part of each session to prescribed activity. If a little is beneficial, why not even more? Part answer to the question comes from our detailed records of children's behaviour while engaged in compulsory tasks. Recall how precise were our records. We didn't note casually that the target/child was engaged in 'groupwork' for a period of so many seconds, or even that the adult was 'giving instructions' about the rules of picture lotto. Instead we focused hard on the child's behaviour. Was he examining his buttons? Was he nudging and whispering to the girl next to him? If so, we called his behaviour *examination* or *social play* and not *structured materials*. Thus, we know in what proportion of time that *structured materials* was on offer the children actually engaged in those activities. If the full truth be known, a not insubstantial proportion of time was devoted to off-task behaviour. Moreover some on-task behaviour was not challenging. Children might wait patiently while instructions were given a second or third time to the slower ones in the group. Or they might be interested in workmen outside but not allowed to go to the window to watch.

Chapter 9 examines more fully the healthy balance between free and structured programmes and documents the sad results when structure becomes too prevalent. We close here by admitting that prescribed tasks did not work as a magic elixir for promoting concentration and imagination. But they appear to contribute towards these goals by helping children sustain attention or master new skills. What surprised us was the fact that the benefit of the structured programme was seen in the free periods as much as in the planned tasks. We looked at this in detail in one of our nursery schools. Each target child, and there were ten of them, was observed once during free play and once during an 'educational' group task. There were no differences in amount of cognitive complexity between the two observations. This was due to the low-level waiting or giggling that occurred during the compulsory task, and the high level return to structured themes when the children were on their own. We think that the reason structured centres score such high marks on measures of cognitive complexity can be found in the *balance* of free and compulsory activity. We stressed earlier that no centre had more than two prescribed activities in a session. Even at that, some children grew fidgety after 20 or 30 minutes. The British nursery school and playgroup is justly famous for the amount of free choice it offers children. Our data do not support a major revolution in this policy – only a shift towards 'punctuating' the free regime with required educational tasks. When this is done, the free play becomes more than a time for letting off steam; it's a period for consolidation and expansion.

The prescription above is part of the stated philosophy of almost every preschool centre. We took pains to review it, however, because many of the preschools we investigated did no more than pay lip-service to it. Most thought they offered a 'lightly structured' programme. They did, however, offer something else. Most had a fixed routine rather than a task-structured programme.

The fixed routine

On many measures, the centres with structured programmes are doing a better job at challenging children at play, getting them to 'use' adults as partners, and encouraging tasks that smooth the way to formal schooling. What is beneficial about such programmes? Is it the *required nature* of certain tasks or is it the *temporal regularity*? In other words, is the secret ingredient for success to be found in the *tasks* themselves or in the *routine*?

To answer this question we again sorted our centres into two camps – those high and low on temporal routine. This time we looked not at compulsory and educational tasks but at the regularity of schedule; doing the same thing each day at the same time. To qualify as having a 'fixed routine' programme, a centre had to conduct three regular activities (including milk and outdoor play) within each session. Play-groups were over-represented in this group.

At first, we hypothesized that a familiar schedule would be comforting to young children, predictable and therefore soothing. As such, we thought it might raise the general level of cognitive challenge. This turned out to be the case, but the reverse was true for older children who seemed more stretched in centres with low temporal structure. Table 7.4 summarizes these findings.

	Percentage of high challenge	Percentage of low challenge	N
Young children			
Centres with free temporal structure	33	67	1820
Centres with fixed temporal structure	40	60	1090
Older children			
Centres with free temporal structure	64	36	2000
Centres with fixed temporal structure	53	47	1490

Table 7.4 *Proportion of time children spent in high cognitive challenge in centres with fixed or free temporal structure (Chi squared, young = 16·4; Chi squared, old = 41·98)*

There were few significant differences between centres in terms of 'favoured' activities, or indeed of social groupings. We did, however, find more dialogue among younger children (both child-child and also adult-child) in the free centres, but this did not hold for older ones. Moreover, centres with fixed routines tended to have more adult-led group activities and this diminished the possibility of conversation.

In sum, then, there is an important difference between the structure that comes about when children are expected to take part in specially planned educational tasks and the structure that is the result of a regular routine which children are free to accept or reject. The first kind of structure, that which is task specific, has a positive effect on children's language and intellectual activity. The other kind of structure, the fixed routine which is neither particularly educational nor compulsory, has little effect. If anything, the centres where there were the same activities day after day inhibited the young children from talking, although the predictable schedule may have increased the cognitive level of younger children.

It may seem that this book constitutes a hymn of praise to structure. Those activities that challenge the intellect possess a clear goal structure and those preschools with healthy proportions of challenging play include prescribed tasks as part of each session. But where is spontaneity? Imagination? Acquiring a motor skill, or letting off steam? The kinds of preschools we favour have plenty of these, but they have the more cognitive activities as well. When we speak of intellectual stretch, we include the imaginative use of materials, the negotiated unfolding of a chat, or the deliberate obstacle course a child might invent on the climbing frame. These are as high in cognitive challenge as 'educational' tasks planned by adults. Based on our limited sample, and recall that we observed only 19 preschools in one county, we believe that the programmes most capable of stretching the child's mind are those with a healthy balance between tight- and loose-goal materials, whose daily routine includes a free-choice as well as 'enforced' activity, and where periods of order are coupled with some of boisterousness.

It's easy to talk glibly about the 'right' balance and every practitioner seeks it, but how to achieve it? Books of this kind usually proclaim findings of research, then close with general exhortations that teachers translate findings into general rules so that practice may be changed. We are more humble here. First, we try to describe the nature of the evidence on which we base recommendations. We wish our readers to understand our methods and results so they can evaluate them fairly in terms of their experience. But this is not enough. Printed tables of numerical data are a far cry from the children and the preschools we studied in detail. To illustrate what we mean by 'a basic diet of free choice punctuated lightly by prescribed educational tasks', we turn to one case study from our sample. It was chosen to illustrate how a flexible, well-planned programme can provide a healthy balance between free and structured activities. In this centre the staff had an explicit conception of the materials and activities that challenge children over time and used it to plan the weekly routine of the centre and the daily 'programme' of each individual. This explicit (but informal) planning constituted an in-service curriculum for staff education and growth.

Case study: a structured programme in practice

The particular school has been given a pseudonym – Bridge Street Nursery School – but the description that follows is accurate in all respects except that David and Polly are not real children. Their experience however is typical. (The reader may wish to compare this nursery school with the composite one called Morris Road in Chapter 6.)

Bridge Street School is large compared with other nursery schools in Oxfordshire. It has 80 children on its roll of which about 20 are full-time. At any one session then, there are 50 children in attendance – 20 full-time and 30 part-time. The plan shows the three rooms where they are housed.

In each room there are both full-time and part-time children, young and old, mostly from the general waiting list but including a few children with special needs. Some of this latter group have little or no speech, some have physical problems such as cerebral palsy, and many show disturbed behaviour such as hyperactivity or aggression.

The school caters for a very mixed group of children of all social classes. The building itself is very much like Morris Road. It has a large garden surrounding it, so that there are inherent problems in the supervision of outdoor play.

In addition to the permanent staff detailed in the plan, parent helpers are encouraged by means of a voluntary rota. In practice this means that there is generally at least one parent attending per session and very often more – particularly for 'adult intensive' activities like cooking, finger painting, or outings, or to give special help to children who require one-to-one support.

The nursery school is very well equipped, much on the lines of Morris Road, but it also has a large storeroom not accessible to the children which holds vast stocks of apparatus, only a selection of which is put out at any one time. The equipment is changed at least weekly, or more often should the need arise, and much thought is given to the potential of each item. For example, one shelf is set aside for 'matching' games; this category includes all the activities that have as their primary or most obvious function the teaching of visual discrimination, an important prerequisite for reading. While some matching games (like the posting box) involve simple shape matching, others involve picture-to-picture matching, and the most complex stage is reached with word-to-word or even picture-to-word matching. Within each category, therefore, there is a clear progression from simple to very complex activities. On the small scale construction shelf are stored both easy-to-manipulate toys like large lego and toys with intricate pieces like meccano, which demands deft fingerwork of the kind necessary for writing.

Staff choose each week's equipment with care to fit the developmental stages of the children in their room and if necessary make materials in school to fit a particular need. Perhaps the most important factor about this storeroom organization is not the accuracy with which staff assess a particular toy's main function – for who has failed to be delighted at an individual child's discovery that lego pieces make intriguing patterns in plasticine, certainly not part of lego's 'primary purpose'? – but the thinking necessary to operate such a system. Some of the best nursery toys are those which would fit into many categories since they are multipurpose, but it may be that the thought required to assign them to a particular category is valuable in ensuring that their use is understood. The other main benefit of this system is that it is an easy matter to ensure at all times a wide range of activities in the rooms since one has only to select one or two items from each shelf to provide for every need.

In addition to this bank of materials there is a separate store of more advanced materials, brought out at special

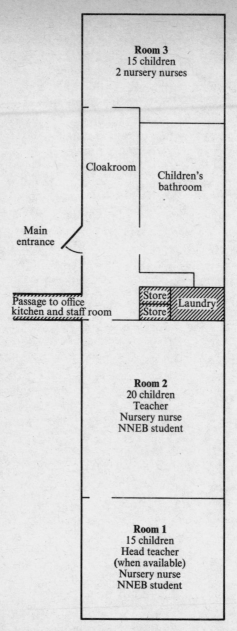

Figure 7.1 *Plan of Bridge Street Nursery School*

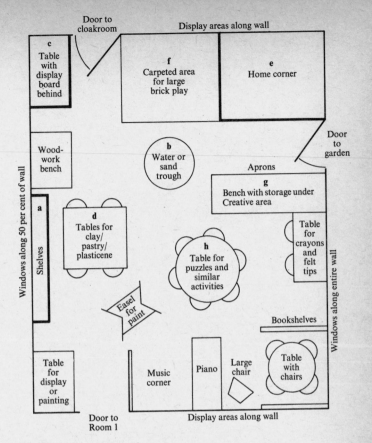

Figure 7.2 *Plan of Room 2*

All fixed areas have thick outline.

a Shelves: contain selection of table activities freely accessible to children.

b Water or sand trough: purpose alternates with Room 1. Sometimes used for scale-version toys.

c Display table: generally nature table but may be special display.

d Tables for clay etc: activity changes each session according to a rota arranged with other two rooms. May also be used for art activities and puzzles, etc.

e Home corner: In this room set up as hospital with nurses' and doctors' outfits and equipment, bed for child and cots for dolls, night clothes, dressing gowns, etc., for all.

f Carpeted area: large bricks stored here but may also be used for railways, road systems, garage, dolls house, floor puzzles, etc.

g Bench: all art materials stored under. Generally used for boxwork, glueing but any activity here or table activities.

h Table for puzzles: always set out initially with table activities but very often used later for group art activities e.g. finger painting. May be extended by inserting two tables (**d**) between the two halves.

Time	Activity	Head teacher	Nursery nurse Room 1	Student Room 1	Teacher Room 2	Nursery nurse Room 2	Student Room 2	Nursery nurse Room 3	Nursery nurse Room 3
9.00 – 9.30	Arrival and settling down to quiet table activities	At main entrance to welcome children	Room 1	Room 1	to welcome children	Room 2	Room 2	Room 3	Room 3
9.30 – 10.00	Milk and chat now available	Room 1 / involved in activities with children	Room 1	Room 1	Room 2	Room 2	Room 2	Room 3	Room 3
10.00 – 11.15	Freedom to move to other rooms or engage in music, sand, water, large brick play etc.	Room 1	Room 1	clearing milk and preparing for outside play	Room 2	clearing milk and preparing for outside play	Room 2	Room 3	Room 3

	Outside	Office	Room 1	Outside	Room 2	Outside	Outside	Outside	Room 3
10.15 – 11.15	play available but indoor play continues in all rooms. Full-time children have concentrated work period followed by wash and group time	Room 2 with full time children from all rooms	clears room and prepares apparatus		clears room and prepares apparatus				clears room and prepares apparatus
11.15 – 12.00	Part-time children have story/songs followed by pre-selected table activities	Then into staff room for group time	Room 1 with part-time children from rooms 1 and 2. Responsible for story then table activities	Room 1 finishes clearing of room and setting out of table activities	Room 2 with full time children from all rooms. Then preparing lunch tables in Room 2	In bathroom for wash. Then preparing lunch tables in Room 2	In bathroom for wash. Then preparing lunch tables in Room 2	Room 3 finishes clearing of room and setting out table activities	Room 3 with part-time children from this room. Responsible for story then table activities

Table 7.5 Location and activity of staff on day 1

sessions only, for the rising-fives. There is also another bank of very new materials with a similar arrangement for the younger children. This equipment is not part of the normal stock so is fresh to the children at their special times. Although it is not necessarily different in nature from the equipment used freely in the rooms at other times, from the child's point of view it is fresh and therefore especially interesting.

Besides this careful structuring of *materials*, the *space* within each room is organized into different activity areas which, although they may change and stray, generally form a clear and reliable framework within which all can organize their world (see Figure 7.2).

Different areas of the rooms are available at different times in the session as demonstrated in the staff/activity plan that follows (see Tables 7.5, 7.6, 7.7 and 7.8). Each session is punctuated by a series of changes of activity. The examples in Tables 7.5 and 7.6 show the movements of staff during typical morning sessions. Times are a guide only, since of necessity the schedule flows from one activity to another rather than abruptly changing at fixed points.

From the child's point of view this routine imposes constraints on choice of activity since he may not at all times please himself. Yet reducing his apparent options may in reality provide him with more freedom to choose, not less. If he knows the sand is available only after milk-time, he is free to concentrate on painting until then, secure in the knowledge that the time will come when he can play with sand. If all activities are available all the time, how can he possibly decide what to do first? Some subtle direction may actually help him to make a choice. Naturally, as with spatial organization, the temporal schedule may be altered to suit temporary needs of both children and staff.

Since much of this structure is behind the scenes and not evident to the untrained eye, the children's behaviour must demonstrate it. We will follow two children through a session at nursery school. As already stated, David and Polly are not real children but their experience is typical. David is a rising

Time	Activity	Head teacher	Nursery nurse Room 1	Student Room 1	Teacher Room 2	Nursery nurse Room 2	Student Room 2	Nursery nurse Room 3	Nursery nurse Room 3
9.00 – 9.30	Arrival and settling down to quiet table activities	At main entrance to welcome children	Room 1	Room 1	Room 2	Room 2	Room 2	Room 3	Room 3
					to welcome children				
9.30 –	Milk and chat now available	Room 1	Room 1	Room 1	Room 2	Room 2	Room 2	Room 3	Room 3
				involved in activities with children					
10.00 – 11.15	Freedom to move to other rooms or engage in music, sand, water, large brick play etc.	Room 1	Clearing milk and preparing outside play	Room 1	Clearing milk and preparing outside play	Room 2	Room 2	Go out on shopping expedition for cookery ingredients	
10.15 – 11.15	Outdoor play available but indoor play continues in Room 2 only	Room 2	Outside	Room 1 clearing and setting up table activities for part time children	Outside	Room 2	Outside	Out shopping	
11.15 – 12.00	Full-time children have concentrated work period followed by wash and group time. Part-time children have story time followed by table activities	Room 2 with full-time children	In bathroom for wash	In bathroom for wash	Room 2 with full-time children	Room 1 story and table activities with part-time children from Rooms 1 and 2	Room 1	Room 3 story and table activities with part-time children from this room	Room 3

Table 7.6 *Location and activity of staff on day 2*

Time	Room 1	Room 2	Room 3
9.00 – 9.30	1 Clay	1 Pastry-making	1 Blue plasticene
	2 Felt tips – paper cut into circles of varying size	2 Crayon leaf-rubbing	2 Coloured pencils – paper cut into circles, triangles, squares and oblongs for children to choose
	3 Paint on easel – primary colours of paint, brushes of varying size and circular paper	3 Paint on easel – primary colours of paint, brushes of varying size and circular paper	3 Paint on easel – black, white, red and blue paint, feathers of varying size, large white oblong paper
	4 Collage – fabric, bottle tops, straws, etc.	4 Boxwork – boxes and cartons, strong glue, paper fasteners, rubber bands, string etc.	4 Collage – different kinds of paper – wallpaper, wrapping paper etc.
	5	Book corner available in all three rooms.	
	6	A selection of table activities available in all three rooms: this is changed at least weekly and includes jigsaw puzzles (various degrees of difficulty), grading, matching, and sorting toys, small-scale construction toys, and scale version toys	
9.30 – 10.00		All previous activities still available and other activities gradually becoming available as milk is finished	

1

2 Sand – dry with sieves, funnels, wheel and lorries to load, containers of various sizes

3

4 Home corner and dressing up

5 Large scale construction – large wooden bricks

6 Roads and garage layout

Milk and chat in all three rooms

2 Water – wooden and plastic boats with small plastic 'people'

3 Music – piano and instruments

4 Home corner – hospital

5 Large scale construction – large wooden bricks, planks and box

2 Water – pouring and filling with graded containers, funnels and tubing of varying diameter

3 Music – instruments

4 Home corner and dressing up

5 Large scale construction – large interlocking plastic bricks

10.00 All previous activities now available and children free to move to other rooms

10.15–11.15 All previous activities continue but outdoor play also available

11.15–12.00 Story for part-time children from Room 1 and 2 followed by a selection of fresh structured materials

Structured materials for all full-time children followed by wash and story in staffroom as Room 2 is prepared for lunch

Story for part-time children from this room followed by a selection of fresh structured materials

Table 7.7 Activities available on day 1

Time	Room 1	Room 2	Room 3
9.00–9.30	1 Pastry	1 Red plasticene	1 Clay
	2 Chalks – black, green and white paper	2 Felt-tips – free choice of paper	2 Crayons and coloured pencils – paper in large and small triangles
	3 Paint on easel – primary colours and black, white; a selection of brushes and paper shapes	3 Paint on easel – pale shades of paint, thin brushes and free choice of green sugar-paper shapes	3 Paint on easel – black, white and primary colours, thick and thin brushes, a selection of paper shapes
	4 Boxwork – cartons and boxes etc.	4 Collage – old birthday and Christmas cards to cut and stick	Sticky paper pictures – pre-cut shapes
	5	Book corner available in all three rooms	
	6	A selection of table activities available in all three rooms: this is changed at least weekly and includes jigsaw puzzles (various degrees of difficulty), grading, matching and sorting toys, small scale construction toys, and scale version toys and other activities gradually becoming available as milk is finished	
		All previous activities still available and	
9.30–10.00	1	Milk and chat in all three rooms	
	2 Water – floating and sinking materials of wood, stone, cork etc.	2 Sand – wet with combs for pattern making	2 Sand – wet with small 'tonka' diggers and lorries etc.
	3	3 Music – piano and instruments	3 Music – instruments
	4 Home corner and dressing up	4 Home corner – hospital	4 Home corner and dressing up
	5 Large scale construction – large wooden bricks	5 Large scale construction – large wooden bricks, planks and box	5 Large scale construction – large inter-locking plastic bricks
10.00–	All previous activities now available and children free to move to other room	Previous activities continue but outdoor play also available	Out shopping – room left ready for group session
11.15			
10.15–	Previous activities continue in Room 2 only but outdoor play also available; this room left ready for group session		Out shopping
11.15			
11.15–	Story for part-time children from Rooms 1 and 2 followed by a selection of fresh structured material	Workbooks for all full-time children followed by wash, and story in staffroom as Room 2 is prepared for lunch	Story for part-time children from this room followed by a section of fresh structured materials
12.00			

Table 7.8 Activities available on day 2

five who has been coming to nursery school for nearly a year. Like all the others of his age he has a full-time place. Polly is in her second term at nursery school. She is just four and attends only for the afternoon sessions. Adults have been given pseudonyms.

David's day at nursery school

9.00–9.30   David arrives. He takes off his coat and hangs it on 'star', his peg picture. Mum dallies to chat to the head teacher who stands by the front door to welcome parents and children. David sees his friend Richard and rushes off into Room 2, his room. Mrs Snow, the nursery nurse, is sitting at the round puzzle table. He sits next to Richard and chooses a clock puzzle. The room is quiet, filled only with the buzz of greetings.

9.30–10.00   David has completed several puzzles and goes to the shelves to choose something different. He sees that the large lego is available today so chooses that and Richard brings the zoo animals. Having cleared a space on a small table, they proceed to build a zoo with separate cages for the animals. Richard puts the crocodile in with the monkeys by mistake and they both giggle. Other children join them and the zoo has snowballed. Mrs James, the teacher, brings over an extra table and it soon covers this too. They enlist her help in constructing some zoo buildings and a long conversation follows with six or seven children comparing notes about zoos and wild-life parks they have visited. Still chatting, they have milk which Mrs Snow has brought in since Sandy, the student, is busy preparing finger-painting on the round table previously used for puzzles.

10.00–10.30   The room is noisier now as hammers bang on the woodwork bench. To the accompaniment of 'experimental' music on the piano by Susan, aged four, David does some finger-painting with three other children. Richard has gone outside to play since Mrs Snow has promised him the rope ladder today for his 'fireman' game. David spends some time finger-painting, making all sorts of curving shapes which he says are roads.

10.30–11.00   David goes to wash off the mess and then goes outside to play in the sand. Lots of buckets and spades are there, all different sizes, some wooden, some metal, some plastic. He chooses the largest metal spade he can find for the serious business of digging down to the bottom of the sandpit. There is great excitement when he reaches the concrete bottom and all the children take turns to stand in the deep hole.

11.15   Time to go in. All the children help to leave toys tidy for the afternoon session. David goes back to Room 2 where all the rising-fives are gathered from all the rooms. (The younger children are in Rooms 1 and 3 for story/music and special table activities.) David is directed by the teacher to a game which involves matching a series of coloured plastic shapes onto a picture on a base card. He completes this very quickly and is called to wash for lunch. When he returns he finds room at the lotto table and Mrs Jones invites him to play.

11.45–12.00   As activities are completed, children put away the boxes and follow Mrs Smith, the head teacher, into the Staff Room. There they play games involving recognition of their names on cards until called to lunch. David's name card is last in the pile and he seems very cross to be last in to lunch.

Lunch   Mrs Snow and Judy, a student, are 'doing' lunch today. Afterwards David enjoys the action songs played on the record player, particularly the one about going to the zoo.

1.00–1.30   David helps to get out the clay for the afternoon session. Children start to arrive. David absent-mindedly pulls at the clay, and looks around the room. Richard is a part-timer, and he has no special friend in the afternoons. At last he persuades the mother helper to read him a story.

1.45   Room 1 is beginning music and movement and David is invited to join in. He begs for assistance with his shoes and socks but after some grumbling removes them himself. Today they do all sorts of things, tiptoeing, stamping, running, walking, creeping. They have to guess what the 'music' is telling them to do.

2.15   David goes back to his own room. Most of the children have gone outside but some are busy at the woodwork bench. David looks for some wood to make an aeroplane and decides he will have to saw a piece off for some wings. He fits the wood in the vice and after a lot of effort cuts through it. He sands the rough edges. Mrs Snow is at hand to give assistance as the tools are full size and dangerous if improperly used. David finds the three boxes of nails – long, medium and short. After some discussion with Mrs Snow he decides that a short nail will be quite long enough. Just as he is finishing off, the children come in for story time.

3.00–3.30   Story time, in the Staff Room for Room 2

children. Today they have one about animals and David, remembering the zoo of the morning, asks whether Mrs James will let him have the small lego tomorrow to improve it.

3.45   David's mum comes to collect him and he proudly shows her his aeroplane, says goodbye, and goes home.

Polly's part-time session

1.15–1.30   Polly arrives and hangs her coat on the 'fish' peg. She waits with impatience for mum to finish chatting to the head teacher and then goes through to Room 1. She seems pleased to take Mrs Howard (a nursery nurse) some shells from her holiday at the sea. They have been talking a lot about the sea recently and have an interesting display table with all sorts of things children have brought. Polly feels the seaweed as she passes it. Lisa, Polly's friend, comes to help sort out the shells and put them on the display. Lots of other children come to watch and talk about the different shapes and sizes.

1.30–2.00   Polly goes to tell Judy, the student who is now preparing the milk, all about the shells. After milk she puts on her apron to go and help with a large picture they are doing for the wall. Mrs Smith, the head teacher, told them all about it at story time yesterday. Today they are painting the sea blue and making wave patterns in it with combs. Polly asks if she may use the big one but Lisa gets it first. After some argument they agree to take turns.

2.00–2.30   Polly washes her hands and goes outside. Some of the children are playing with empty milk crates and Polly joins in. Yesterday they made a house but today they are putting the crates in a long line to make a road. This takes a long time since they all have their own views as to the arrangement but eventually they agree on a plan.

2.30–3.00   A game with the crates – they have to walk along them and if they fall off they are in the sea and eaten by crocodiles! Polly manages to stay on a long time but eventually falls off and is 'eaten'.

3.00–3.30   Story time for all Room 1 children together (full- and part-time). It's the story of Noah today. Polly looks at the sea picture on the wall. Tomorrow they are going to cut out some shell shapes to stick on and her mum is coming to help. After the story they all go to the tables which are set out with puzzles and games. Polly chooses a lovely new puzzle. Mrs Howard sits at Polly's table with four children and encourages them all in turn. Polly's mum arrives and they go home.

A key factor in this is the *continuity* that can be offered in developing games which continue from day to day and which challenge the child at his cognitive level. The organization behind the scenes is important in ensuring this.

A note on democracy

It can be seen from the daily schedules (pp. 146–8) that the day is not a haphazard and casual progression from one activity to another. All members of staff take part in every activity. Rotas operate for specific tasks such as responsibility for outdoor play or supervision of wash. These, like all other policies *can* be changed for particular purposes but are otherwise in force. An atmosphere of cooperation ensures that there is no task too menial for anyone to perform nor so demanding that some are excluded from participation. This general policy among the staff serves as a model for parental helpers who feel free to assist with any and every activity. If problems or suggestions arise, they are generally discussed not at formal weekly/monthly staff meetings but immediately at daily conferences round the lunch table or pre-work cup of tea. Thus all staff play an important role in decision making and the forming of future policies.

Formal meetings *are* conducted with new parents and parents of rising-fives who are about to take up a full time place. These meetings are held to explain what goes on and why. What does a jigsaw puzzle teach? Why is finger painting important when it's so messy? In this way the nursery school aims to enlist from the start parents' understanding and cooperation – with obvious benefits for the children.

8

How many children? How many adults?

If the reader were to put down the book at the end of chapter seven he would conclude that structure is the key to good preschool practice. High marks have gone to materials with clear goal potential, programmes with the 'right' amount of choice and requirement, and activities that bring together adults and children in spiralling elaboration. This is not the whole story.

The special quality of a preschool, its immediate feel to the 'regular' who attends or the visitor who comes frequently, is a consequence of many factors. We have discussed the ones having to do with the statutory status and the kind of programme in force on the ground floor. Other important influences contributing to the character of a preschool are overall size of the centre and the relative number of adults. We turn first to ratio of staff to children, as this has been discussed most fiercely in the professional literature as well as the popular press.

In the 19 centres we studied, there was an abundance of adults. Most of them were formally there as 'staff', although there was occasionally the odd visitor from the neighbourhood or the mother who stayed on for a chat or to help settle her child. The observations and recommendations that follow are made on the basis of centres richly endowed with staff, for in not one observation did we see a centre dreadfully short of hands. For convenience sake, we divide our centres into those with good staff-to-child ratios (1:8, 1:9, 1:10) and those with excellent ones (1:7, 1:6, 1:5). As anyone who has ever visited a preschool knows, it's very difficult to decide who is staff and who is not. In one nursery school, the kitchen was a focus of activity and the cook regularly supervised the children as they assisted in all manner of culinary tasks. And what of the mother helper who appears regularly each Friday to sit in the book corner? We had to draw the line somewhere between staff and visitor and decided on the following criteria: staff members are (1) paid for their responsibility for education or child care services, or (2) student teachers, or (3) volunteer helpers who serve at least two sessions per week. By these criteria, sadly, we could not count the cook or the Friday mum in the reading corner. Still, it enabled us to achieve some comparability between nursery schools, classes and playgroups so that we could look at the effect of staffing ratios in all types of centre.

First, we look at the effect of staff ratio on the kinds of activities children engage in. Good-ratio and excellent-ratio centres have about the same amount of washing, eating and drinking, even outdoor play. But there are major differences in the kinds of activities that go on indoors. Centres with excellent ratios specialize more in small scale construction, art, and structured materials. These, of course, are the activities that were found to be most challenging to the intellect. Centres with ratios that are only good had higher proportions of pretend, manipulation, and rough-and-tumble play – all less challenging. In addition, centres with the poorer ratios had more adult-led activity, the usual means of preserving order and productivity when adults are in short supply. The data appear in Table 8.1 below.

	Good ratio	Excellent ratio
Structured materials	3	6
Art	6	11
Small scale construction	3	6
Pretend	12	9
Manipulation	13	11
Rough-and-tumble	4	2
Adult-led group activities	10	6

Table 8.1 *Percentage of total time spent in selected activities according to staff ratio*

The varying kinds of activity give clues to the effect of staff ratio on the intellectual level of children's play. Table 8.2 shows clearly that children in the richly staffed centres spend a greater proportion of their time in activities that are challenging of the mind.

	Good ratio N = 3138	Excellent ratio N = 2977
High challenge	40	53
Low challenge	60	47

Table 8.2 *Percentage of time spent in challenging activity according to staff ratio (Chi Squared = 115·92)*

Once again, we have included only those activities on which we felt able to make a reasonable judgement as to the amount of intellectual challenge involved. Thus the 'standard fare' are included here, but not milk, washing, walking about or staring at something.

Lastly we examine the influence of staff ratio on children's conversations and social relations. Children in centres with excellent ratios are more prone to conversation. Interestingly, they speak less to one another but twice as much with staff members. The magnitude of the difference is surprising, as there were not twice as many adults around to serve as conversational partners. Table 8.3 summarizes these findings nicely.

	Good ratio N = 5170	Excellent ratio N = 4400
Dialogue with other child or children	15	12
Dialogue with staff member	5	10
No dialogue	80	78

Table 8.3 *Percentage of time in which children engaged in conversations according to staff ratio (Chi Squared = 141·22)*

We can conclude our analysis of the effect of staff numbers with the rather bold statement that ratio makes a large impact on children's behaviour. Centres with many adults serving in staff capacity are able to offer more educational activity, more conversations between children and adults, and more cognitively challenging play on part of the children. The more adults the better the centre.

Must the adults be members of staff? Why not occasional visitors or the odd mum with a free morning? In our observations we found that children interacted overwhelmingly more with staff; in fact, only one eighth of the interactions with adults were with people not there in a formal capacity as teacher, play leader, 'official' mother-helper, student teacher or nursery nurse. In other words, the people with whom the children come into daily contact are those formally responsible for them. This was even true in playgroups, despite their explicit policy of inviting parents into the centre. (It is fair to say, however, that we saw twice as many non-staff taking part in playgroups as in nursery schools or classes. Still, the overall number of non-staff interacting with target children was remarkably low. It is fair to say that the child at preschool is 'sheltered' from adults in the community.)

The relative number of adults seems to affect children's activities, and that is no surprise. But what about *absolute* number of people – not ratios? Some centres appear crowded with different faces and voices; others seem intimate and peopled by a stable few. Contributing to these impressions are factors other than the number on the roll. First, there is the total amount of space available inside and out. Then too the arrangement of furniture and equipment can create small, 'roomlike' spaces or open, 'barnlike' areas. Lastly, organized activities with little racing about may contribute to the feeling of size of the centre.

Looking at only 19 centres, we found it impossible to divide them into groups of similar spatial size. Clearly the feeling of bigness or smallness must be related to this. But some 'little' playgroups had regular access to larger rooms.

Should they be classed with the centres with generous space or not? And some 'barnlike' centres made a regular practice of room dividing on certain days of the week. How to group these? In the end, we decided to look at the effect of absolute number of children, that is – enrolment size, on the kinds of activities children were seen to pursue.

For the purposes of this analysis, we grouped together centres with fewer than 26 children per session (calling them small) and those with more than 26 (calling them large). In general, nursery schools and classes tend to be large and playgroups small. This is not uniformly true, however, as a few playgroups in our sample had 30 children and a few nursery classes only 25. Still, it is fair to conclude that playgroups tended towards the smaller and the State sector towards larger groups, many in the latter group numbering forty or more on the register of each session.

The first difference to emerge from the data is the greater frequency of pretend in small, intimate-sized centres. While there are no differences in the amount of structured play, there is more physical play in the large centres.

	Manipulation	Pretend	Gross motor	Social play
Young children				
Small centres	13	12	9	2
Large centres	12	7	14	4
Older children				
Small centres	16	13	8	1
Large centres	18	10	7	6

Table 8.4 *Percentage of time spent in various activities according to size of centre*

Not surprisingly, there was a difference between small and large centres in the intellectual level of children's play. Again, confining analysis to those categories which could be divided into high and low challenge, we see that there is a definite advantage to the small centres. Table 8.5 shows this, and it is especially marked in the case of older children.

	Small centres	Large centres
Young children	N = 1213	N = 1697
High challenge	39	33
Low challenge	61	67
Older children	N = 1799	N = 1691
High challenge	70	49
Low challenge	30	51

Table 8.5 *Percentage of challenging activity according to size of centre (Chi Squared, young = 11·19; Chi Squared, old = 162·76)*

Last, we found differences amongst older children on the social side as well. There was much greater contact between children and adults in the small centres, and fewer children (again, older only) were seen alone in them. Differences were not great in amount of peer interaction. Table 8.6 shows all this.

	Small centres	Large centres
Young children	N = 2000	N = 2800
Child alone	14	15
Child in contact with adult	47	48
Child with a peer (no adult present)	39	38
Older children	N = 2399	N = 2399
Child alone	9	15
Child in contact with adult	47	32
Child with a peer (no adult present)	44	47

Table 8.6 *Percentage of social groupings according to size of centre (Chi Squared, young = 405·01; Chi Squared, old = 101·51)*

We might conclude with the simple statement 'the smaller, the better'. This is not to say that all our highly populated centres fared poorly, only that – in general – it is more difficult to create both an exciting and a secure place in a centre with a large population. Recall that many of the large centres catered to upwards of 50 children per session. Although there was ample space and materials for so many, and often each child had 'his' room as home-base, still there was the inevitable wandering from room to room and the general hubbub of so many young voices. Instead of encountering 20 young faces each day, children in the largest centres came into at least glancing contact with 50 pairs of eyes. We would argue that the child under five thrives in smaller groups. Imagine how difficult it must be for a four-year-old to know the names of 50 children. Imagine also how difficult it is for staff members to know the habits or the problems of 50 sets of parents.

Although we have praised the small centres for their atmosphere of intimacy and camaraderie, remember that the large (fifty children per session) Bridge Street Nursery School described in Chapter 7 managed to create a place where children talked to peers and staff, engaged in cooperative play, and stretched their minds each day. We argue here that large centres have a harder row to hoe. They *can* create an atmosphere of smallness and steadiness, but this feat requires careful planning of programme and arranging of space. These centres are not home-like in nature, yet they are intimate. Homes are places of fewer children, rarely more than four. Furthermore, tasks of economic importance are conducted there and adults are only partly 'present' for the children's comfort or pleasure. Small preschools are successful because they are different from homes yet offer intimacy. It is this that encourages conversation with adults and diminishes the overly frequent occurrence of physical play. With fewer people, projects and sounds to accommodate, children are able to focus on the more challenging and imaginative play. Neither small nor large centres are homelike. They offer, instead, another kind of intimacy – one easier to achieve with fewer on the roll.

9

When structure becomes a corset

What can we learn from preschools elsewhere? Or what can we tell them? The difficulty with most comparisons across distant settings is that information is not gathered by a common method. We, however, were able to attempt a second study where it would be.

In 1979, under the auspices of the Department of Early Childhood Education at the University of Miami, Marjorie Walker conducted a target child study in preschools in the area of Greater Miami. It followed closely the Oxfordshire study, and every effort was made to ensure that results would lend themselves to direct comparison. Carolyn Roy trained the Miami team to observe and to code and herself served as one of the principal observers there. (Reliability was measured between observers on both teams and also *across* teams through their one common member.) (Results of these statistical tests are discussed in Chapter 10.)

Since some ground had already been explored in the Oxford study, the Miami study could afford to have narrower objectives from the outset. Pilot observations in Miami had revealed important differences from Oxfordshire in terms of organization and 'curriculum'. Therefore the second study was designed to investigate further the nature of structure and its consequences.

Who attends, and where?

Miami centres were chosen to represent state, full-fee paying, and voluntary sectors. Ten children were observed in each of 12 preschools: five day care centres, three Montessori schools, two half-day nursery schools, one public kindergarten (attached to a school) and one cooperative. (The last type relies on voluntary aid and is the most similar to a British playgroup.)

The one cooperative, both half-day nursery schools, one of the day care centres and two of the Montessori schools are all completely self-supporting, their fees ranging from $65 to well over $100 per child per month. The third Montessori school obtains federal funds for certain 'needy' children while the rest pay fees, and in the kindergarten attendance is free and publicly financed. The remaining four day care centres obtain some state funds and charge fees mostly on a sliding scale. The children at these centres thus span a wide range of backgrounds. Some are equivalent to the Oxford-shire social services referrals, some are from professional or wealthy families, and a fair number of both children and teachers are from Cuban or black families. Because of the large Cuban population, Spanish is taught in several of these centres. The teachers in this sample are all highly qualified, and they are also, like the *aides* that work with them in some centres, highly experienced. Even the voluntary-sector cooperative has a permanent professional teacher along with temporary parent-helpers organized in much the same way as the playgroup 'rota mums'. Regardless of how the centres are funded, all staff except the cooperative's parent-helpers receive regular professional salaries.

Only one of the centres could be called cramped for space. Most have either several rooms or a single very large room (the Montessori schools falling in the latter category). The exception is the public kindergarten, which has only one medium-sized room. The single-room units tend to be class-rooms within a main school, while the others are self-contained. Unlike many of the British playgroups, all centres have their own premises. Only one centre (Montessori) has no outdoor space attached to the building, and this school compensates by daily excursions to a public children's park. For the rest, outdoor space ranges from the medium (relative to their Oxfordshire counterparts) to the enormous – with paved, grassed and wooded areas.

When we consider the numbers of children in attendance, however, the space sometimes appears less generous. Enrolment per session ranges from 30 at the cooperative to 50 in the kindergarten. The day care centres stand slightly apart in that, although their total enrolment is high, the children are grouped by age (infants, toddlers, younger and older preschools) into various rooms, with, for the preschoolers, usually around 30 or 40 in a room. At the time of the study, one of these centres had as many as 120 preschoolers on the roll, but these were free to roam over several rooms.

Miami centres, then, are large by Oxford standards – and they have relatively fewer adults. Staff-child ratios vary widely there, the voluntary cooperative, like the playgroups, faring better than its 'professional' counterparts because parent-helpers bring its ratio to one adult for seven children. The Montessori schools provide one adult for roughly 10 children, the half-day nurseries operate with a ratio of 1:15 and the kindergarten 1:25. The day care centres vary among themselves, with a typical ratio of 1:8 to 1:10 for younger preschoolers and up to 1:15 for older.

Recall that some of the larger centres in Oxfordshire are able to create an intimate, 'home-like' atmosphere comparable to that in the smaller ones. They achieve this through careful arrangement of rooms, rotation of activities and locations, and division of the space by, say, shelving to form some secluded areas.

With two exceptions (the kindergarten and the largest day care centre), all of the Miami centres attempt just the same. While all have an open area of floor space for adult-led groups, there are also corners for books, a home corner, blocks and the like. Some, in particular the Montessori schools, the cooperative and a few others, divide their rooms into alcoves for the activity tables too, though in other centres activities are conducted in the middle of the room at tables that are either small and close together or extremely large, seating 12 or more children. In most of the centres, in any case, the enrolment size coupled with available space means that children working at tables are crowded together elbow-to-elbow. Moreover, as we shall see later, even in those centres where there *are* sheltered corners, the children spend most of the day either in adult-led groups on the floor or in groups around the tables, rarely having the opportunity to choose to go to a less busy spot. So it is a moot point whether, from the child's point of view, there is much chance to find a quiet corner in many of the Miami centres examined here.

Because all the centres in the Florida sample have their own premises, furniture and equipment can be permanently laid out. Almost all rooms are geographically fixed, the block area is always the block area and tables are always in the same locations. Further, table-top activities are not rotated in the same manner as in Oxford. Equipment is similarly stationary in the outdoor areas, mostly consisting of swings, climbing frames and the like, permanently anchored in the ground. Where there is variation, it takes the form of whether a particular space contains its materials or not, rather than of which materials are available in which locations. Thus on some days a particular corner of the room will contain a painting easel; if the easel is not out, the corner will be empty.

Equipment

One of the most noticeable differences between Oxfordshire and Miami preschools lies in the accessibility of equipment, in whether a child is free to select what he wants when he wants it. Only in the Montessori schools is the full range of materials available on tables, shelves or in cupboards to which children have more-or-less free access. In most of the other centres, although a wide range of materials lies visible on shelves and tables, the children cannot always help themselves; and in a few, many of the materials are housed in closed cupboards.

Activities are not rotated as in the Oxford system,

whereby, typically, the same selection of a fairly wide range of table-top and floor materials will be laid out for about half, if not a whole, session before being rearranged. In Miami, by contrast, many centres (though not the Montessori's nor the cooperative's) tend to lay out only a rather limited subset, such as three Rs materials, at any one time. These are used for a specific task, and when it is completed they make way for another subset. Choice is thus firmly controlled by the teachers for large parts of the day – even during free play periods in some cases.

Outdoors

Miami playgrounds are generally spacious and richly equipped. Sandpit, swings, slides, tunnels, balancing beams and several types of climbing frames – sometimes very elaborate ones custom-built at great expense – are standard. A few centres have less usual apparatus such as a tree-house or spring-ride rockers (typically a fibreglass animal on a stout spring; one child at a time sits on the animal's back and rocks with the spring). Wheeled vehicles such as tricycles, pedalcars, carts, are less common. The Miami centres of this study have no two-child rockers or see-saws, and no movable equipment such as tressles, ladders or planks. Balls, hoops and the like are rare, though occasionally brought out for adult-led games. Large scale construction materials are not used outdoors.

The emphasis in the Miami outdoor 'physical movement' apparatus is on the 'prepackaged' and the 'fixed'. Very little is flexible, moveable or adjustable; most of the equipment was designed to be used in one particular way and is not adaptable to other purposes.

Two of the centres, however, have in addition to the playground a room indoors devoted to large apparatus. Here the equipment is more flexible; it can be moved or dismantled, some of the items have removable or adjustable parts such as ladders, and different bits of equipment can be combined. Thus one climbing frame could be pushed against the slide to offer more than one way of climbing up, and a barrel added to make a tunnel at the foot of the slide.

Indoors

There is a striking absence in Miami of materials associated with the 'loosely structured' activities such as *manipulation* and *pretend*. The Oxford staples of sand and water troughs and clay or dough appear, and not usually daily, in only three of the 12 Miami centres – the cooperative and two of the day care centres, where shop-bought plasticene is used for dough rather than home-made flour-and-water paste. Other manipulative materials, like boxes of buttons, sandmills, or pulleys or cranes with buckets of bottle-tops, are never seen. The three Montessori schools, however, have an area for 'sensorial' activity which can include, for instance, trays of assorted substances or objects for exploration by touch.

For pretending, only the centres attached to a main school (that is, Montessori and kindergarten) are without home corners, though the children are often not given free access. Moreover, the local name for these – not *home* but *house-keeping* corners – speaks to a slightly different emphasis: their contents often stop at dolls, cushions, cots, and pots and pans (real rather than scaled-down models), and do not always include miniature first-aid kits, nurse's outfits, or telephones, such as are found in the Oxford home corners.

Some other materials seen in Oxford are rare in Miami. Permanent art tables or painting easels appear in exactly half of the centres (the three with manipulation materials also having art corners). One further day care centre actually possesses easels, sand troughs, and so on, but prefers not to use them because of the mess (which, in view of the numbers of children and staff ratios, may be one of the reasons for their absence in other centres). Scale version toys are generally limited to small transport toys; zoo, farm, fort sets and doll's houses are never seen, and full sets of garages or train tracks only rarely. Large scale construction materials consist only of prepackaged (and expensive) sets of wooden blocks – never of crates, planks, ladders, or tyres. Small scale construction does appear, but without woodwork materials and implements. And the miscellany of oddments brought from home (bottle-tops, wool and cloth, wood-shavings, egg-cartons, toilet-roll tubes) to the Oxford centres for junk construction are totally absent. So, as with the outdoor equipment, Miami centres make use of the prepackaged and inflexible, of materials designed to be used in one specific way.

The Miami target child study

We turn now to a closer look at how the research was carried out in Miami. Children were selected as in Oxford and the age-sex composition of the sample was identical. A total of 120 children were selected at random from various preschool centres. Half the children were in the younger age group ($3\frac{1}{2}$ to $4\frac{1}{2}$ years) and half in the older ($4\frac{1}{2}$ to $5\frac{1}{2}$) with equal numbers of boys and girls in each group.

On the basis of preliminary trial observations, we decided not to follow the Oxford method of observing at random times over the child's day. An important distinction was made between periods of 'teacher-directed activity' (TDA) and 'free play' (FP) times. TDA is prescribed, mandatory activity where the child is assigned a task by the adult, whether or not the adult remains to direct him. It amounts to 'work time', although not all of the activities were educational and some might be regarded as play. In free play, in theory, the child has freedom to choose what to do, although in practice it was not uncommon for an adult to lay out materials in front of him or to lead an activity. We further divided free play into outdoor and indoor. Each target child was observed once during TDA, and once during free play, *either* indoors *or* outdoors.

There was one main difference between the two methods

of observing children. Whereas in Oxfordshire the observation consisted of a narrative record by a live observer, in Miami videotape recordings were made. One of the researchers was on hand, but filming was done by a professional camera-operator.* The taped observation was later watched and coded by half-minute intervals in the same manner as the Oxford narrative records.†

Despite these few variations between the two studies, in all essential respects the method of gathering the information, the types of information sought, and the way it was coded and analysed, were the same across the continents. So we can safely make direct comparisons between the two sets of findings.

How children spend their time

We have seen, in Chapters 3 to 5, what happens in the

* The use of videotape meant that observations could not cover all of the child's day entirely at random. For reasons of the child's privacy and the cumbersomeness of camera equipment, the child could not always be followed immediately. Certain periods of time spent washing, toiletting and in rapid movement (for instance, from indoors to out) were not captured. Further, filming usually took place between 9 a.m. and 5 p.m., although some centres were open for longer hours, and was suspended also during lunch and sleep times. Thus the Miami observations do not wholly represent the preschool day, though they do reflect a wide range of 'work', 'play' and 'domestic' activities.

† Tape recording techniques were perfected during the preliminary study, and coders were trained on these trial tapes by Carolyn Roy, of the Oxford team. Each tape was analysed by two coders who watched the tape several times and entered category names directly on the coding sheet. Coding and the categories used followed the Oxford method almost to the letter. The main codes in each half-minute interval included activity, social setting, language, and play bout theme. Some 'extra' information in the Oxford study was here replaced. For instance, contact with non-staff adults was replaced by the child's distraction by the video equipment and operator because in Miami centres we rarely saw adults who were not staff members. Because of differences in the way in which certain activities were conducted in Miami, two of the activity categories previously regarded as highly challenging by definition (*Three Rs* and *adult-directed art and manipulation skills*), and one of the former 'ordinary' categories (*organized games with rules*) could now be deemed either challenging or ordinary. In all other respects, coding was as in the Oxford study. Definitions of codes are to be found on pages 31–5.

Oxfordshire preschools. We now know, for example, which types of activities are most common and which highly challenging; and we know that these challenging activities are conducive to sustained spells of concentration. We also know which social settings are likely in various contexts; and where talk occurs. We can have a fair idea, then, of what to expect in the Miami findings. How does reality match our expectations? Are things the same as in Oxfordshire?

We look first at the various activities themselves. Table 9.1 shows which are the most frequent (though bear in mind that not quite all activities in the child's day were recorded in Miami).

We can see immediately that there are a number of differences between the American and British centres in the most common activities. For one thing, time is slightly more evenly distributed in Oxfordshire: several 'common' activities here occupy middling amounts of time (5–10 per cent), while in Miami a few activities take up a lot of time (watching and passive adult-led groups taking up between them nearly 25 per cent) so that less room is left over for others.

But there are also differences in the types of activities that occur most often. Although manipulation is very common in both settings, Miami centres 'specialize' in passive or 'unison' adult-led group activities (listening to stories or records, singing, and so on) or, indeed, in inactivity – watching, waiting, and so on. The Oxford children, by contrast, appear much more active – they engage in pretend, for example, over two and a half times as often as their Florida counterparts, have twice as much construction, and more art and play with scale-version toys. On the other hand, Miami children are not always passive; in their turn, they have far more (though still little) three Rs activities than occur in our Oxford centres, where these are rarely seen except at nursery schools.

Table 9.2 groups these activities together to highlight the gross differences. There are like amounts of goal-structured activities in both countries, but where Oxford children

	Miami	Oxfordshire
Very frequent	Watching Adult-led group activities Manipulation Aimless standing around, wandering or gazing	Manipulation Pretend
Common	Gross motor play Non-playful interaction Art	Gross motor play Watching Art Adult-led group activities Aimless standing around, wandering or gazing Group routine, Individual physical needs and Distress Non-playful interaction
Less common	Structured materials Social play with spontaneous rules, and Rough-and-tumble Pretend Three Rs activities Group routine, Individual physical needs and Distress Construction	Social play with spontaneous rules, and Rough-and-tumble Construction Structured materials
Rare	Adult-directed art and manipulation skills Organized games with rules Scale-version toys Examination, and problem-solving Music	Scale-version toys Examination, and Problem-solving Three Rs activities Adult-directed and manipulation skills Music Organized games with rules

Table 9.1 *Order of frequency with which activities were observed in Miami and Oxfordshire*

engage more in the loosely structured activities that are the standard nursery fare, Miami children are less often actively engaged.

If preschool children in Miami are doing different things from those in Oxford, what do they find stretching? Which of the activities offer them intellectual challenge? In Table 9.3 we rank activities from 'highest yield' of challenge to 'lowest

	Miami	Oxfordshire
Goal structured: Construction, Structured materials, Art, Adult-directed art and manipulation skills, Three Rs, Problem-solving	20	19
Loosely-structured: Gross motor play, Pretend, Manipulation, Scale-version toys, Music, Social play with spontaneous rules, Rough-and-tumble, Non-playful interaction, Examination	39	49
Passive/non-engaged: Adult-led group activities, Watching, Waiting, Aimless standing around, wandering or gazing, Cruising, Distress	33	22
Other: Group routine, Purposeful movement, Organized games with rules	8	10

Table 9.2 *Percentage of total time spent in 'goal-structured', 'loosely-structured' and 'passive' activities*

yield'. (For easy comparison across the two countries, parts of Table 4.1 are reproduced here). Categories where challenge cannot be judged are excluded from this analysis.

Here we see much greater similarity between the two profiles. Miami children most exert themselves intellectually in the same sorts of task settings as do the Oxford children. Recall from Chapter 4 that these 'high yield' activities are those that have inherent structure, are overtly goal-directed, and provide tangible feedback about how the task is progressing towards a goal. That loosely-structured tasks and flexible materials are less intellectually stimulating, while activities with little or no built in goal structure offer little in the way of challenge, is found to be just as true for children in preschools far removed from Oxfordshire.

Inasmuch as both groups of children engage in these goal-structured tasks equally often, the Miami children appear to be leading as intellectually demanding lives as

	Miami	*Oxfordshire*
Highest yield of challenge	Three Rs Music	Three Rs Adult-led art and manipulation skills
High yield	Large scale construction Art Small scale construction Pretend	Music Art Small scale construction Large scale construction Structured materials
Moderate yield	Adult-led art and manipulation skills Structured materials Organized games with rules Manipulation	Pretend Scale-version toys Manipulation
Low yield	Social play with spontaneous rules Non-playful interactions Gross motor play	Non-playful interaction Social play with spontaneous rules Gross motor play
Lowest yield	Scale version toys Informal games	Informal games Organized games with rules

Table 9.3 *Activities that challenge and those that do not in Miami and Oxfordshire*

those in Oxford. But recall that in Miami the moderately-structured activities are less frequent, and are replaced by inscrutable or 'low level' activities in which we cannot judge challenge or which are definitely not challenging.

In fact, we can refute outright the claim that the Miami children are stretching themselves as much as the Oxford ones. In Table 9.3, we presented only the rank order of the various action categories according to yield of cognitive challenge. Table 9.4 shows these same categories but includes the actual proportion of minutes that were highly challenging in each activity.

The intellectual yield from even the most challenging activities is very much less in Miami than in Oxford. If we consider the overall proportion of time spent in challenging

Activity	Miami	Oxfordshire
Three Rs	60	100 (by definition)
Adult-led art and manipulation skills	32	100 (by definition)
Music	55	73
Art	42	71
Small scale construction	38	71
Large scale construction	49	70
Structured materials	29	69
Pretend	38	50
Scale-version toys	11	50
Manipulation	25	47
Non-playful interaction	18	32
Social play with spontaneous rules	21	28
Gross motor play	18	22
Informal games	6	2
Organized games with rules	28	0 (by definition)

Table 9.4 *Percentage of highly challenging minutes in selected activities in Miami and Oxfordshire*

activity for only those action categories that can be judged as high or low level (12 categories in the Oxford study, 15 in Miami), we find Miami lagging far behind Oxford, as shown in Table 9.5.

	Miami	Oxfordshire
Challenging activity	29	47
Ordinary activity	71	53

Table 9.5 *Percentage of total time spent in challenging activity in selected categories for Miami and Oxfordshire*

So, given that the same types of tasks and materials afford cognitive challenge to the children in both countries, they spend their time in preschool in strikingly different ways. Why? In Chapters 6 to 8 we looked at some characteristics of the Oxford centres in relation to the children's activities in them. We were interested in which characteristics fostered cognitive complexity, concentration, social interaction, conversation, and so on, and we saw that these included both physical ones, such as size, and curricular ones, like time-table. Could the different tasks and reduced cognitive challenge found in Miami be at least partly explained in terms of differences in the physical environment and pro-gramme?

Size and staffing

Space and how it is filled

In terms of the physical characteristics of the centres, we can already guess that in some ways the children in the Miami sample may be disadvantaged in comparison to those in Oxfordshire. In Chapter 8 we saw that within the Oxford sample more time is spent in challenging activity in centres with 'excellent' staff ratios (1:7 or less) than in centres with 'good' ratios (up to 1:10). Since in Miami just one centre of the 12 selected has an excellent ratio, and six of the centres, indeed, have only fair or even poor ratios (over 1:10 and up to 1:25), it is not too surprising to find these children engaging less of the time in challenging tasks and more of the time in adult-led group activities, passively or in unison. Similarly, Table 8.5 told us that small Oxfordshire centres yield a greater proportion of challenging activity than do large centres. Again we are not suprised that fewer minutes are spent in intellectually demanding activity in Miami, for not one of these centres is 'small' by the Oxford standards.

Materials and how they are used

Prepackaged, inflexible equipment preponderates in Miami: no item readily lends itself to more than one type of activity. Creative, intellectually taxing play outdoors is perhaps inhi-bited by the very nature of the equipment. But other conditions too may hinder challenging activity outdoors.

As a result of the large numbers in most of the centres,

children often have to queue for turns in the playground. A tree-house, for example, was in such demand in one centre that a rule was established that children enter by climbing up the ladder and exit by sliding down the pole; it became just another bit of climbing equipment, with children sliding down as soon as they had climbed up rather than spending any time in the 'den' at the top. To reduce squabbling over turns, rules extend to other items too; for the spring-ride rockers, for example, children had to wait in line and count to ten – the supposed duration of each child's turn. In practice, of course, they counted so fast that no sooner had a child climbed onto the rocker than he had to concede it. Thus not only is the equipment not generally capable of more than one use, children rarely have time or opportunity to explore that use to the full. That the children in the Miami centres are not making the most of their time outdoors is reflected by the fact that the proportion of challenging activity indoors is about double that of outdoor free-play. The picture looks remarkably similar if we exclude all activity categories except gross motor play – that is physical movement tasks – from consideration. We find that although the children do six times as much physical activity outdoors as in during free play, relatively little (15 per cent) of their outdoor body movement involves intellectual challenge; they are stretching themselves physically but not mentally in the playground. By comparison, the Oxfordshire childred acted with challenge in 22 per cent of their physical activity.

Prepackaged materials extend to the indoors too. While all the centres are well-stocked with structured materials inclined towards school-like activities, fewer unstructured materials are on offer, and in some centres less than in others. The children's behaviour reflects the fact that these materials are scarcer in Miami than in Oxford, for as Table 9.6 shows, Miami children spend less time in activities that make use of them.

But even though tasks grouped under the heading 'structured materials', say, might appear equally often in both sets of preschools, it does not necessarily follow that the activities

	Miami	Oxfordshire
Manipulation	10·6	12·0
Pretending	4·0	10·4
Art	7·2	8·3
Scale-version toys	1·3	2·3
Construction	2·7	5·2
Total time spent in the above 5 activities	25·8	38·2
But:		
Adult-directed art and manipulation skills	2·2	0·6
Structured materials	4·8	4·5
Three Rs	3·4	0·6

Table 9.6 *Percentage of total time spent in selected activity categories in Miami and Oxfordshire centres*

are alike. We need also to look at how such materials are used, which sorts of tasks are done with them. Once again, there are certain consistent differences between the Miami and Oxford centres.

The most noticeable is a heavy gearing in Miami towards preparing the child for school. Whereas the Oxford centres focus as much on emotional and social aspects of development, many of those in Miami regard themselves very much as *preschools*. The exception again is the cooperatives, which, like playgroups, aim to create a home-like atmosphere and a chance for children to play with peers.

As might be expected, school readiness activities are prominent in the Miami centres. Three Rs activities are found far more often in Miami than in Oxford, where indeed they hardly feature at all. Moreover, almost all instances of three Rs activity observed in Oxford were spontaneously initiated by the *child* – for instance writing a name on a birthday card. Sometimes in Miami this happens too, as when a child counts objects he is laying out. But far more often the context is a teaching one: in adult-led group games of bingo or the Montessori 'bank game'; in parallel groups where the children have to copy down sentences from the blackboard;

or with adult and child working in a one-to-one tutorial with reading or counting materials. For this reason, three Rs activities, which in Oxford are always judged to be highly challenging, can be quite mundane in Miami. While for some children to copy a sentence can be intellectually demanding, for others it is executed so easily that it ceases to challenge. Or sometimes it is the other way round: a child still struggling to read numbers may be so unable to keep up with others in a bingo game that he abandons the attempt.

The emphasis on school readiness extends into the structured materials category. Along with jigsaw puzzles, shape-posting boxes and picture-lotto, 'ditto' work-sheets, designed specifically for tasks of matching and copying letters and numbers, are much used in Miami preschools (we classified these as belonging to structured materials rather than three Rs because they do not require actual knowledge of letters and numbers, focusing instead on matching outlines as in any shape-matching task.) The child normally completes these sheets on his own, and hands them to the teacher for correction. Table 9.5 has shown that, as with three Rs activity, these tasks may be too repetitive to present much challenge.

Art for its own sake is slightly less common in Miami than in Oxford, though there is more adult-directed art and manipulation. Free art tables, where they occur, have less variety of materials, lacking the range of types of papers, paints, pens, crayons, paste, Sellotape, staples and junk modelling oddments found in Oxfordshire centres. Sometimes, in fact, a tin of water-colours and a beaker of water are set in front of a child, who is told to 'draw an animal', though tables with 'dry' materials (crayons, scissors) may also be available for truly 'free' art. In directed art, where freedom is curtailed by the nature of the materials and/or by the adult's instructions, the children may do finger-painting, but more often they are given prepared bits of material (cut-out paper shapes, and so on) for pasting or modelling, or prepared drawings to cut out, or they may be told exactly what shape to draw and how to colour it. In this respect, although no group art projects were seen in Miami, they resemble their Oxford counterparts' directed group collage work, where the children are sometimes heavily instructed in how to cut out and paint their parts and exactly where to stick them on the frieze.

In much of what we have said about equipment and its usage, however, the Montessori schools are a special case: indoor equipment is always accessible and the rooms are subdivided into work areas called 'practical life', 'sensorial', 'maths' and 'language'. Many materials are found in these schools that do not often appear in other types of centre – an aquarium for instance, a set of handbells tuned to the notes of the scale, special counting and geography materials, and so on. And the teachers are highly trained in the use of these things in specific tasks.

Finally, certain activities that require little equipment are seen more often in Miami than in Oxford – those activities performed in large groups supervised by a teacher – organized games, or passive adult-led group activities. In Oxfordshire, organized games (when they occur, which is rarely) are typically traditional – for example, Hopscotch, spontaneously initiated by a few children, or Farmer's-in-his-den organized by an adult. Although traditional or spontaneous games do occur in Miami (such as Ring-a-roses), there are also complicated circle games new to the children and directed by a teacher; these sometimes happen during free

	Miami	Oxfordshire
Unison adult-led groups (story, song, etc.)	10·9	7·7
Organized games (circle or traditional games)	1·5	0·1
Watching (without doing)	13·6	9·4
Total time accounted for	26·0	17·2

Table 9.7 *Percentage of total time spent in passive and organized group activities in Miami and Oxfordshire centres*

play periods. Other adult-led group activities take much the same form as in Oxford, with the children parallel in passive roles attending to a common focus (listening to a story for instance, or watching popcorn being made). See Table 9.7 for comparisons.

In sum, as in the playground, the prepackaged indoor materials designed for specific tasks are used in somewhat stereotyped ways not conducive to intellectual challenge.

We have dealt at some length with the physical environment of the Miami centres, for it may seem foreign to those accustomed to the British (or at least Oxfordshire) nurseries and playgroups. But what about other, less tangible, characteristics?

Programme structure

By calling a centre 'structured programme', recall, we mean that its daily sessions include two or more prescribed tasks, at least one of which is educationally-oriented and in which most if not all of the children are required to join.

The reader will have noticed many clues that Miami is again very different. The dominance in the programme of 'preparing the child for school' means that many of the tasks are educational in nature – we have already seen the heavier emphasis on school readiness materials and activities. In fact, a number of the teachers talk specifically of *work* time, and both adults and children often talk about 'handing in work', just as in school. Individual tasks are described as 'math' or 'language' or 'science' – terms often not encountered until relatively late in the school career in Britain.

How much 'work' is done in the Miami preschools? In Chapter 7 we said of the Oxfordshire establishments: 'When we call a centre 'high' on task structure we *do not mean* that the centre regimented the children throughout each session, requiring them to sit at tables all morning then militarily marching them outdoors at noon.' Then: 'all of the centres allowed free play for the greater part of the session. . . .

However, some time during each session they [the children] were expected to take part in a compulsory, structured activity, often lasting no more than 10 or 20 minutes.' In the Miami centres of this study, structure went much further. Prescribed, compulsory tasks, whether assigned to the children as a group or as individuals, took up much of the day, again just as in school. We outline here the daily schedule provided by one of the centres:

a.m. 7.30–9.15	Arrival – free play indoors
9.15	Circle time (large adult-led group on floor)
9.35	Snack (set at tables)
9.45	Tasks at learning centres (same seats as for snack)
10.45	Clean up
11.00	Story/music/singing (large adult-led group on floor)
11.30	Free play outdoors
12.00	Lunch
p.m. 1.00	Sleep
3.00	Snack (set at tables)
3.15	Task at learning centres (same seats as snack)
4.15	Free play outdoors
5–5.30	Continues until departure.

Most of the children selected from this centre attended from 8.30 a.m. until 5.30 p.m. – a session of nine hours. Of this, an average of two and a half hours are spent in free play, nearly three hours in teacher-directed tasks or group-times, and more than three and a half hours in (compulsory and teacher-directed) group routine activities such as eating or tidying up. Centres with a wide age range often stagger activities for younger and older preschoolers (so that, for example, young children are outdoors while older ones work and *vice versa*) but the mix is usually about the same for both age groups. Centres with shorter sessions, of course, have less of the last category of activities (group routine), for the children do not need a rest-period or go home before lunch. Thus in the six-hour day centres, three and a half hours is teacher-directed work or groups and the rest equally divided between free play and group routine; and in the three-hour session ones, task time occupies up to two hours, though in some centres for some of this time the children are not teacher-directed but have free choice. The cooperative, with its less school-like orientation, is the one centre of the 12 that has no teacher-directed table-top activities or tasks (and one of the few that offers 'unstructured' manipulation materials, and so on). Here, over an hour is spent in adult-led groups (such as story, or singing) and the rest of the three-hour session is free play, 15 minutes of it outdoors. Unlike in the Oxford centres, where some children choose to remain indoors when the playground is available, even if outdoor access is relatively scarce, in Miami it is usual for all children to be expected to go outdoors when outdoor play is scheduled, and in this sense their choice of what to do is restricted even in free play. (Fluctuations in weather conditions, of course, rarely impose constraints on outdoor activity in Miami!) So, with the exception of the cooperative all of these centres are, by Oxford standards, *extremely* high on task structure.

Table 7.2 showed us that children in the Oxford centres high on task structure acted in complex, challenging ways more often than did their peers in low structure centres; we had high praise for task structure. No, not quite; for we stressed throughout Chapter 7 that all of the Oxford centres offered not just structure but 'a steady diet of free play "seasoned" with a few mandatory tasks'. We stressed that mandatory activities were brief, usually just 10 or 20 minutes at a time, and that few were conducted during the day even in high structure centres. And we stressed the importance of a *balance* between free and compulsory activity, with occasional prescribed, educational tasks scattered in a basically free programme. That is not all, for we noted also that the challenging behaviour observed in structured-programme centres was, for various suggested reasons, as likely to occur during free play time as during one of the mandatory educational tasks.

We can look at this directly in the Miami findings, for there each child had one observation during time in teacher directed activity and one during free play, either indoor or out. And the Miami children, as Table 9.8 demonstrates, act in ways that agree with the earlier observations. Since almost all teacher directed activity takes place indoors, we compare it here only with free play indoors. This analysis excludes the inscrutable categories where we cannot judge whether the activity is challenging or not.

	Challenging activity	Ordinary activity	Time units included
Teacher-directed activity	33	67	2285
Indoor free play	34	66	1892

Table 9.8 *Percentage of challenging minutes spent by Miami children in selected activities during teacher-directed activity and indoor free play.*

Miami children are certainly not stretching themselves intellectually in the structured teacher-directed tasks any more than in their free play. Besides, as we already know, they are stretching themselves less than their Oxford peers (see Tables 9.4 and 9.5, for instance). And this despite the general emphasis on school-like activities and the greater frequency of prescribed work than of free periods than in Oxfordshire. What is 'seasoning' in Oxford becomes the main course in Miami. The children are so constrained by 'structure' that they cannot savour the richness of the (sometimes sophisticated and intriguing) materials in their own way and in their own time.

As is evident in the sample timetable on page 185, however, centres with highly structured, compulsory task programmes also, in Miami, are high on another kind of structure – that of temporal routine.

Temporal structure

The Miami centres vary widely in the hours of their sessions. In general, the half-day nursery schools and the cooperative held three-hour sessions only, those attached to a main school (Montessori and kindergarten) had five- or six-hour sessions, while day care centres offered full-day provision (nine hours or more). Such long days, obviously, need thoughtful planning if the children are not to be exhausted or bored, and the Miami teachers certainly give careful consideration to the timetable, interspersing table-top task periods with circle time on the floor, with indoor free play and with outdoor physical activity, as illustrated in the sample schedule. The extensive planning, however, tends to lead to a quite rigid schedule in a number of centres. Although there are a few minutes lee-way in each case, the same *type* of thing (though not the same activity itself) is normally done at roughly the same hour every day. Only one of the 12 centres indicated in its schedule that it was highly flexible over the timetable. We cannot therefore make any fair comparison with regard to effect of regularity of timetable on the children's behaviour in the Miami centres, since they have about equal extents of temporal routine. We can only recall that for the Oxfordshire schools task structure seemed more important than temporal routine as far as cognitive challenge was concerned.

We may, however, note briefly that there are differences among the Miami centres in terms of how the timetable is implemented with respect to compulsory teacher-directed tasks, even though they are done at fixed hours. Three typical programmes for conducting these activities were observed: in one, the entire class (or a large subgroup) sat at tables in parallel and all the children were assigned the same task with the same materials at the same time. When the task

SUMMARY OF CENTRE CHARACTERISTICS

Day care centres (N = 5)	*Montessori schools (N = 3)*
Permanent self-contained premises	Permanent premises within main school
Number of rooms varies; all have outdoor areas, but vary in size and facilities; access restricted by timetable	One large room divided into sections; usually have playground; access restricted by timetable
Fair range of equipment, some unstructured materials; only a subset available at one time; permanent geography	Wide range of Montessori and other materials, little unstructured; always accessible, timetable permitting; permanent geography
Hours about 8 a.m. – 5 p.m. but may offer more	Hours about 8.30 a.m. – 2.30 p.m.
Timetable inflexible, unvarying daily	Timetable rather inflexible
Compulsory activities; mixture of tasks in class parallel and at learning centres; group times; free play time indoors and out	Compulsory activities; longish work periods mainly in individual projects; group times; outdoor free play; indoor free play not scheduled but possible
Enrolment 40–120 children (preschoolers only), divided into rooms by age; adult ratio 1:10 to 1:15	Enrolment about 40 children; adult ratio about 1:10
Mostly a mixture of federal plus graded fees	Mostly private, fee-paying
Occasional voluntary helpers	

Half-day nursery schools (N = 2)	*Kindergarten (N = 1)*
Permanent self-contained premises	Permanent premises in main school

Number of rooms vary by enrolment; large, well-equipped outdoor areas; access restricted by timetable

Wide range of materials, some unstructured; only a subset available at one time; permanent geography

Hours about 9 a.m. – 12 noon but may offer more

Timetable planned but may be flexible; may vary daily

Compulsory activity; longish work period at learning centres (though may be free to choose work); group time, free play outdoors but little indoors

Enrolment 45 per room (up to 90 altogether); adult ratio 1:15

Privately funded from fees

Cooperative (N = 1)

Permanent self-contained premises

Several rooms, divided into sections; outdoor area; access restricted by timetable

Wide range of materials, including unstructured; always accessible, timetable permitting; geography fairly permanent

Hours 9 a.m. – 12 noon

Timetable rather inflexible, unvarying daily

Some compulsory group times; the rest free play

Enrolment 30 children; adult ratio 1:7

Voluntary, funded from fees

Run by teacher with voluntary parent help

One room; school playground with little equipment but large grass area; access restricted by timetable and school

Fair range of materials, little unstructured; only a subset available at one time; permanent geography

Hours 8.15 a.m. – 1.45 p.m.

Timetable inflexible, unvarying daily

Compulsory activities; longish work periods at learning centres; group times; some free play indoors and out

Enrolment 50 children; adult ratio 1:25

Public funds (no fees)

was completed after, say, 20 or 30 minutes, the materials were cleared away and fresh ones put out for a new task.

In another programme, the children sat in small groups around separate tables known as 'learning centres'. Each table was given one activity, different from that at the next table. Again after a fixed interval such as 30 minutes, the tasks were changed; either the children rotated to another table or they stayed put and assignments were rotated.

In the third programme, again the entire group had a fixed work period but this time longer – one to two hours. Within that period, children as individuals or *small* groups were assigned tasks to perform in their own time. When a child finished what he was doing he went to the teacher for a new assignment. Few schools operated with just one of the types of system, in fact; most had some time in parallel large groups and some with the children working on individual projects, though each school did tend to favour one programme over another. For ease of future reference to these three types of work settings, we call the first the *class parallel,* the second the *learning centre* and the third the *individual projects* settings.

Pages 189–90 show a chart summarizing the details of the physical and programme characteristics that we have encountered in the various centres in Miami. A comparable chart for the 'composite' Oxford centres appeared in Chapter 6, p. 117.

Social setting

In many of the Miami centres, the number of children in relation to the available space and adults entails a considerable amount of compulsory activity in large groups where the children are elbow-to-elbow. Moreover, when the prescribed task is an 'educational' one, a degree of discipline is required – discipline in the sense of getting heads down to work and not disrupting the activity by running around, giggling or talking noisily. Much activity, then, is conducted with the class quietly in parallel rather than in smaller groups or with the children interacting. Table 9.12 illustrates that 'parallel in large group' is indeed the most common setting. In the Miami preschools, the children are side-by-side without interacting for 42 per cent of the time, as against 30 per cent in Oxfordshire.

Very common	Parallel in large group
Fairly common	Alone Parallel with one child or a few children Interacting in a child-child pair Interacting in a small group
Rare	Interacting in an adult-child pair Interacting with adult in small group Interacting in large group with or without adult

Table 9.9 *Most and least common social settings in Miami preschools*

In fact, the children interact with one another in free play periods rather than in compulsory teacher-directed activities. Table 9.10, which excludes the very infrequent social settings, shows this.

	Teacher directed activity	Free play
Parallel in large group	X	
Interacting in adult-child pair	X	
Interacting in small group		X
Interacting in child-child pair		X
Alone		X
Parallel with one or a few child(ren)		X

Table 9.10 *Social settings that occur (marked X) during teacher-directed activity or during free play (indoor and out) in Miami centres.*

It is not too surprising that the children sit quietly beside each other during the compulsory activites. We expect them to be listening to the story or busily matching picture cards, not jostling each other and talking. In Chapter 6, we learned that children in Oxfordshire, too, talk less with each other in the goal-directed activities than in loose-structure ones. That is, in Oxfordshire the children interact least during activities of high intellectual yield but much more in activities of 'moderate' yield. What about Miami? In Table 9.11 we consider overall the amount of highly challenging activity seen in each setting. It appears that, most often, challenging work is done by a child when one-to-one with an adult – not unexpectedly, since we already know that this is a 'fruitful' setting for Oxford children (p. 74) and that in Miami this setting happens during teacher-directed 'work' activities (Table 9.10). But remember that this adult-child pair actually occurs very infrequently. The other setting, by far the most common, for teacher-directed periods is 'parallel in large group'. But note that Table 9.11 classes as 'ordinary' those 'inscrutable' categories where challenge cannot be assessed. In story- or song-time, for instance, we cannot tell from the child's overt behaviour whether or not he is being intellectually stimulated. And these, along with waiting and the like, also take place in parallel group settings.

	Challenging activity	Ordinary activity
Interacting adult-child pair	38	62
Parallel with one child or a few children	27	73
Interacting with adult in group	20	80
Alone	17	83
Interacting with one child or a few children	17	83
Parallel in a large group	10	90

Table 9.11 *Percentage of time in various Miami social settings spent in challenging activity*

Overall, then, large groups do not go hand in hand with intellectual stretch. But to make a fair comparison among the various settings in terms of how much 'good work' is accomplished, we must confine analysis to only those activity categories that can be judged 'high' or 'low' on challenge. This is done in Table 9.12.

	Challenging activity	Ordinary activity
Interacting adult-child pair	42	53
Parallel in large group	36	64
Parallel with one child or a few children	34	66
Alone	33	67
Interacting with adult in a group	26	74
Interacting with one child or a few children	22	78

Table 9.12 *Percentage of time in various Miami social settings spent in challenging activity during selected tasks.*

The rare adult-child pairs are still well ahead; nearly half of the activity done there is challenging. But now parallel children are clearly also engaging in more challenging activity than are interacting children. On the few occasions when children in large groups engage in tasks that *can* provide challenge, they often make the most of them. The children in Miami, then, are quite capable of working on their own. This is reflected also in the amount of challenging activity done by children alone. The Oxford children, by contrast, fare relatively less well when alone (p. 72). Miami children are encouraged, and with some success, to work independently.

Where are the adults?

As a result of the school-like nature of the Miami centres, adults there (except in the cooperative) typically occupy roles very much managerial and pedagogic – as in main schools. The relatively poor staff-child ratios means that the teachers have little spare time for 'just a chat'.

The amount of adult attention that an individual child receives varies across centres according to the type of setting which the programme follows. In 'class parallel' settings, where all or most children do the same thing at the same time, the teacher's time may be taken up with the 'administrative' side, handing out materials, taking in work, making sure that children understand the instructions, or arbitrating in a dispute over who gets to use the scissors first. In the 'learning centres' situation where subgroups of children work on different tasks, again much time is required for management of the work period. But in between, the teacher may join in at one of the tables. In the last setting, one of 'individual projects', the teacher has many pots to keep boiling at once. She makes sure that every child has an assignment, and then settles with a single child to work closely with him in a one-to-one tutorial for a while before moving on to someone else; or she joins in a small group of children. During this time, of course, other children bring work to show her, or come to ask questions, or make requests for new tasks. Thus in this last regime a few children have a longish, intensive spell of working with the adult while the rest have little or no adult contact – their turn will come later. In general, then, the talk between adult and child during 'work times' concerns management, services and instruction, with only a few children at any one time having a longer talk with the teacher designed to further their expertise with the materials and to elaborate the activity.

Free play time contrasts strongly with 'work'. This is seen as an opportunity for the children to get on with whatever they want on their own without adult 'interference'. Some teachers take this time to set up the rooms ready for the next activities, while others stand on the sidelines monitoring the children's play, checking that no-one harms himself or others. Much of the adult-to-child talk here has to do with mild reproof and arbitration: 'Let Vick have a turn,' 'Don't roll in the sand.' Only occasionally were adults observed to participate in the children's activity – joining in a pretend tea-party in the home corner, helping a child to swing along the beams, or opening a coconut and discussing it with the children who flocked around. In fact, adults rarely feature in free play situations, particularly outdoors, in comparison with in prescribed tasks. And this despite the fact that some 'free play' activities are actually teacher-directed, in that the adult may lead group games or supervise all the children in 'free' art.

What does the setting and routine mean for the children?

Looking back to the morning timetable in the sample schedule on page 185, we find that the children are sitting down indoors with little freedom to move about for one and a half hours, have 15 minutes' clean-up, then sit again for another half-hour before having a half-hour's free play outside. Remember that this routine is quite typical of many of the centres. For rather long spells, the children have little opportunity to stretch their legs – they often do not even get up to fetch snack or materials, having everything set before them. After a morning spent in this sedentary fashion, the children are ready to let off steam when they go outdoors. And since for much of their time indoors they are engaged in mandatory educational tasks, in their free play periods they are happy to stretch their bodies rather than their minds. Earlier, we suggested that the inflexible equipment of the playground might be partly responsible for the Miami children's relative absence of challenging activity outdoors – that is, that little is provided to challenge. Now we may guess that it is not just the type of equipment but its combination with the need for sheer body movement that is likely to preclude intellectually challenging behaviour in the playground. The children are not interested in thinking up new ways of getting up the climbing frame; as they appear to be in Oxford. Instead they want just to swing, run, slide, cycle – all the repetitive but energetic activities. Surely the children need these spells of physical exercise.

There are other ways in which setting affects the children. Remember the 'class parallel' work setting in which the children carry out the same task for a given short period. It is difficult to manage such a setting, for some children work faster than others. One way for staff to ensure that children work at roughly the same pace is to hurry them along. This may occasionally have unfortunate consequences. Consider the following observations of two children in a group for an adult-led art activity. They were instructed to 'draw a circle and a square and colour it in very hard with these crayons'. The paper was later to be covered in finger-paint so that the areas shaded in wax crayon would stand out. (This was not made clear to the group at the outset, though some children realized it.) Jo-Anne rapidly drew one circle, one square and one triangle in a row on the paper. She scribbled with the crayon to fill in the shapes, often missing the edges of the outlines, and was one of the first to finish. She called to the teacher, who praised her for 'doing it so quickly' and for the 'nice drawings', and went off to the finger-paint table after getting the teacher to fasten her apron. Actually, none of her drawing was judged to be challenging by the coders. She drew so easily and coloured too carelessly that the task for her was quite routine.

Jason, meanwhile, was still working. He had drawn an elaborate curved sausage for his circle. In another corner, he drew a rectangle, paused to look at it, then added another rectangle overlapping the first. He chose a variety of colours to fill in the outlines, and tried out several different strokes with the crayon, making sure that all of the shape was filled but without going over the edges. When he was still colouring, the adult came up: 'That's not what I told you to do. That won't show when you paint it. Hurry up or you won't be able to paint it.' Jason fetched an apron and struggled to put it on himself, working out how to tie the tapes behind his neck. The child next to him was having difficulty with his apron, and Jason helped to tie it. The teacher, unaware of this, again called to him to hurry up. Yet despite receiving no praise, Jason's time was spent in intellectually complex activity throughout: not only in the drawing task, where his care, creativeness and planning earned a high challenge code, but also in his 'problem-solving' with the apron-ties. Unfortunately, in this sort of regime there just isn't time for individual children to 'hold up the group' by elaborating on the assigned task. Speed and conformity are the ways to get through the day.

But there are sometimes other consequences of this sort of

'class parallel' setting too. At the starts and ends of tasks, materials are handed out and collected by the teacher or by a child appointed to the job. Consider the length of time it takes for this person, teacher or child, to set down all the bits and pieces on the table in front of each child separately, for a class of 30 or so individuals. An art task, for example, may require first 30 sheets of paper, then 30 beakers of water (or perhaps 15 if the children share), then 30 palettes of water colours . . . . Soon, one or two children will be calling out that someone hasn't got a palette, that Denise is missing the red colour that her neighbour has, that Matt has spilt his water. The teacher has to go back to sort things out before setting out the 30 paintbrushes. There is quite some time between the *announced* start of the art activity and its *actual* start. The ritual is repeated at the end of the task as all the materials are gathered and fresh ones set out. During these 'preparing' and 'ending' intervals, the group is already (or still) seated at the tables. Further, as already noted, not all children finish the task at the same time. But in this 'class parallel' regime, a child who completes his task ten minutes before a new one is scheduled to begin may not immediately receive another set of materials. Remember that the target child coding notes what the child is actually doing in any half-minute and not, for example, what he is supposed to be doing. The activity category cannot be, say, *art* if the child has not yet begun or has already completed his drawing. He might be giggling with a neighbour or crawling under the table during the interlude. But we have already said that a number of the centres discourage the children from leaving their seats or 'fooling around' in work times. On the other hand, quiet talk or examination of materials not distracting to others is certainly not prevented. Yet the children rarely engage in such activity while off-task in such a setting; they simply sit and wait patiently. Perhaps they don't talk, even softly, to each other at these times because of conditions in the centre. That is, it takes some time for a young child to get to know 40 others as well as four adults. And since much of his time is spent in compulsory, parallel, large groups, he may not have much opportunity to get to know the individuals. It is difficult for a four-year-old, as yet unarmed with a repertory of small-talk, to make the overtures with the 'stranger' sitting next to him. So, as we might expect given the frequency of this kind of setting, the activity category *waiting* appears quite often in the coding. In Miami it is four times more frequent than in Oxfordshire.

Such periods of pure waiting, however, occur mainly in the school-like 'class parallel' setting. Fortunately, no centre operates with this regime all of the time. When the children are engaged on individual projects or in *small* groups in their own time, waiting is virtually eliminated. The adult works alongside one or a few, giving other children tasks to perform on their own which they bring to the teacher when completed or when a problem is encountered. Not that the child then invariably knuckles down immediately to his assignment and stays with it until finished. On the way to his table or instead of just waiting for the teacher to be free to attend to him, he may pause for a chat or to look at something another child is doing. Pure waiting is particularly rare in the Montessori schools, one of the few types of centre to leave materials lying accessible to the child at most times. There, the child snatches moments of 'illicit' free play in between, although, strictly speaking, he is in a teacher-directed work period. Provided he accomplishes a 'reasonable' amount of work, he has considerable freedom, and he makes full use of it to explore the wealth of interesting materials lying about. Thus a child sent to trace around a template of Alaska on the map he was making of North America first spent several minutes examining all the map sections in the drawer and discussing them with a friend. Or another stopped by the hand-bells and carefully arranged them in order of pitch, sounding each one in turn.

In Montessori schools, however, another type of 'non-work/non-play' activity is rather common in place of waiting but still connected with preparing for and ending tasks. There is a focus in these centres on a sort of routine not yet mentioned: the order for doing things and placing things. For example, a child set the job of dusting the room is expected to begin at a certain point and work around the room in a given direction. This routine is most obvious in the assembly and clearing up of equipment. The (usually complicated) materials needed in most tasks have to be fetched one by one in a predetermined order. Consider another example from the observations. Ossie was about to conduct a task matching picture cards and writing down numbers corresponding to the pictures. The teacher was seated on the floor where the activity was to take place. First, Ossie went off to the shelf at the side of the room, fetched a small, rolled-up rug, brought it back to his place on the floor. He knelt down holding the rug in a prescribed fashion and unrolled it on the floor. He went off to the shelf, fetched a sheet of paper, laid it at the top right-hand corner of the rug. He fetched a pencil, laid it next to the paper. He fetched the set of picture-cards, laid them on the left-hand side of the rug. He fetched the counting-beads, laid them beside the cards. When he was ready, the teacher began the task with him. He was quite adept and finished it rapidly. Then he returned the various materials one by one to their proper places, taking them from the rug in reverse order.

The task itself occupied exactly two minutes of the observation (and at that was not challenging to the boy). The preparation took four and a half minutes and clearing away a further three and a half minutes. Although, of course, not all activities required as many pieces, spells of routine assembly and clear-up (the activity category *group routine*) regularly took longer than the task itself in these centres. Nevertheless, it is also in these types of 'individual projects' settings that the child is likely to receive individual attention from a teacher. And we have already shown the benefits of interaction with an adult for highly challenging activity (Table 9.12).

Suggestions for experiment

Two aspects of life in Miami preschools have dominated

discussion so far: heavy use of prepackaged equipment and materials of fixed design and single purpose, and the relatively large proportion of the day given over to compulsory tasks. This is not due to happenstance for all the American centres engage in careful planning, devoting much energy and thought to choice of equipment and materials. Although we know that preschools in the two countries inherit varying educational traditions and that their influence is great, a discussion of history is beyond the scope of childwatching. We therefore conclude with a summary of observed similarities and differences in the two samples, venturing at the end a few tentative proposals.

1 Children in Oxfordshire devote more time to challenging play than their counterparts in Miami.

2 On both sides of the Atlantic children's play is most stretching when devoted to activities with clear goal structure. These include constructing things, drawing things, solving puzzles. Compared to Miami, Oxford children devote a greater part of the day to self-initiated play (high and moderate structure combined) and have available for it more flexible materials. Further, when Oxford children participate in structured activities, they do so in ways that are more complicated and usually self-chosen.

3 Miami children spend more time in passive and organized group activities.

4 In both samples children perform at their intellectual best when part of an adult-child pair. Adults are scarce resource in all preschools, but scarcer still in Miami where the staffing ratios are poorer.

5 Children in Miami play in less challenging ways when part of an interacting pair or group than their counterparts in Oxford. In Miami, children fare better, at least intellectually, when acting parallel to one another.

6 From the Oxford study we know that children engage in cooperative, chatty play when participating in

activities of loose or moderate goal structure, such as pretend, manipulation and social play. These are less common in Miami, where children are found in parallel activity, often in a large group. Further, child-child conversations require intimate settings such as dens or cosy corners, which are rare in Miami, or where they *do* exist (as, for example, the tree house described earlier) are not used for friendly chat.

7 In Oxfordshire, where children are usually free to begin and end activity at will, there is a strong relationship between intellectual complexity and bout length. This is not the case in Miami where children engage in very long bouts of teacher-directed activity which is not especially challenging.

In view of the heavy emphasis on 'school readiness' in Miami, teachers might take a hard look at what actually occurs in the many teacher-directed 'education' activities. Children who are 'officially' part of a three Rs 'ditto' worksheet exercise are often found to be engaged in waiting, staring aimlessly, or less frequently, in social play. Even more to the point, they engage in behaviour of equal challenge when allowed free play. And this *despite the fact that more staff time and energy are devoted to planning the 'educational' side to the curriculum*.

It may be that Miami children would match the higher intellectual achievements seen in Oxfordshire if they were allowed more time for self-initiated activity, more flexible materials, and given greater opportunity to play in interacting pairs or small groups. Cooperative peer play, at least in Oxfordshire, had an additional benefit of increasing the amount of dialogue.

These proposals would involve teachers less in directing activities and distributing materials and more in acting as resource and companion to the children's own play. This would, of course, require a greater investment in materials, although not necessarily a bigger cash outlay. Materials suggested here to expand the current range of structured materials include games such as picture lotto, constructional materials such as woodworking, tyres, crates, ropes and planks, as well as a richer array of props for make-believe. All of these can be used by children without the supervision of adults, leaving staff to respond to children rather than direct them.

Chapter 7 argued against a totally self-expressive regime where materials were rich in inherent challenge but children given free reign. The loosening of structure suggested here is a far cry from free reign. It would require (a) a change in spatial layout with more quiet corners, 'messy areas', and multi-purpose spaces, (b) a widening of free-choice materials while retaining emphasis on high and moderate structure materials, (c) a loosening of daily schedule and lessening of adult-led activities.

These recommendations are tentative, for it's impossible to graft one system onto another. Further, it is possible that the present staffing ratios would prohibit a programme as free as Oxford – perhaps such programmes are possible where preschool provision is available only for the few, and not – as it should be – for all. Still, the more imaginative materials actually cost less, and might easily be acquired. Then too the teacher-directed activities take up a great deal of time and energy in preparation. Could this same time be devoted to 'tutorial work', even playful chats with children? When conferring together, Oxford teachers discuss the *possibilities* of free play materials and children's individual needs; they don't produce worksheets or correct them.

One related doubt concerning the possibility of loosening the Miami regime is the large American enrolment size. Should there be more, smaller, centres? Or, barring this, could more be done, as at Bridge Street, to create an intimate atmosphere where children are members of smaller groups within the centre?

In the final analysis, we do not know for certain whether differences in children's behaviour are due to differing preschool regimes or to differences in the two cultures. However, if we confine conclusions to the Miami observations only, we still state with certainty that free play is as stimulating to the children as their much-touted educational curriculum. And this despite the rather restricted array of materials and (outside the Montessori schools) the limited access to them.

Miami preschools might benefit from a few experiments in the Model 2 research mode described in Chapter 2. We are aware that what is suggested here may not bring about the desired effect. We venture to make recommendations because so many of the Miami staff told us that the goal of the adult-led activities was 'educational' whereas the free-play periods allowed children to 'let off steam' or 'express themselves'. Surely they are wrong, and just as surely this is a case where informed and caring observation, followed by experiment, could make preschools 'matter' more.

To this point we have written descriptively of our research into preschools. We have given the figures that establish our arguments but have not discussed the statistical base that supports them. The next chapter is for those who wish to examine that statistical base in detail. Nothing new is presented by way of content; rather, it turns what have been descriptive statements into a statistical model.

10

Combining factors in a statistical model

Although scores of numeric tables have been presented, the social scientist will have noticed, certainly to his surprise, the absence of statistical tests. We have chosen to discuss them in this final chapter so that readers uninterested in the statistical enterprise can study proportions and probabilities without details concerning formal tests or models.

In this chapter we ask two sets of simple questions. The first concerns agreement amongst our observers as to what they observed and how they coded it. We need to know if observers A, B and C (for we had three in each study) would produce identical coded records if they were to observe the same child. Further we wanted to know if the 'Target Child Coding Manual', describing our procedure for observing and coding, could be followed by others in such a way that their coding was similar to ours. (Other workers in this field are concerned that there is no 'drift' when observers code over time, but we did not consider this.)

The second set of questions concern the generality of the findings to other samples of the preschool population. Do the results enable us to make predictions about children in other places and how certain are we about these 'informed guesses'? Only the data from the Oxford study is presented here.

Reliability of observing and coding

In practice, agreement on observing and coding is tested simultaneously since only the coded records were used in numeric analysis. There is individual style in the kinds of records made, as for example, one of the observers had a better ear for the precise wording of children's talk, or perhaps she was just better at writing it down. Differences in observation details are more or less wiped out in the process of coding, however. In other words, the fact that Observer A might have recorded the complete utterance of a child, or Observer B drawn a detailed diagram of a meccano, made little difference in the final analysis if both agreed that, in the first instance the target child addressed one utterance to a mate, or in the second that he engaged in small scale construction of a challenging level.

Some observational studies give as a measure of observer-coder reliability the raw percentage of agreement for each category. Cohen (1960) developed the Kappa statistical test for agreement because '[many people] assume that the distribution of proportions over the coding categories was known and equal for both observers. Generally neither of these assumptions is met in observational research.' Cohen's Kappa measure is simply the proportion of agreement *after* chance agreement is removed from consideration.

Kappa $= (P_o - P_c)/(1 - P_c)$
where P_o is observed proportion of agreements and P_c is chance proportion of agreements.

Although Cohen designed Kappa for independent observations, Hollenbeck (1978) suggests its usefulness in measuring agreement between observers of continuous behaviour. We have used it because we concur with Hollenbeck that it is a good measure of agreement but would note that its expected sampling distribution under sequential observation is ill-defined. Nevertheless its use will enable comparison with similar studies, and, insofar as its calculation notes 'near-misses' in coding as equivalent to 'misses', it provides an unduly pessimistic picture of agreement. But of course for agreement measures, pessimism as a virtue.

The most common context for measuring agreement between observers-coders is that in which they observe or score (or, as in our case, both) the data from a set of common 'subjects'. Because it is difficult for several observers to watch one live child in the busy preschool without disturbing either him or the routine, we used filmed records of children's behaviour to estimate agreement amongst coders. Subjects were drawn randomly from the Miami file of videotapes ($N = 240$ observations) and observers made narrative records while viewing. After this, they coded their records and the Kappa test of agreement was made on the coded records. This came as near as possible to replicating live observation in the classrooms, followed by coding.

Table 10.1 summarizes the agreement for the most important behavioural categories. In it we show agreement between the one observer-coder who participated in both target child studies, and another member of the Oxford team.

Behavioural category	Kappa	N
Activity name	0·92	200 intervals
Activity level (first 12 categories only)	0·89	184 intervals
Contact with adults	0·86	200 intervals
Social participation	0·85	200 intervals
Presence of utterance	0·80	200 intervals
Nature of utterances (up to seven in any one interval) excluding instances where there is disagreement concerning presence	0·81	84 utterances
Nature of utterance (up to seven in any one interval) including instances where there is disagreement concerning presence	0·75	96 utterances

Table 10.1 *Inter-observer agreement*

Even the rather stringent Kappa test shows how much agreement there was between the observer-coders in the Oxford study. The pattern is similar amongst the Miami team except that their agreement is *even higher* because the American observers were more familiar with watching and scoring video records than the Oxford team.

Would there be similar findings in another study?

There are several reasons for caution concerning transfer to other contexts. One might concern the adequacy of the sample. After all, though we have 9,600 half-minutes, these are a small fraction of the possible half-minutes (and fresh half-minutes are generated every minute as you read – the 'Tristram Shandy problem' that life takes longer to write than to occur).

The other concern is that there may be some crucial variables which affect outcome, which would vary from sample to sample and affect the impact and interpretation of the variables which we have here analysed singly. We can get some leverage on this second problem by defining and estimating models which include a plurality of predictors. Provided we include variable 'A' (and provided that our model is correct) then results should be stable over samples which might vary in their scores on variable 'A'. This more usual research procedure is the application of formal tests of significance to the returned coefficients of effects of interests. We have chosen to restrict these to this chapter, preferring to examine them in the context of a relatively 'full' explanatory model.

The strongest counter to the doubt of sampling stability is a non-formal argument – which is not to say that it is either informal or casual. The best evidence that our findings would *be* stable across varying samples is to observe that they *are* stable across samples. We put this argument here because we believe that the simplistic sampling structure assumed by formal tests maps uneasily onto our data. Stability is the best evidence for stability. In this book we report two samples, one in Oxford and another in Miami. The patterning of information from the two of them shows remarkable stability, and will be discussed in numeric terms elsewhere (Walker, in preparation).

Multiple regression analysis

A quick glance at the research literature reveals that most studies of preschool examine one or two independent variables, for instance, the extent of 'on-task concentration' in terms of precise independent variables such as size of room. In the earliest studies, simple t-test were performed whereas most recent work has adopted analysis of variance as the favourite statistical tool. We rejected this approach as so many of our variables were related in ways that could not be unravelled easily. We chose, instead, to analyse the data with multiple regression because it allows us to look at the simultaneous 'operation' of a host of variables.

In target child studies, regression analysis permits answers to two kinds of questions:

(a) If we know only predictor variable X (say social participation) how good are we at predicting dependent variable A (say, level of challenge)?

(b) If we already know predictor variables X and Y, how much better are we at predicting dependent variable A if we add to the equation another predictor, variable Z?

Obviously question (a) concerns the effect of the predictor variable on its own and is usually investigated via analyses of variance. But question (b) examines the effect of Z on A in *conjunction with* information from other variables and is best handled for non-independent variables by regression.

It is the second question that concerns us most because it allows a more complicated model whose explanatory power is increased by looking at the effect of one variable while holding the others constant. Note that we used a simple additive model, except in special cases where we had reason to believe it inadequate. In these exceptional instances, the regression equations allowed us to express the interaction effect of variables X and Y on A where the effect of X varies according to its conjunction with Y.

Our estimation procedure has involved representing the categorical predictor variables by sets of dummy variables (each 'k' category predictor is represented in the estimation by 'k-1' dummy variables). 'Dummy variables', despite their name, are perfectly respectable animals and are simply 0/1 variables. We can include them as interval level predictors, since on no grounds can they be denied access to the interval-level club. Regression with categorical predictor variables converted to binary form is formally equivalent to an additive model analysis of variance, and we can (if we have theoretical grounds) also include interaction effects.

The classical analysis of variance requires equal category membership in the predictor variables; it requires this in order to ensure that the source predictor variables are independent of each other. This enables exact allocation of variance amongst the predictors, with each responsible for a determinate percentage. But for many social situations the model is not apt, and random experimental allocation produces a world other than the one we wish to understand. It makes little sense to ask 'what is the independent contribution of activity type and adult contact to cognitive challenge when these are allocated completely independently of each other?' when in the real world there may be systematic patterns of association between activity and interaction. It is here that regression estimation procedures prove useful. For whilst they are, for independent variables, formally equivalent to the analysis of variance, they extend very readily to handle non-independent predictors. With such predictors we cannot provide unique allocations of variance (because our model requires that the variables act jointly) but we can, as we saw in the last paragraph, ask clear questions about the increments in explained variance (or, if you will, knowledge) obtained when adding information about one variable to an equation already containing others. The order of this 'addition' is not determined by the data; it is determined by our perception of the data and the questions we wish to ask of them. Different questions will, quite properly, yield different answers.

There is a further problem when predicting binary dependent variables such as the presence or absence of dialogue, or greater or lesser cognitive challenge, and that concerns heteroscedasticity which may lead to inefficiency of the coefficient estimators. There is, however, a dispute over the magnitude of the resulting inefficiency and it is not clear that the more sophisticated estimation strategies are to be preferred to the ordinary least squares. Because of the interpretive advantages, we have chosen to use ordinary least squares as our method. The reader with doubts about this choice should recall that ordinary least squares with binary dependent variables is equivalent to two-category discriminant analysis and can read the results that follow as an exercise in locating the predictor function of two groups of half minutes – as, for example, minutes of ordinary or high challenge.

There are other ways of analysing contingency tables, especially log-linear models, but the basic predictive structure assumed by log-linear models (i.e., row effect + column effect + interaction effect) is formally identical to that assumed by regression analysis. Each can be regarded as a particular estimation strategy for the general linear model and each has its advantages.

The unit of analysis in most of the target child analyses is usually the half-minute interval. (With the important exception of the bout-theme for which we calculate the length of time that children stick to one activity). Of course the many half-minute intervals are not a simple random sample of all possible half-minutes. They are the product of a multi-stage random sample. Therefore the intervals are not independently drawn for, in fact, they are drawn in clumps which are really children. This is no different from most of social science research where simple random sampling rarely occurs.

In the equations that follow, we speak of the 'predictive' value of a variety of predictor variables. This of course refers to prediction within our sample, and not, in the technical sense, to other samples.

On the basis of the Oxford study, for example, we cannot

make an unequivocable prediction to other samples because (1) the sampling of children was not totally random, (2) the half minutes are not independent of one another, (3) the predictor variables are not really independent as for example activity categories such as 'social interaction' are definitionally dependent on certain social participation categories. However, the regression analyses allow us to explore *within our own sample* the relative effect of the predictor variables. The findings provide a good estimation as to how children in other places might act when confronted by similar circumstances, but we do not claim to know for certain.

One way to estimate the generalizability of research findings is to divide the original sample in half and treat each with separate regression equations. If the patterns in the data are similar, one is more convinced that the pattern of results is 'general' rather than 'particular'. We did just that in the Oxford target child study and found much similarity between the pattern of coefficients for older children, drawn from one set of centres, and younger children, drawn from another. (We did not expect a large difference between the two age groups as the age range in the total sample was not wide.) Results of this split-sample procedure will be reported in Table 10.4.

Predicting level of challenge in children's play

The factors that foster children's thinking have already been discussed in Chapter 4, but they are presented here in terms of a formal model. Our first step was to look at the effect on level of play of 'demographic' factors such as *age, sex, time of day,* and statutory *type* of centre. This group of variables turned out to be rather poor at predicting challenge. Although some of them were 'significant' in the statistical sense, they were not very powerful as predictors. Next, we added to the equation the effect of the social setting, including the *grouping* of the child and whether or not he was in *contact with an adult*. We also included as predictors whether or not there was *dialogue*.

Table 10.2 presents the coefficients for the factors just named and yields an R^2 of 0.11, rather low considering that we have used as predictors demographic information, centre type, and details about social participation. Before examining its content, we describe briefly its form.

The coefficients are unstandardized regression coefficients and each 'k' category predictor (such as 'adult contact') has been represented by k-1 dummy variables.

The 'zero' point on the resulting scale is a purely arbitrary reference point (a result of our particular choice of dummies) and the 'zero' point can be reallocated by simple adjustment of the constant term. What is of substantive (and statistical) interest is the relative pattern of effects amongst the categories for a particular predictor (such as 'adult contact') and this is unaffected by the representational choice of dummies. For example the 0.10 coefficient for dialogue in Table 10.2 says that the presence of dialogue (as against its absence and holding everything else constant) gives 0.1 units of expected increase in cognitive challenge. In Table 10.2, where we are allowing the effects of 'adult contact' to vary by age the total impact of being 'old and alone' is given by adding the 'old' effect from 'age' to the appropriate adult contact effect; in other words the 'age' effect gives the difference in baseline between the 'adult contact' effects for the two age groups, the 'adult contact' variable itself gives the differing patterns of effects for the two age groups. Differing aggregations speak to differing substantive equations.

As we have noted, the zero point on our scales of categories is a numerical convention. Since the straightforward regression tests of significance are tests of significant difference between reported category and this base point (and there are a very large number of possible comparisons) we have chosen not to report individual F tests for variables with many categories. However, for some variables, such as social code (where our base line is 'child alone') or an 'adult

Variable	Category		Effect coefficient		F
Sex:	Boy		0·00		
	Girl		−0·04		12·38
Age:	Young		0·00		
	Old		0·17		24·23
Time of day:	Morning		0·00		
	Afternoon		0·00		0·10
Dialogue:	Absent		0·00		
	Present		0·10		53·25
		Youngs		Olds	
Social	Alone	0·00		0·00	
participation:	Pair	−0·04		0·01	
	Group	−0·09		−0·06	
	Parallel	0·04		0·09	
Contact with	None	0·00		0·00	
adult:	Near	0·05		0·13	
	Interacting	−0·06		0·10	
Centre type:	Nursery school		0·00		2·80
	Nursery class		0·03		
	Playgroup		0·17		112·82
Constant:			1·29		$R^2 = 0·11$

Table 10.2 *Predictive effect of demographic, social and centre variables on cognitive challenge (ordinary challenge = 0; high challenge = 1) N = 3357 units*

contact' (where our base line is 'no adult around') the straightforward comparisons are of substantive interest (is being in a 'pair' different from being 'alone'?). In Table 10.4 we report some F tests, which tell whether being in the named category is significantly different in effect from being in the 'zero' category.

Returning to the content of Table 10.2, we find that it merely echoes what has been reported in Chapter 4, namely that having a conversation is associated with challenging play and that for older children contact with an adult is positively related to challenging play. But recall that one of the striking findings of the target child studies is the influential effect on level of play of the child's activity type. Table 10.3 examines the effect of this on level of challenge while holding constant all the factors included in Table 10.2. By the addition of this one variable, the proportion of explained variance is doubled.

Variable	Category	Effect coefficient		F
Sex:	Boy	0·00		
	Girl	−0·04		13·78
Time of day:	Morning	0·00		
	Afternoon	0·05		15·46
Dialogue:	Absent	0·00		
	Present	0·09		37·73
		Youngs	Olds	
Social	Alone	0·00	0·00	
participation:	Pair	−0·02	0·13	
	Group	−0·03	0·16	
	Parallel	−0·02	0·10	
Contact	None	0·00	0·00	
with adult:	Near	−0·05	0·08	
	Interacting	−0·13	0·08	
Activity:	Non-playful interaction	0·00		
	Gross motor play	−0·03		
	Large construction	0·39		
	Small construction	0·20		
	Art	0·23		
	Manipulation	0·14		
	Structured materials	0·42		
	Pretend	0·42		
	Scale-version toys	0·40		
	Music	0·45		
	Social play	−0·28		
	Informal games	−0·00		
Constant		0·24		
				$R^2 = 0·22$

Table 10.3 *Predictive effect of demographic, social and activity variables on cognitive challenge*

The regression equations have enabled us to see the relative effect of the many factors associated with cognitive challenge. By far the most powerful single factor in terms of prediction is the activity in which the child engages. Many others were significant (when compared to the category set at

0) but their overall predictive effect is not nearly so strong as that of activity. Adding knowledge of activity when we already know social participation (which doubles the amount of explained variance) constitutes a stringent test because the effect of social setting has already been incorporated into the model. The different activity categories fluctuate markedly in their effect on challenge, in fact the range between lowest and highest is 0·7 (in a 0–1 scale).

In incorporating age we have already departed from a simple additive model. There is some further argument about the use of simple additive models and this concerns the possibility that some variables may interact differently with one another. For example, social participation may affect the level of challenge in a child's play in one way for pretend but in another way altogether for manipulation. To test for this, we designed an equation in which the interactions between context and activity in the individual categories were tested as well as the main overall effect. We found, in the example above, that including these individual interactions did not add noticeably to the amount of explained variance. So, although it's true that being alone while playing with dough is different from being alone on the swings, the *overall relationship* between social participation and level of challenge in the child's activity is for social interaction to increase cognitive level. In science there is always a tension between fine detail and powerful, parsimonious explanation. There is no way to have the best of both worlds; we chose additive regression, (except when looking at age effects and social categories) because it enables us to look at the simultaneous effect of many independent variables. We believe this approach to represent an improvement over analysis of variance, while not producing so many complicated interactions that our interpretive powers would be over-taxed.

Conducting the split-half analysis

One might wonder why we have included separate age-group

coefficients for the social categories but not for the activity ones. In other words, we combined ages for some variables and not for others. We decided to do this only after looking at the two age groups separately. The full regression analyses, separate for each age group appear in Table 10.4 and show why we included separate age effects on social categories but not on others.

Variable	Category	Effect coefficient		F	
		Youngs	Olds	Youngs	Olds
Sex:	Boy	0·00	0·00		
	Girl	−0·02	−0·05	2·26	13·03
Social participation:	Alone	0·00	0·00		
	Pair	0·03	0·12	1·54	15·41
	Group	0·01	0·13	0·12	21·69
	Parallel	0·02	0·05	0·37	3·00
Contact with adult:	None	0·00	0·00		
	Near	−0·06	0·08	3·99	8·26
	Interacting	−0·12	0·07	31·48	13·38
Activity:	Non-playful interaction	0·00	0·00		
	Gross motor play	−0·08	−0·03		
	Large construction	0·20	0·45		
	Small construction	0·21	0·18		
	Art	0·21	0·24		
	Manipulation	0·10	0·25		
	Structured materials	0·48	0·36		
	Pretend	0·42	0·38		
	Scale-version toys	0·34	0·41		
	Music	0·47	0·36		
	Social play	−0·23	−0·36		
	Informal games	−0·20	0·10		
Constant		0·23	0·29		
		$R^2 = 0·16$	$R^2 = 0·16$		

Table 10.4 *Predictive effect of sex, social participation and activity on cognitive challenge: old and young samples*

Note that the coefficients associated with the various activity categories are in almost identical rank order with regard to their predictive efficiency. This is all the more remarkable when remembering that children in two age groups were drawn from different centres and also that some of the Ns in individual categories (such as problem solving) were low, and the two age-specific samples are drawn from different schools. We would expect that the effect of some variables (in particular the effect of adult contact and social setting) would vary systematically by age. But it is surprising and comforting to find the effects for activity type stable across the groups. This says that our findings are stable across two samples which, were sampling instability rife, would be expected to yield different results. It is, of course, possible that there are peculiar social groupings or contexts for which our findings do not apply (these can never be ruled out). But our own trust in the conclusions reported here comes from their remarkable stability across differing sample conditions. This, more than the formal measures we also provide to demonstrate 'significance', is what legitimates the recommendations we make in the concluding chapter. We believe our results to be replicable because we have replicated them.

Predicting the presence of dialogue

The effect of various factors on children's talk was formally investigated in ways identical to that presented for level of challenge. To begin, we asked questions about the role of the various activity settings in fostering dialogue. Table 10.5 shows the effect coefficients when we use sex, age, time, and activity as predictors of dialogue. The R^2 of only 0·07 shows that the relationship between categories with loose goal structure and dialogue is statistically significant, but not of great magnitude.

To these predictive factors above, we next add the social ones of *grouping* and *contact with an adult*. The results appear in Table 10.6 whose R^2 is 0·22.

One might wonder whether the better prediction in Table 10.6 requires knowledge from *both* sets of factors. In other words, does information about social setting on its own

Variable	Category	Effect coefficient	F
Sex:	Boy	0·00	
	Girl	−0·02	6·15
Age:	Young	0·00	
	Old	0·01	4·07
Time of day:	Morning	0·00	
	Afternoon	0·03	8·96
Activity:	Non-playful interaction	0·00	
	Gross motor	−0·03	
	Large construction	−0·10	
	Small construction	0·23	
	Art	0·01	
	Manipulation	0·11	
	Structured materials	0·01	
	Pretend	−0·00	
	Scale-version toys	0·02	
	Music	−0·14	
	Social play	0·13	
	Informal games	0·16	
Constant		0·16	
			$R^2 = 0·04$

Table 10.5 *Predictive effect of demographic, and activity factors on dialogue (no dialogue = 0; dialogue = 1) N = 9577*

provide a good predictor? The answer is yes, for Table 10.7 shows that social information by itself is a good predictor of dialogue. Information about activity helps in the prediction as one might expect but we know that it's usually the pair

Variable	Category	Effect coefficient
Sex:	Boy	0·00
	Girl	−0·01
Age:	Young	0·00
	Old	0·01
Activity:	Non-playful interaction	0·00
	Gross motor play	−0·19
	Large scale construction	−0·24
	Small scale construction	−0·01
	Art	−0·16
	Manipulation	−0·08

Variable	Category	Effect coefficient	
	Structured materials	−0·13	
	Pretend	−0·16	
	Scale-version toys	−0·10	
	Music	−0·26	
	Informal games	−0·12	
	Social play with spontaneous rules	−0·12	
	Three Rs	0·15	
	Examination	0·01	
	Problem-solving	0·06	
	Adult-directed art and manipulation skills	−0·15	
	Rough-and-tumble	−0·40	
	Organized games	−0·20	
	Adult-led groups	−0·33	
	Watching staff	−0·18	
	Watching peers	−0·15	
	Watching events	−0·15	
	Waiting	−0·19	
	Purposeful movement	−0·17	
	Cruising	−0·18	
	Aimless	−0.16	
	Individual physical needs	−0·18	
	Group routine	−0·15	
	Distress	−0·09	
	Other	−0·00	

Variable	Category	Young	Old
Social participation:	Alone	0·00	0·00
	Pair	0·30	0·30
	Group	0·27	0·21
	Parallel	0·04	0·00
Contact with adults:	None	0·00	0·00
	Near adult	−0·05	−0·05
	Interacting with adult	0·06	0·10
Centre type:	Nursery school	0·00	
	Nursery class	0·04	
	Playgroup	−0·04	
Time of day:	Morning	0·00	
	Afternoon	0·00	
Constant:		0·18	

$R^2 = 0.22$

Table 10.6 *Predictive effect of selected variables on dialogue*

Variable	Category	Effect coefficient		F
Sex:	Boy	0·00		
	Girl	−0·01		0·04
Age:	Young	0·00		
	Old	−0·01		0·32
Time of day:	Morning	0·00		
	Afternoon	0·00		0·01
Type of centre:	Nursery school	0·00		
	Nursery class	0·06		37·01
	Playgroup	−0·05		23·28
		Youngs	*Olds*	
Social	Alone	0·00	0·00	
participation	Pair	0·34	0·36	
	Group	0·31	0·25	
	Parallel	0·06	0·03	
Contact	None	0·00	0·00	
with adult:	Near	−0·10	−0·08	
	Interacting	0·06	0·10	
Constant		0·04		$R^2 = 0·19$

Table 10.7 *Predictive effect of demographic, centre, and social variables on dialogue*

(slightly more than the group) that's associated with conversation.

The effect of activity setting in Table 10.6 varies slightly from the tables presented in Chapter 4 because there we separated dialogues with adults from those with peers and here we lump together both kinds. Still the overall pattern of effects is similar with the tightly structured activities (art, structured materials) being less conducive to conversation than the more loosely structured ones, manipulation and social 'horsing around.'

Effects of sequence

It may appear that we are cavalier about the sequential

nature of behaviour. The analyses presented so far have concerned the relationship of factors *within* time intervals, yet commonsense tells us that the way we behave right now is influenced by what has happened in the past. Recall that data were presented in Chapter 4 showing that children were more likely to shift up in challenge if they had been interacting with an adult in the previous half-minute. With the exception of very limited interactions such as this, we were disappointed with the predictive efficiency of information from the half-minute before the interval being explained. In the main, most of the information needed to predict level of challenge or dialogue (or other behaviours not reported here) was contained in the interval for which the prediction was made. As an example, if we wish to predict a child's level of challenge and know only his age, sex and current social participation, we can explain 3 per cent of the variance. If we were to add to this information concerning the very same categories but taken from the preceding interval, the R^2 is only marginally increased.

Why? A child enjoying the beneficial effect of a peer interaction was usually enjoying the same benefit in the preceding interval. Then, too, half a minute is rather long in a child's life and whatever 'helped' him to more complex play may well have occurred in the half-minute for which the prediction is being made.

To investigate sequence effects, we added to many equations what we call 'lagged' variables. A lagged variable is one which describes the interval before the one being predicted. By using lagged variables, we discovered the strong relation between the interacting adult in the previous interval and the shift in level of challenge. As a further example of lagged variables consider Table 10.6. If we add to these predictor variables a set of lagged ones (that is if we look at the effect of being a member of a pair in both the present interval and the one preceding, of being alone in both present interval and preceding, etc. for all the variables) the R^2 is increased by only 0·02. This small increase in explained variance shows the half-minute variables to be minimally related to that which precedes them. It may be that half-minutes are too large to see the precise effect of sequential information and that only robust effects such as that of the interacting adult can be seen in them. Whatever the reason, we report our disappointment that the continuity analyses did not bear more explanatory fruit.

The task in the preceding analyses has been to describe some factors regularly associated with the occurrence of cognitive challenge and dialogue in the behaviour of children at preschools. There are countless reasons why children act as they do and many are idiosyncratic. Therefore it is not surprising that the factors investigated here, such as activity type or presence of adult, 'explain' only part of the variance. Instead of investigating one factor at a time, we have looked at the effect of several in conjunction. By holding constant the effect of other relevant variables, we obtain a precise estimation of the effect of a given predictor when others are constrained. There are, however, questions for which the appropriate assessment of effect would allow the intervening variables to vary. If we were interested in the effect of social participation on cognitive challenge, we might think of it as affecting activity type and hence, through that, affecting cognitive challenge. If this is the question, a measure of total effect can be obtained from a reduced model omitting activity type, and so allowing it to vary (Macdonald, 1979). The tabular analyses in earlier chapters can be seen in this light as proper estimations, not poor approximations to regression.

Full description of the regression models used in analysing the target child studies will be reported elsewhere. Here we have attempted to sketch its major outlines so that readers will know our arguments for using regression analysis for sequential data of this kind, our reservations about it, as well as the congruence between the analyses in this chapter and those in earlier ones.

11

The compleat pedagogue

We have stressed the kinds of materials, programmes and centres that are regularly associated with positive actions in children, such as concentration, imaginative and complex play, conversations with others, and cooperation between peers. We have not measured children's happiness at school nor how well they got on with one another. In our studies we were struck by the capacity of some children to comfort those who weep, laugh at their own mistakes, and walk bravely into the dark. Surely these are virtues and surely the preschool affects them. But they are difficult to measure and, as we argued earlier, there is no agreement as to the form they should take or their order of importance. So we stuck to bread-and-butter skills, ones we thought were the core of competence.

In the end, we argue that competence is fostered by activities with clear goal structure because they concentrate the mind and instil confidence in one's own power . . . the childish version of 'by Jove I did it'. But lest people toss away the sand and dough, we feel we should emphasize the importance of these unstructured materials for the way they encourage chatting amongst children and provide moderate scope for complex thought. Pretending comes in for special mention for while some of it is the tired 'home corner litany', it provides practice in the social negotation of goals and that is why children stay at make-believe games for long spells of time.

The most difficult task facing the teacher or play leader is to decide which of all the 'important' and 'worthwhile' things she might do have highest priority.

Courtney Cazden (1975) reports on her experience upon returning to the classroom after teaching more than a decade at a teacher-training college. Faced with a roomful of five-year-olds, she was forced to put into practice an array of methods that had heretofore been the subject of lectures. Her problem, she said was not in knowing the right thing to do – it was rather in knowing *too many* 'right things'. It would seem that training courses send forth practitioners filled with ideas and techniques but possessing no good means of choosing amongst them in 'real life'. For example, the hard-pressed practitioner wishes to speak daily with every child, yet knows that sustained conversations are the ideal. She wishes to provide materials with clear goal structure but knows that the less structured ones encourage chatting amongst the children. She may know that small, intimate centres are best for young children but be stuck with an enrolment of eighty odd. We have tried with the case studies from Oxford, as well as the contrast provided by Miami, to be explicit about staples and spices in the preschool diet. And we have tried to make concrete the findings from numeric data.

But of course this is not all there is to say about good practice. While we have been trying to establish the programme and setting the practitioner needs to create, we have not been able to include in our analyses one of the most crucial variables – the practitioner herself. We have seen her behind the scenes ordering materials, planning the day, having 'conversations' with fellow staff. What is she (and it has been 'she' in our studies) really like? What really makes a good teacher or playleader? These questions are explored in Wood, McMahon and Cranstoun (forthcoming). Surely it has to do with liking children. Warmth and zestfulness go a long way towards making a preschool hum with productive cheer. Equally important are fondness for talking with children, listening to children, and even sharing in their play. In addition to these (almost banal) conclusions about warmth and caring, we found that the best practitioners had about them an air of self-confidence. They knew what they did well and were open about their limitations. This last is important as it most often leads to improving deficiencies or finding ways to circumvent them. This leaves one further characteristic vital to preschool work – a willingness to learn.

A well-known and successful tutor in the Pre-school Playgroups Association network once said despairingly, 'Why bother to teach courses on how to run playgroups? If they're good with people, they don't need a course and if they're not, there's no way we can improve them.' It seems to us that statements such as these assign an omnipotence to adult personality that denies the equal power of challenging materials, exciting activities, and well-planned routine. These things do indeed matter. However, everyone knows a mother whose kitchen provides a marvellous curriculum for two children but who fails as playgroup supervisor. Perhaps she cannot cope with twenty children, nor order supplies enough in advance. We agree that 'liking children' or 'being positive' are essential ingredients in the skilled preschool worker but argue that they are additive in the equations we have discussed throughout the book. They don't magically nullify the 'rules' concerning materials, programme or size; they enter the equation and subtly lighten or change their shape. The rules are not prescriptive ('thou shalt not') but merely statistical ('generally, it's better to').

Appendices

Appendix A is a guide for practitioners who wish to conduct observations on their own. Its structure is identical to the more complicated research instrument described in Chapters 3 and 4, although it employs fewer categories for behaviour, a shorter observation span, and applies codes to full minutes. It is interesting to contrast this practitioners' guide with the research manual, an excerpt from which appears as Appendix C.

Appendix B is an excellent example of the fruits of participatory research in the Model 2 vein. Although a short excerpt from the complete handbook, it shows how playgroup courses can benefit from structured observations and how research can be turned to practical ends.

Appendix C is an excerpt from the complete coding manual used for the target child studies in Oxfordshire and Miami. It shows the fine detail used in assessing cognitive challenge in pretend play.

Appendix A

Observing Children

Kathy Sylva, Marjorie Painter, Carolyn Roy

Why observe?

Watching is commonplace behaviour; we do it surreptitiously when in public, more openly when we believe that we, the observers, are not ourselves observed. There are countless motives for watching others. First, there is ordinary curiosity. But we also watch to gain information useful in achieving specific goals. One such goal might be the creation of rich environments for children and there follow suggestions for observing them in their preschool habitat.

The 'target child' method of observing has been stolen – in a respectable, scientific way – from people who study animal behaviour. Curious as to the ways animals adapt to both the physical and social environment, ethologists donned sturdy field-gear and followed individual animals around woodland, plain and desert. They recorded minute aspects of behaviour, making notes on social interaction, feeding habits, cooperative and defensive activity. They learned the peculiar habits of individual animals, but equally valuable were the pictures they pieced together of how animals in various categories (e.g. young infants, mothers, or male juveniles) behaved in everyday situations.

Formal observation of animals and preschool children is a far cry from casual watching. To begin, the observer makes notes and pores over them after observation. Field notes are then coded and quantified. No one, even the most innocent, watches with a completely open mind. We select certain bits of activity as 'interesting' or 'important' and exclude the rest. We are often unaware of the process of selecting and interpreting but it is always with us. The 'target child' technique makes explicit its ways of filtering and interpreting. You may query its methods, or even change them, but it will make you confront the preconceptions that you bring with you to the task.

How to observe?

Decide *which child* to observe. You may have a reason for choosing a particular child. Perhaps you simply don't know him well, or maybe his behaviour causes difficulty, or you suspect some abnormality. Otherwise it is a good idea to start by choosing a child at random. Pick a name randomly from the register, or choose, say, the first child you see wearing blue, or the first child to cross a particular spot on the floor or at a certain activity.

Before you start observing, make sure that *members of the staff* know what you are doing and that they understand that you will not intervene unless there is danger to children or property. This is particularly important if you work in the group where you are observing. Ask them to carry on normally, trying not to avoid the child you are watching nor spending an unusual amount of time with him.

When observing, try to become '*a fly on the wall*', as inconspicuous as possible. If you can, get close enough to hear what the child says, but without his realizing that you are watching him. It is a good idea to sit or crouch sideways on to the child, not directly facing him. Try to avoid meeting his gaze. If he or another child speaks to you, of course answer him, but as briefly and kindly as possible.

How long to observe? Aim at observing for 10 minutes. Later you may want to observe for longer, say 20 minutes, to get a fuller picture of what the child does.

Recording your observation

Use a ready drawn-up recording sheet as in Figure A1.1.

CHILD'S INITIALS:	SEX:	AGE:	DATE AND TIME OBSERVED:		
ACTIVITY RECORD		LANGUAGE RECORD		TASK	SOCIAL
1					
2					
3					
4					
5					
6					
7					
8					
9					
10					

Figure A1.1 *Blank recording sheet*

Have a watch, preferably with a second hand, so that you can record minute by minute. Observe for several minutes before you start to write anything down.

Write down *what the child does* in each minute in the ACTIVITY column. For instance, 'Pulls small lump off large piece of dough, squeezes it, watches child opposite.' Write down exactly what happens without adding any interpretation. Also jot down a note about the activity and materials and whether other children or adults are present. For example, 'Table with 2 large lumps of blue dough, 2 other children, helper sitting there.'

Write down what the child says and what other children or adults say to him, for each minute, in the LANGUAGE column. It is often impossible to write down the exact words spoken, but record the gist of comments if you can.

It is helpful to use the following abbreviations as a sort of short-hand to help you note down quickly what is done and said:

TC   Target child (the one you are observing)
C   Other child
A   Any adult (such as staff member, mother-helper, teenage student, the observer (you))
→   Speaks to

These abbreviations are especially useful in noting the language; here are some examples:

TC	Sings to self
TC→C:	'I'm the father and you're the mother.'
C →TC:	'You're not coming to my birthday party.'
A →TC:	Comforts him
TC→A:	'Will you tie my apron please?'
TC→C:	Conversation
TC unison	Sings
A →Group	Announces milk-time
A →TC+C	Reads a story

Note: The LANGUAGE column does not include instances where the child is listening-in to another conversation without participating or being included. This would be written down in the ACTIVITY column.

If you are interrupted for a short time whilst observing, don't worry. Just note it as 'interruption'.

After your observation is finished, make a note of what the

child does next. This may help you to make better sense of what he was doing at the end of the observation.

Looking for 'themes'

When you have finished writing down your observation, go over it and divide it into separate spells of coherent activity; look for the themes in the child's activity. By a 'theme', we mean a continued stream of activity where the child is 'following a thread'.

Draw double lines across the page of your observation where one theme ends and another begins, so that you can readily see the start and end of each spell of activity.

The theme *may* be based on the materials which the child is using, or on the other children or adults that he's with. But sometimes the start and end of a theme do not coincide with what on the surface looks like a change in the type of activity itself.

Some examples:

(1) A child leaves the milk table and goes to the woodwork bench where he constructs an aeroplane, then he moves off to do a painting. From his movement towards the woodwork until his completing of the aeroplane and leaving the bench, is one theme. The painting begins a new theme – it is not connected with the woodwork.

But:

(2) A boy makes an aeroplane at the woodwork bench, then takes it to a table to paint it. Although he's using some different materials and changes from construction to painting, this is all one theme centred around the aeroplane.

(3) A child climbs up and slides down the slide, goes over to a large barrel and wriggles through it, then goes off to climb along a raised plank. All of this sequence

involves body movement, but there are three separate themes.

But:

(4) A boy is with two friends playing 'follow-the-leader'. He follows his friends up and down the slide, through a barrel, along a plank. Here there is only one theme, with the different movements tied together by the flow of the follow-the-leader game.

Sometimes a child engages in a spell of sustained activity that has short interruptions in it. If an interruption lasts for only a minute, then ignore it when drawing the double lines for 'theme'.

An example:

A child spends several minutes painting, but stops for a minute to go over and talk to a friend before returning to her painting. Note this as all one theme, ignoring the brief chat.

Ignoring these small interruptions gives you a better idea of how long a child stays with an activity. Similarly, preparation for an activity (such as putting on an apron before water-play, fetching a helmet to pretend at being a fireman), or completing an activity (such as hanging up a painting), can be counted as part of the main theme.

The sample observation (Figure A1.2) may make this clearer.

Marking the start and end of the themes like this will give you an idea of how long a child sustains a theme in his play and how many themes may occur in an observation. You may then be able to see what it is that makes for long themes of play (interesting materials? other children? adult presence?) and what brings themes of play to an end (completion? lack of ideas? distractions? interruptions?). You may want to see how often a child returns to a theme from a previous spell of play in one observation, or to see whether a child finds some themes more absorbing than others.

CHILD'S INITIALS: A.N. SEX: boy AGE: 4/11 DATE AND TIME OBSERVED: 18/11 10·50 am			
ACTIVITY RECORD	LANGUAGE RECORD	TASK	SOCIAL
1 TC at woodwork table, hammers nail into wood. Goes round table & looks at small metal pieces. Offers nail to A.	TC → A: Will you bang this? A → TC (bangs nail in)		
2 Watches A carefully. Gives A a bottle cap to hammer on for him	A → TC (about hammering) TC → A (asks her to hammer on cap)		
3 Watches A hammering his bottle cap & milk bottle top into wood with nail. A finishes - hands TC his wood. (Looks like			
4 Carries woodwork outside, back indoors. Takes it to paint. Paints it blue, with brush			
5 Paints his woodwork. Paints, wipes thumb on paper, on wood.			
5 Paints his woodwork.			
7 Takes coat off - gets apron and puts it on. Continues to paint	A → TC: Not with your coat on, you'll get it all over		
8 Paints woodwork	A → TC: Now finish that and come and have your milk. TC → A: No! A → TC: We'll save some then		
9 Looks at hands - goes to washbowl in corner (leaves woodwork on paint table) . Washes with 1 C	TC ⟷ C TC ⟷ C A → TC + C (about washing)		
10 Washes hands, dries them Goes to sit at milk table, next to twin brother. Helper gives him cup	TC → A: Where's mine? I haven't got a cup. TC → C: I got a blue one		

Figure A1.2 *Sample record*

Coding your observation

Each minute's observation can be looked at in three different ways. They are:

The social code (whom the child is *with*)

This code analyses the observation in terms of the child's social interaction, or lack of it. For example, the *task code* tells us the child was, say, engaged in manipulative play, while the *social code* tells us he was chatting with a friend throughout it.

The language code (what the child *says* and what *is said to* him)

This code shows who spoke to whom and what it was about. A quick glance at the coding in the LANGUAGE column tells you whether the child spoke much or little. The coding tells you how much he was talking with other children and how much with adults, and whether he initiated talk or mainly responded to others.

The task code (what the child *does*)

These categories describe the child's behaviour – what he was actually doing each minute. They include play behaviour such as *pretend*, *art*, or *manipulation*, as well as non-play behaviour such as *watching* or *cruising*.

Why code?

You may think that your narrative records in the ACTIVITY and LANGUAGE columns might be enough for you to see what went on in your observation. But the coding is a way of *summarizing* these large amounts of detail about what was done and said. It enables you to see at a glance the *structure* of a child's activity over the observation. With just the narrative record there is so much detailed information that you may not be able to see the wood for the trees!

So from the coding you can read off rapidly what activities the child engaged in, how long he spent in each one, whether he was alone or with other children or adults for most of the time, whether he was speaking with the others or just silently playing beside them. And you may be able to see whether being alone tends to go with some kinds of activity, while interacting with others goes with different activities.

How to code

Go through your observation and for each minute choose the appropriate categories from the coding lists – these lists are given in the following pages. Look at the sample observation (Figure A1.3) at the end for help with the layout. Make sure that you have completed the coding for each minute, in each of the three types of code.

Using the social code

For each minute, code whether the child's activity was:

SOL   Solitary.
PAIR Two people together (target child plus one other child or adult).
SG   In a small group of three to five children.
LG   In a large group of six or more children.

Sometimes, in a group of two or more children, the child appears to have little contact with the others. If he is playing or working on his own, despite the others around him, add a /P, for 'parallel', to the *social code*.

For instance:

PAIR/P means that the child is near another but not playing or talking with him.

CHILD'S INITIALS: A.N. SEX: boy AGE: 4/11 DATE AND TIME OBSERVED: 18/11 10.50 am

	ACTIVITY RECORD	LANGUAGE RECORD	TASK	SOCIAL
1	TC at woodwork table, hammers nail into wood. Goes round table & looks at small metal pieces. Offers nail to A.	TC → A: Will you bang this? A → TC (bangs nail in)	SSC	(PAIR)
2	Watches A carefully. Gives A a bottle cap to hammer on for him	A → TC (about hammering) TC → A (asks her to hammer on cap)	SSC	(PAIR)
3	Watches A hammering his bottle cap & milk bottle top into wood with nail. A finishes – hands TC his wood. (looks like →		SSC	(PAIR)
4	Carries woodwork outside, back indoors. Takes it to paint. Paints it blue, with brush		ART	SOL
5	Paints his woodwork. Paints, wipes thumb on paper, on wood.		ART	SOL
6	Paints his woodwork.		ART	SOL
7	Takes coat off – gets apron and puts it on. Continues to paint	A → TC: Not with your coat on, you'll get it all over	ART	(SOL)
8	Paints woodwork	A → TC: Now finish that and come and have your milk. TC → A: No! A → TC: We'll save some then	ART	(PAIR)
9	Looks at hands – goes to washbowl in corner! (leaves woodwork on paint table) Washes with 1 C	TC ⟷ C TC ⟷ C A → TC + C (about washing)	DA	(PAIR)
10	Washes hands, dries them Goes to sit at milk table, next to twin brother Heifer gives him cup	TC → A: Wheres mine? I haven't got a cup. TC → C: I got a blue one	DA	LG

Figure A1.3 *Sample record, coded*

LG/P   means that the child sits or stands in a large group of children but does not interact with any of them.

Note that the children may even be doing the same thing, but call it /P if they are not interacting with one another.

Special mention of the adult:

Put a circle around the *social code* if the child is interacting with, or is very near to, an *adult*. So,

(PAIR) would be the code if the child is chatting with a helper.

(SG/P) might be the code if the child is sitting next to an adult who is supervising a group activity.

If the child's social situation changes within the minute, decide which was the longest type of interaction and code the whole minute as that. For example, if the child has a short chat with a friend but plays alone for most of the minute, code this as SOL and not PAIR.

However, it is useful to make a special note of *any* contact with an adult, even if it is very short – you still put a circle around the *social code*. (This helps you keep track of the effect of the adults.) So if the child was playing alone except for a brief exchange of greetings with a passing helper, the *social code* would be (SOL) for that minute.

Using the language code

The method of coding the language has already been explained under 'Recording your observation' in the LANGUAGE column. If you have already used the abbreviations listed on page 3 (TC→C; S→TC: and so on), then you have already coded the language! So just make sure that you have indeed completed this coding.

Using the task code

For each minute of observation write down the appropriate *task code* category. There is a list of these categories and their abbreviations on the following pages.

As in the *social code*, you note only the more prominent behaviour if the child engages in more than one category of behaviour in a minute. If, in a minute, a child shows two different sorts of behaviour one after the other, decide which was the longest and code it all as that. If the child engages in two sorts of behaviour at the same time (for example, *manipulation* together with *watching*), decide which seemed the main one and code it all as that.

You have already marked the start and end of the themes in the child's activity by drawing double lines across the page. Often the theme and the *task coding* coincide, so that when you change to a new *task code* category the theme changes too. But sometimes one theme could include more than one *task code* category, or one *task code* series could contain more than one theme. Look at the fully-coded sample observation at the end, and at the examples given under 'looking for themes' on page 233, where the themes and *task code* categories overlap each other.

The task code categories

Each of the categories below may include talk. Sometimes it may appear that social interaction is more important to the child than the task, but this is acknowledged in the *social code*. If there is an appropriate task code, it should be used.

Large muscle movement (LMM): Active movement of the child's body, requiring coordination of larger muscles, such as running, climbing

Large scale construction (LSC): Arranging and building dens, trains, etc., with large crates, blocks, etc.

Small scale construction (SSC): Using small constructional materials such as lego, meccano, hammering and nailing

Art (ART): 'Free expression' creative activities such as painting, drawing, chalking, cutting, sticking

Manipulation (MAN): The mastering or refining of manual skills requiring coordination of the hand/arm and the senses: e.g., handling sand, dough, clay, water, etc. Also sewing, gardening, arranging and sorting objects

Adult-directed art and manipulation (ADM): The child is mastering and refining skills and techniques under adult direction, and sometimes with an adult-determined end-product; e.g., tracing, directed collage

Structured materials (SM): The use of materials, with design constraints, e.g. jigsaw puzzles, peg-boards, templates, picture or shape matching materials, counting boards, shape posting boxes, bead-threading and sewing cards

Three Rs Activities (3Rs): Attempts at reading, writing or counting. It includes attentive looking at books

Examination (EX): Careful examination of an object or material, e.g. looking through a magnifying glass. It differs from *manipulation* in that the looking, smelling or tasting is more important than the handling

Problem-solving (PS): The child solves a 'problem' in a purposeful way using logical reasoning; e.g., looking to see why something won't work and then repairing it

Pretend (PRE): The transformation of everyday objects, people or events so that their 'meaning' takes precedence over 'reality'

Scale-version toys (SVT): Arranging miniature objects, e.g., dolls' houses, farm and zoo sets, transport toys, toy forts. It does not include use of toys such as prams, dolls and dishes. If miniature objects are used in pretend play, use previous category

Informal games (IG): A play situation, with or without language, where the child is playing an informal game with another child. These are spontaneously and loosely organized; e.g., following one another around while chanting, hiding in a corner and giggling, or holding hands and jumping

Games with rules (GWR): Includes ball games, skittles, circle games including singing games, and board games such as snakes and ladders, dominoes, noughts and crosses, etc.

Music (MUS): Listening to sounds, rhythms or music, playing instruments, singing solos and dancing

Passive adult-led group activities (PALGA): A large group of children, under the leadership of an adult, listen to stories, rhymes or finger plays, watch television, watch a planned demonstration (e.g., nature table, making popcorn), etc.

Social interaction, non-play (SINP): Social interaction, with another child or with an adult, verbal or physical, but definitely not play, with another child or with an adult. E.g., chatting, borrowing, seeking or giving help or information to someone, aggressive behaviour (not play-fighting), teasing, being cuddled or comforted by an adult. Note that *social interaction, non-play* is used only when the child is not engaged in another task code category; e.g., if he is doing a puzzle while chatting to a friend, code it as *structured materials*

Distress behaviour (DB): Seeking comfort or attention from adult or other child. He must show visible signs of distress or make a visible bid for comfort; e.g., prolonged crying, wanton destruction of materials, social withdrawal

Standing around, aimless wander or gaze (SA/AWG): The child is not actively engaged in a task or watching a specific event

Cruise (CR): Active movement around from one thing to another, or purposeful looking around, when the child appears to be searching for something to do

Purposeful movement (PM): Purposeful movement towards an object, person or place: e.g., searching for an object, going outdoors, crossing the room to another activity

Wait (W): The child's time of inactivity while waiting, for adult or child

Watching (WA): Watching other people or events. The child may watch a specific person or activity, or look around in general. Includes listening-in to conversations without participating

Domestic activity (DA): Includes going to the toilet, hand-washing, dressing, arrival and departure, rest, tidying up, milk, snack or meal

Appendix B

Extract from *Learning from Observation: a Guide to Using 'Observing Children' in Playgroup Training and Support*

Avril Holmes and Linnet McMahon

Suggestions for using target child observations with a student group

The tutor has to decide how much time can be spent on observations during a playgroup course. This will depend very much on how well it is integrated into the whole pattern of the course, and if everyone is finding it a helpful way of looking at children and playgroups.

It can also be useful to base a short series of meetings on this observation method, particularly for experienced people who would appreciate this more detailed analysis of observation. At the end of the handbook is a detailed account of one way in which the method has been used, including, for example, the use of photographs as a way of introducing observing.

The first attempts will probably be trial runs to familiarize everyone with the technique. One way to encourage further attempts is for the tutor to read through these first observations and pick out points for discussion. Students may not always realize how much can be got out of observations unless they are given individual comments. As the observations are discussed and examples are shown, it will become easier for the students to understand the method and the reason for it. It is also possible to gain acceptance and better understanding of the categories, *Language*, *social*, *task*, if the group discuss what they hope to gain from observations. Discussion usually centres on:

1. 'Really seeing what the child is *doing*.'
2. 'What is the child *talking about?*'
3. '*With whom* does he play?'

If the group accepts Doing, Talking, and With Whom? as a summary of their discussion, it is much easier for them to accept and use the formal categories of *task* – *language* – *social*. Another way is to arrange for the students to share their observations in small groups. Try a short session at first (ten minutes) with just a few questions to aid discussion. For example:

What was the child doing? *Task code*.
(a) Did he spend much time watching?
(b) Did the child do the same thing for five minutes or several different things?
(c) What made him start – stop?

Discussing one observation in detail has also proved to be very useful, particularly if everyone has the same observation. It helps to clarify the coding if the group share their individual reasons for choosing a code. It may also reveal the limitations in the written record which make it difficult to decide what code to choose. This indicates what is important to record if it is to be of help when looking through an observation later. Tutors could use the observations in the *Observing Children* manual, one they or their students have done, or one included in this handbook. If the group get interested and want to look in more depth they can make several observations and might move on to doing 20 minutes, or even record in half-minute intervals. A few general questions may encourage people to think more carefully about their observations, once the technique has been mastered, as it is important that they can be made use of in playgroup work and not become just an interesting exercise.

From your coded observations can you tell:

1. How satisfying the activity was to the child? What evidence have you in your observation to support your views?
2. Were other people (adults or children) important in sustaining the child at the activity or did they distract him?
3. Does the activity encourage the use of language? What do they talk about?
4. Has your observation given you any fresh insight, either to the child or the provision in the playgroup?

Making graphs

A more detailed approach may not appeal to many but one or two may like to try the following ideas.

A series of observations can provide more information than a single one and therefore a student could combine the information from all her observations, perhaps presenting it in graph form. This can also be done with a single observation. Imagine an observation of a child at an adult-directed activity . . . It could be presented graphically in the following ways.

Adult-directed manipulation	Aimless wander or gaze	Adult-directed manipulation	Watching	Adult directed manipulation	Watching	Manipulation	Task code categories
1	2	3 4	5	6	7	8 9	10

This shows what the child is doing over ten minutes. It uses the *task code*. . . . You might ask, 'Is this typical? or unexpected?', 'Is the child absorbed in her activity or not?' etc.

A similar diagram could be used to show the *language* or *social coding*.

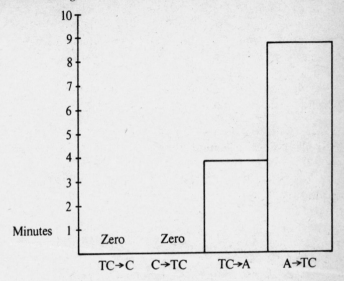

This shows the number of minutes in the observation in which the target child spoke to someone or someone spoke to her. (This is not the same as the total number of interactions. Instead, you ask, for each minute, in that minute did the child speak to someone or not?)

The *task code* and *social coding* could be portrayed in the same way.

A similar kind of graph could be made from a series of observations of one child. For example, graphs of the coding (task, social and language) observations made during the term in which a child is settling into playgroup could be compared with graphs based on observations made in the child's second term.

Observation of a child settling into playgroup

This particular subject is most suited to the longer

foundation-type course as it monitors the child's development and integration over a period of time. It can be used to reinforce group discussion on the different practices of introducing children to playgroup and can help to create a more 'open-minded' atmosphere than when discussion depends on an exchange of established opinions. Relating the evidence of the observation to the way in which children are introduced to the playgroup can help to identify practices which give most support to children and parents.

Why observe the new child?

Playgroup workers sometimes need a way of getting to know the new child in order to develop a relationship. Watching what the child actually does helps further understanding and *helps identify needs so that proper provision can be made*. This is a positive contribution that playgroup workers can make to improve their own playgroup.

A series of observations of a new child, for example, over *two terms*, will provide a great deal of information on how a child gradually adapts to a new experience and behaves in the group. The advantage of a two-term series of observations is that the child who regresses is 'picked up'. It is possible to look back at the initial introduction to see if this could have been improved. There is also the satisfaction of having a record of a developing child, and the coding can highlight the structure of the child's play.

Suggestions for observing the new child:

This would have to be undertaken in the student's own playgroup for practical purposes of keeping in touch with the child, and so that any changes based on the observations may be carried out.

Relevant background information would be:

(a) How many prior visits were made to the playgroup?

(b) Did the mother stay to settle the child and for how long?

(c) Were siblings or friends also at the playgroup?

(d) Any previous experiences which might hinder the introduction? Such as recent hospitalization, moving house, etc.

(e) Experiences which might help? Such as attendance at a mother-toddler club in the same building.

Make a continuous record over two terms.

Handout for students: Observation of a child settling into Playgroup

The objective is to see if by close observation you can identify what helps a child settle into playgroup.

Method. Make a record over two terms – this could be:

Once a week for the first half-term, three observations in the second half-term, then four or five during the second term. The observations will make you more aware of the child's behaviour and will be useful in checking if your impressions are correct. Choose any new child, not necessarily a very young one: any age will be interesting and provide a comparison with other course members' observations. The cooperation of your colleagues will be needed in order for you to withdraw from your usual responsibilities for the period of observation.

Helpful background information

1. Has the child attended a mother-toddler club (in the same building)?
2. How many prior visits were made to the playgroup?
3. Did the mother stay, and for how long?
4. Are siblings and friends also at the playgroup?
5. Any experiences which may influence the child's behaviour (such as recent hospitalization, moving house, new baby, etc.)?

From your coded observation, abstract the following information:

1. Identify themes – how many?
2. *Use the Social code* to find out how the time is spent on social contacts.
   (a) *With adults:* how many?
       If it is one particular person, who?
   (b) *Children* – has he a special friend?
   (c) How often does he play alone – in a pair – *small group or large group?*
3. *Use the Task code* to find out what he does.
   (a) Which activities attract the child – which does he avoid?
   (b) How long does he spend at his chosen activity?
   (c) What changes can you see in the child's tasks over the two terms?
4. *Use the Language code* to find out the amount of talk with:
   (i) Adults:
       (a) Are they regular staff? if not, whom?
       (b) Is it mainly one particular person?
       (c) Does the adult ask questions, give instructions, information or comfort?
       (d) Does he respond verbally?
   (ii) Children:
       (a) Does he start conversations with other children?
       (b) Are they mainly siblings or friends?
       (c) Does he use language to request help? Gain attention or information?

Questions which you might like to discuss with other course members using your observation data:

1. Does the new child spend much time in making social contacts? To whom does he direct his attempts – adults or other children?
2. Is friendship an important aspect of the settling-in period?
3. Is there any evidence to suggest that children need rewarding social relationships before they can develop their play?
4. What kind of adult support is most helpful to the new child? Does language play an important part in the developing relationship?
5. Is there a difference in the chosen activity of different ages or sexes?
6. What are the preferred activities? Are they usually available?
7. Can you identify positive procedure which enables the child to enjoy playgroup and settle well?

Observing an activity

The target child observation was not devised to study activities but with some modification can be used for studying groups as well as individual children. People have found it a valuable way of evaluating what is provided, how it is presented, the amount of interest shown by the children and the need to create fresh stimulus from time to time.

What can be discovered from observations

1. What makes an activity attractive to the children? Is

position in the room an important factor? Can several children play together? Is an adult usually present? Is it challenging or emotionally satisfying?

2. Does the activity encourage long spells of concentrated play? How long did a child spend at an activity? Did he give effort and thought to what he was doing? Did he complete what he was doing or give up in frustration? (The equipment provided may be inadequate.)

3. Does it encourage cooperation between children? Do they give each other ideas to develop their play? Do arguments develop over equipment? Has the child room to carry out ideas?

4. Does it encourage conversation? What is the child talking about: the activity, pretend situation, past events or social chatting?

What implications does this information have for provision in the playgroups?

One observer discovered that a group of children at the dough table intended to continue a birthday party after milk-time. Normally the activity would have been changed at milk-time but on this occasion it was left and the children returned and continued their pretend play for the rest of the morning.

If the observed activity is a silent, repetitive manipulative experience you could consider what might be added to encourage a 'shift in gear' – *not a chatty adult!* – but something which stimulates the children, something which demands a change in approach, something worth talking about and which encourages a different way of handling. For example: a squeezy bottle with holes in the water play may provide a surprise factor; dinosaurs in the sand tray may encourage questions! Providing a cooker at the dough table may allow play to develop.

A way of improving provision could be to do 'before and after' observations. That is, an initial observation in the playgroup and the second one after a session on the course when the activity has been presented and discussed in detail. For instance, first observation may show children having ideas which are hampered by the resources available (observed needs).

The second observation would be done after the addition of what seemed to be lacking. It is possible to find water trays so full that the children cannot see the water. A separate container for spare equipment may enable play to develop. This is probably obvious to most people but an observation may make it still clearer.

A collection of observations made during the course, whether made by one student or a group of students, could show how successful different activities were. You might want to pick out different task code categories such as pretend, manipulation, etc. to see where these occur and what the child was learning. For example, the observation might reveal that (*task code*) *pretend* appears more frequently *away* from specifically designed areas such as the home corner.

A similar approach, the making of a collection of observations, can be used to study other subjects, for example rising-fives. What sort of things do children who are rising-five find most absorbing and extending? – and so on.

The following handout is a general guide to looking at activities but you may want to devise some of your own for a specific activity; for instance, when studying water play you may wish to have more information on the design of the water tray, aprons and a list of equipment.

The questions you decide to ask will perhaps be influenced by a particular aspect you are considering. For example, language, developing skills, or group play. The suggestions on the activity handout may give you some ideas.

Handout for students – Observing an activity

Objective: to find ways of improving the provision of materials and equipment and the management of activities in the playgroup.

Choose the activity you wish to study and arrange a time when you think children will be engaged in it. Observe *one child* at the activity for at least ten minutes if possible. If she/he leaves, continue observing another child who seems similar to the one who just left, in the same age group, sex – at a later time if necessary.

It would be best to do at least two observations as children may use the activity in different ways.

Make a note of the site of the activity in relation to other activities. Describe the activity and equipment provided. Also the number of children allowed to play at one time. How is this organized? – e.g., four aprons for water tray – two paint easels – four chairs at the table.

Do at least two ten-minute observations on different occasions. From your coded observations can you see:	*For your notes*
1. *What attracts* the child to the activity? An adult – other children – curiosity – familiarity – a place of refuge?	
2. *What keeps him* at the activity? An adult – other children – enjoyment – exciting discoveries?	
3. *What was he doing?* Learning skills – trying out new ideas – problem-solving, repetitive manipulation – pretend play?	
4. *Does he talk about the activity?* Directs himself or others? – does it remind him of past events, or the future?	
5. *How does his play come to an end?* Satisfactory climax – interruption – lack of ideas?	
6. Was there anything provided which was not used by the children?	

Conclusions: Think of ways in which the activity could be extended so as to continue being relevant to children at later stages of development.

For your notes

Appendix C

An excerpt from the 'Target Child Coding Manual'

Carolyn Roy

There are four categorization systems for describing children's behaviour: activity, social setting, language, and play bout (thematic sequences of half minutes). The 'Target Child Coding Manual' is too lengthy to be included here in full, but we include one example, taken from that part of the manual dealing with activity.

Pretend

The transformation of everyday objects, people or events, so that their 'new' meaning takes precedence over their literal meaning. Pretending may take place with or without props, and with or without language. Many pretend sequences involve one or more of the following types of transformations:

> *pretend objects:* e.g., food, medicine, telephone
> *pretend events/actions:* e.g., fire, party, shopping, fighting
> *fantasy roles:* e.g., family (mother, father, sibling); occupational (fireman, doctor, policeman); fantasy person (Batman, Bionic Woman, Superman).

Objects used in pretend may be those provided in the preschool setting (doll, crockery, toy train, home corner); they may be constructed or altered by the child (house made from furniture, blankets; train made from large crates; gun made from lego bricks; bracelet made from dough); or, of course, they may be entirely imaginary (drinking from an empty cup; eating from an empty plate; shooting with a non-existent gun).

We do not infer that a child is pretending unless he provides clear, *observed behavioural or verbal evidence* of pretending. It is often, in fact, obvious from the child's language that he is pretending, especially when he is with others. In particular, there may be discussion of the roles that participants are adopting ('You be Mummy,' 'I want to be the doctor,') discussion of props required or of what objects are to represent ('You need a helmet,' 'This is my starship,'), or announcement of the pretend theme ('Let's go shopping,' 'I'm having a tea-party,' or even 'Let's pretend ...'!). Frequently the child accompanies his pretend actions with appropriate sound effects, making the noise of a vehicle (engine running, screeching brakes, siren of police car/ambulance), of a gun firing, etc.

At other times, however, there is no guidance from talk, and the observer must rely on the child's overt behaviour alone to decide whether or not he is pretending. But again, there are usually clear indications when the child is taking objects, people or actions as representations going beyond their literal meaning. Consider the following example:

> A girl goes into the home corner, takes a doll, undresses it, tucks it up in a cot; takes a toy stethoscope, places one end to her ears and the other to the doll's chest; fetches an empty cup and spoon, dips the spoon into the cup and then puts it to the doll's lips ...

Although not a word is spoken, it is obvious that the girl is taking the doll to represent something more than just a plastic doll; it is clear that with the stethoscope she is 'listening to the doll's chest', and that she then 'feeds' something to the doll.

Notice that pretending incorporates a host of other activities such as body movement, fine manipulation, and so on: yet we do not simply code the activity as, say, *gross motor play* or *manipulation*, when the dominant theme is clearly that of the pretend play, as in the above example. (By contrast, had the girl spent all her time simply undressing and dressing the doll, we would have no clear behavioural indication of pretending in the absence of talk, and we would be unjustified in coding her activity as anything other than *manipulation*).

Notice too that it may not be clear at the start of a new theme whether or not the child is pretending. Again, we do not just guess! If initially you are unsure of the activity category, look ahead in the written activity record of your observation. If there is later evidence that the child *is* pretending and suggestive that he has been all through the sequence, then 'score backwards' to the beginning of that episode, coding the entire theme as pretend. If, on the other hand, there is no clear indication of pretending, the entire sequence is coded otherwise according to the activity that the child is actually observed to be engaged in.

Examples of ordinary pretend:

1. Child is in home corner. He sets out plates on the table, announcing, 'Let's have tea.' He draws chairs up to the table, then leaves the home corner to join another activity, without having done anything towards acting out a meal, nor going beyond the materials provided.

2. Child announces he is going to take Baby for a walk. He fetches a doll, puts it in a pram, then wanders around the room pushing it.

3. Child has been engaged in manipulating dough, pounding it, cutting it, rolling it; in the middle of this sustained dough-kneading activity, the child spends two minutes cutting out several small circular pieces, putting them on a plate, then offers them to other children at the table, 'Would you like a cake?',

before resuming the kneading. This brief transformation of dough, plasticine, clay, etc., into 'cakes' during manipulation activity is commonly observed among young children, and is virtually a ritual part of the manipulation. When the play does not develop beyond this stereotyped element, e.g., when there is no further acting out of cooking or eating the cakes, it is low level. Compare with Example 9.

4. Child is in playground in a group of boys. TC waves arms briefly, saying – 'I'm Batman!' C shoots him with imaginary gun (hand) saying, 'Bang. Got you!'

Examples of pretend with cognitive complexity (× pretend)

Pretend play that shows original, novel and imaginative interpretation of play materials and situations, often with combination of different elements, such as props and roles. The child goes well beyond the literal meaning of the materials and context into the realms of fantasy and make-believe. The play shows structure and organization, for instance, with respect to the development of a plot, which may include evidence of planning in advance by the child, perhaps in the prior assembly of props or preparation of costume. Roles are fully acted out, with the child adding something of his own to the character he is playing, and in role-play, he may change his tone of voice or style of speech to fit the character. If his character is adopted from a television series or film, he goes beyond the stereotyped, familiar image to add new features, possibly in acting out a story.

5. Child is with others out of doors. They are in two groups, hiding behind opposite walls of large crates and 'shooting' at each other. Some are 'injured' and the others help them. Child creeps round the side of the building to try to invade the enemy from a new

angle while the others 'cover' for him. The children go well beyond ritual play-fighting to develop a plot.

6. Child has built a 'fire engine' with large-scale equipment – boxes, planks, etc. He is joined by others, all don plastic helmets and board the fire engine. Child 'drives' the engine, turning an imaginary steering wheel, making noises like a siren, calling out, 'Out of the way, look out. We've got to find the fire, we're going fast.' He stops driving, 'Here's the fire,' jumps off and takes the ladder off the fire engine, talking about 'rescuing the burning people'. The child elaborately acts out the role of fireman, incorporating it in a plot.

7. Child makes a construction with connector rods, holds it up: 'This is my starship.' He 'flies' it around, 'It's shooting the sun ... now it must go to the farthest star ...'. He is joined by a friend with another rod construction, 'Look at my moon-ship.' They continue flying the 'ships', talking about planets, having battles in space.

8. Child is at the toy garage set; he takes a car out of the garage, runs it along the floor, during which a friend comes up and takes off another car from the garage. Child runs his car back to the garage: 'Help, one of the cars has gone – it's been stolen when the petrol-man wasn't looking. Come on, we'd better find it.' He runs his car along, following his friend's route and making noises like a police-car siren: 'Look, there it is. Faster, faster, we've got to catch the robbers.' The child turns the car's disappearance into a fantasy. (See also the activity category *scale-version toys*.)

9. Child has been kneading dough, in the course of which he has cut out dough circles, put them on a plate and placed them in a toy oven. He now brings the plate back to the dough table: 'My cakes are ready now. Now we can have tea.' Another child

joins in, 'It's John's birthday party.' 'John, you have to wash your hands before you sit at the table.' All pretend to wash hands. Child offers round the plate of cakes: 'Now you have to be careful 'cause the cakes are very hot ... they've just come out of the oven so watch you don't burn your tongue.' Turns to another child who is pretending to cram cakes into his mouth: 'You're greedy – you'll get a tummy-ache if you eat too fast.' (See Example 3; the 'cakes' theme here is much elaborated and far from stereotyped.)

Notes

A spell of pretend play is often preceded by a period of preparation for the pretend – assembling materials, dressing up in costume, constructing something with large or small scale materials that is subsequently used in pretending (as in Examples 5 and 6 above). If the preparation lasts for less than a minute, it is treated as part of the pretending and is entered in the activity column as (*x*) *pretend*. If it lasts for more than a minute, it is coded separately in the appropriate activity category, such as (*x*) *large scale construction* or (*x*) *small scale construction* for construction or arranging of props. However, although it now takes a separate activity category, the preparatory activity belongs to the same theme as the subsequent pretending itself; so unless there is a break between the preparation and pretend periods, the double lines for theme-change are not drawn until after the entire preparation-plus-pretend sequence ends.

Sometimes, although the child announces or argues over a particular role, he actually does nothing further to suggest that he is playing that character. This happens particularly in situations such as described where a group of children are milling around in high spirits. Often the child, announcing he is Batman, will briefly wave his arms up and down as if flying, or 'shoot' at another child, acknowledging the stereotyped role (low level *pretend*). If however, the observed behaviour consists of the child's merely shouting, 'No, *I* want to be Batman,' accompanied by excitable jumping around among the others but without even a cursory gesture towards *being* Batman, then the behaviour is not coded as pretend at all. In this illustration, it would be *rough-and-tumble*, the code for 'milling around' in an interacting group.

Short bibliography

ARMSTRONG, G. and BROWN, F. (1979) *Five years on: a follow-up study of the long term effects on parents and children of an early learning programme in the home*. Oxford: Social Evaluation Unit, Department of Social and Administrative Studies.

ALTMANN, J. (1974) Observational study of behaviour: sampling methods. *Behaviour*, **49**, 227–67.

AUSTIN, J. L. (1962) *How to do things with words*. Oxford and New York: Oxford University Press.

BERREITER, C. and ENGELMANN, S. (1966) *Teaching Disadvantaged Children in the Preschool*. Englewood Cliffs, N. J.: Prentice Hall.

BERNSTEIN, B. (ed.) (1971) *Class, codes and control: Vol. 1 Theoretical studies towards a sociology of language:* London and Boston: Routledge & Kegan Paul.

BLURTON–JONES, N. (1972) Categories of child-child interaction. In Blurton-Jones, N. (ed.) *Ethological studies of child behaviour*. Cambridge: Cambridge University Press.

BRADLEY, J. (1976) Playgroup Survey (Oxfordshire). Oxford Preschool Research Group mimeo.

BRUNER, J. S. (1975a) From communication to language: a psychological perspective. *Cognition*, **3**.

BRUNER, J. S. (1975b) The ontogenesis of speech acts. *Journal of Child Language*, **2**, 1–19.

BRUNER, J. S. (1978) *Child Care: Science, Art and Ideology*. The Gilchrist Lecture.

BRUNER, J. S. (1980) *Under Five in Britain*. London: Grant McIntyre; Ypsilanti, Michigan: High/Scope.

CLARKE, R. V. G. and MARTIN, D. N. (1975) A study of absconding and its implications for the residential treatment of delinquents. In Tizard, J., Sinclair, I. and Clarke, R. V. G. (eds) *Varieties of residential experience*. London and Boston: Routledge & Kegan Paul.

CAZDEN, C. B. (1975) personal communication.

CAZDEN, C. B. (1976) Play with language and meta-linguistic awareness: one dimension of language experience. In Bruner, J. S., Jolly, A. and Sylva, K. (eds) *Play: its role in development and evolution*. Harmondsworth and New York: Penguin.

CHERRY, L. (1974) Sex differences in preschool teacher-child verbal interaction. Doctorial dissertation, Harvard University.

COHEN, J. (1960) A coefficient of agreement for nominal scales. *Education and Psychological Measurement*, **20**(1), 37–46.

DONALDSON, M. (1978) *Children's Minds*. London: Fontana; New York: Norton.

GARLAND, C. and WHITE, S. (1980) *Children and Day Nurseries*. London: Grant McIntyre; Ypsilanti, Michigan: High/Scope.

GARVEY, C. (1977) *Play*. London: Fontana/Open Books; Cambridge, Massachusetts: Harvard University Press.

GOODALL, J. VAN LAWICK (1968) The behaviour of free-ranging chimpanzees in the Gombe Stream Reserve. *Animal Behaviour Monographs*, **1**, Part 3. London: Bailliere, Tindall & Cassell.

GOODALL, JANE VAN LAWICK (1976) Mother chimpanzees' play with their infants. In Bruner, J. S., Jolly, A. and Sylva, K. (eds) *Play: its role in development and evolution*. Harmondsworth and New York: Penguin.

HALSEY, A. H. (ed.) (1972) *Educational priority: Vol. 1; EPA problems and policies*. London: HMSO.

HOLLENBECK, A. R. (1978) Problems of reliability in observational research. In Sackett, G. P. (ed.) *Observing Behaviour*. New York: University Park Press.

HOLMES, A. and MCMAHON, L. (1978) *Learning from Observation*. London: Pre-school Playgroups Association.

HUDSON, L. (1966) *Contrary imaginations*. Later published 1974, Penguin.

HUGHES, M. (1977) Egocentrism in pre-school children. Unpublished doctoral dissertation, Edinburgh University. Reported in Donaldson, M. (1978) *Children's Minds*. London: Fontana; New York, Norton.

HUTT, C., FOY, H., TYLER, S., DEAN, A. *Play, Exploration and Learning*. D. E. S. interim report, Department of Psychology, University of Keele.

ISAACS, S. (1933) *Social Development in Young Children*. London: Routledge & Kegan Paul.

LABOV, W. (1970) The logic of nonstandard English. In F. Williams (ed.) *Language and Poverty*. Markham Press.

LAZAR, I. and DARLINGTON, R. (1979) *Lasting Effects after Preschool*. Consortium for Longitudinal Studies, U.S. Department of Health Education and Welfare Office of Human Development Series, Department of Health, Education and Welfare publication No. (OHDS) 73-30179.

LELAURIN, K. and RISLEY, T. R. (1972) The organization of day-care environments: 'Zone' versus 'man-to-man' staff assignments. *Journal of Applied Behaviour Analysis*, **5**, 225–32.

LUNZER, E. A. (1959) Intellectual development in the play of young children. *Educational Review*, **11**, 205.

MACDONALD, K. I. (1979) Interpretation of residual paths and decomposition of variance. *Sociological Methods and Research*, **7**, 289–304.

MCGREW, W. C. (1972) *An Ethological Study of Children's Behaviour*. New York and London: Academic Press.

MONTES, F. and RISLEY, T. R. (1975) Evaluating traditional day care practices: an empirical approach. *Child Care Quarterly*, **4**, 208.

PARRY, M. and ARCHER, H. (1975) *Two to Five: a handbook for students and teachers*. London: Schools Council and Macmillan Education.

PETERS, R. S. (1966) *Ethics and Education*, London: Allen & Unwin.

PIAGET, J. and INHELDER, B. (1956) *The Child's Conception of Space*. London: Routledge & Kegan Paul.

PRESCOTT, E., JONES, E., KRITCHEVSKY, S., MILICH, C. and HASELFOEF, E. (1975) *Who Thrives in Group Day Care?* Pacific Oaks College, California.

RICHARDS, M. P. M. (1974) *The Integration of a Child into a Social World*. Cambridge: Cambridge University Press.

ROPER, R. and HINDE, R. A. (1978) Social behavior in a play group: consistency and complexity. *Child Development*, **49**, 570–79.

ROY, C. Coding manual for scoring cognitive challenge in Target Child Observations. Unpublished manuscript. Available from Sylva, K., Department of Social and Administrative Studies, University of Oxford.

RUTTER, M., MAUGHAN, B., MORTIMORE, P. and OUSTON, J. (1979) *Fifteen Thousand Hours*. London: Open Books; Cambridge, Massachusetts: Harvard University Press.

SACKETT, G. P. (ed.) (1978) *Observing Behaviour, Volume II: data collection and analysis methods*. NICHD Mental Retardation Research Centers Series. New York: University Park Press.

SMITH, G. and JAMES, T. (1975) The effects of preschool education: some American and British evidence. *Oxford Review of Education*, **1**(3), 223–40.

SNOW, C. E. and FERGUSON, C. A. (eds) (1977) *Talking to Children*. Cambridge: Cambridge University Press.

SYLVA, K. D., BRUNER, J. S. and GENOVA, P. (1976) The role of play in the problem-solving of children 3–5 years old. In Bruner, J. S., Jolly, A. and Sylva, K. (eds) *Play: its role in development and evolution*, Harmondsworth and New York: Penguin.

TIZARD, B. (1975) *Early Childhood Education*. Slough: Social Science Research Council/National Foundation for Educational Research.

TIZARD, B., PHILPS, J. and PLEWIS, I. (1975) Play in preschool centres: I. Play measures and their relation to age, sex and IQ. *Journal of Child Psychology and Psychiatry*, **17**, 251.

TIZARD, B. (1979) Language at home and at school. In *Language and Early Childhood Education*. Cazden, C. B. (ed.). Washington, D.C.: National Association for the Education of Young Children.

TIZARD, J. (1976) Psychology and Social Policy, *Bulletin of the British Psychological Society*, **29**, 225–34.

TOUGH, J. (1977) *The Development of Meaning*, London: Allen & Unwin.

TURNER, I. F. (1977) Preschool playgroups research and evaluation project. Final report submitted to Government of Northern Ireland Department of Health and Social Services. Department of Psychology, The Queen's University of Belfast.

WALKER, M. (in preparation) Unpublished doctoral dissertation, University of Miami, Department of Early Childhood Education.

WEBB, L. (1974) *Purpose and Practice in Nursery Education*, Oxford: Blackwell.

WEIKART, D. P., EPSTEIN, A. S., SCHWEINHART, L. and BOND, J. T. (1978) The Ypsilanti Preschool Curriculum Demonstration Project: Preschool years and longitudinal results. Ypsilanti, Michigan: High/Scope.

WOOD, D., BRUNER, J. S. and ROSS, G. (1976) The role of tutoring in problem solving *Journal of Child Psychology and Psychiatry*, **17**, 89.

WOOD, D. and HARRIS, M. (1977) The Oxford Preschool Research Group: An experiment in psychological intervention. *Prospects*, UNESCO.

WOOD, D., McMAHON, I. and CRANSTOUN, Y. (in preparation) *Working with Under Fives*. London: Grant McIntyre.

ZIVIN, G. (1974) How to make a boring thing more boring. *Child Development*, **45**(2), 232–6.

Index